IKE AND MAMIE

IKE AND MAMIE

The Story of the General and His Lady

Lester David and Irene David

G. P. Putnam's Sons
New York

Grateful acknowledgment is extended to John S. D. Eisenhower for permission to reprint a number of the letters written by Dwight D. Eisenhower and quoted in this book; to John F. Six McDonnell and Katherine G. Howard for permission to quote from their oral histories at the Eisenhower Library; to the Washington Press Club, Ann McFeatters, president, for permission to reprint recipes from *Second Helping*, published in 1962 by the Women's National Press Club; and to the Congressional Club in Washington, D.C., Norma Lagomarsino, president, for permission to reprint Eisenhower recipes from the *Congressional Club Cookbook*. Excerpts from the oral history memoirs of Lucius D. Clay and Robert Sherrod, copyright 1976 by The Trustees of Columbia University in the City of New York and used by permission.

Library of Congress Cataloging in Publication Data

David, Lester.
   Ike and Mamie, the story of the general and his lady.

Bibliography: p.
   Includes index.
   1. Eisenhower, Dwight D. (Dwight David), 1890–1969. 2. Eisenhower, Mamie Doud, 1896– 3. Presidents—United States—Biography. 4. Presidents—United States—Wives—Biography. I. David, Irene. II. Title.
E836.D37   1981   973.921'092'2 [B]   81-7379
ISBN 0-399-12644-9   AACR2

To Michael and Nettie Neer,
who would have been so proud

Acknowledgments

WE OWE DEBTS of gratitude to many persons who had worked with Dwight and Mamie Eisenhower at various times in their lives and who shared their invaluable recollections with us. We wish to thank General Alfred M. Gruenther (ret.); the late James C. Hagerty, Ike's press secretary; the late Dr. Kevin McCann, his aide and speech writer; Maxwell M. Rabb, Secretary of Ike's Cabinet; Bob Hope, who played golf with him and swapped jokes; designer Mollie Parnis; banker Gabriel Hauge, an adviser; his personal secretary Ann Whitman; Ellis D. Slater, the industrialist who was a close friend and bridge partner; Mary McCaffree Monroe, Mamie's social secretary; Katherine G. Howard, who was secretary of the GOP National Committee; journalists Walter Trohan and Mary Ellen Murphy, who had unique information to impart; and so many others. Our apologies for not mentioning them all here but their names appear in the text in appropriate places.

Immeasurably helpful, too, were those who served with the General in his "Army family," the men and women in his headquarters who went where he went during World War II. Special appreciation, then, to Captain Harry C. Butcher (ret.), Ike's naval aide; to former Sergeants Michael J. McKeogh and Pearlie McKeogh, who met and married while on Ike's staff; Lieutenant Colonel Mattie Pinette, his confidential secretary; and to former Sergeant Leonard D. Dry, his driver. Our deepest gratitude to Anthea Saxe, a former Englishwoman, for coming forward and setting the record straight on a matter which has already gone into the history books and must now be erased, and to Dr. Carver Livingston and his wife, Carol, of Southampton, Long Island, for new insights into the life (and death) of Kay Summersby.

We also wish to thank the military historians who gave unsparingly of their time to help us shed light on crucial points, among them Dr. Forrest C. Pogue, director of the Marshall Research Center and the Marshall Library; Dr. Stephen E. Ambrose, who was associate editor of Ike's official papers; and Dr. Francis L. Loewenheim of Rice University. Thanks, too, for valuable information provided by Colonel C.S. George (ret.), who was Marshall's aide-de-camp.

Not quickly forgotten will be the gracious reception we got from the people of Abilene, Denver, and Gettysburg whose lives had touched those of Ike and Mamie. Our special thanks are extended to Henry B. Jameson, editor and publisher of the *Abilene Reflector-Tribune,* and all the others of the plains city where Ike grew up; to Mrs. Arthur Nevins, widow of General Nevins, who still resides in Gettysburg; to Mrs. Ethel Wetzel, Ike's secretary in his retirement days; to Dr. W. N. Sterrett, Mamie's personal physician; and, certainly not least, to the Reverend Dr. Robert H. MacAskill, Ike and Mamie's pastor in Gettysburg. In Denver, our gratitude is unbounded to the staff of the Fitzsimons Army Medical Center and particularly David Potts, the public-affairs officer. To Donald L. Kortz and his wife, Bonnie, who purchased and now dwell in Mamie's childhood home on Lafayette Street, we are grateful for the privilege of visiting it and seeing, in mind's eyes, how the President and First Lady lived there and—a thrill indeed—of standing in the room where they were married. Thanks, too, to Eileen Archibold, who still lives nearby, for sharing with us her childhood memories of Mamie. In Washington, the staff of the Walter Reed Army Medical Center was immensely helpful.

Grateful appreciation is also extended to Director John E. Wickman and the staff of the Dwight D. Eisenhower Library in Abilene, particularly to James W. Leyerzapf, supervising archivist, and Kathleen Struss, archivist. Most helpful were the staffs of the Western History division of the Denver Public Library and the State Museum of Denver. For their patience and assistance, we also thank Margaret Brown Klapthor and her staff at the Museum of History and Technology of the Smithsonian Institution in Washington and John R. Earnst, superintendent of the Eisenhower National Historic Site at Gettysburg, and his aides, Kathy Georg and Laurie E. Coughlan. We are indebted, too, to Mrs. Elizabeth B. Mason, acting director of the Oral History Research Office at Columbia University.

Finally, and surely not least, our unlimited thanks to our editor, Phyllis E. Grann, for support and guidance all the way.

Lester David and Irene David

Woodmere, New York

Contents

MR. AND MRS.

A Kind of Prologue

Precisely at four o'clock on a snowy February afternoon, Dwight D. Eisenhower, in full military uniform, walked down the aisle in the Great Rotunda of Low Memorial Library at Columbia University to receive an honorary degree of doctor of laws. The year before, in 1946, he had returned triumphantly as the victorious Supreme Commander of the Allied forces in Europe and next year he would assume the presidency of Columbia.

As the procession of scholars, university heads and academic officials marched in slow cadence toward the canopied rostrum, the audience of 650 persons, dignitaries from all across the nation, rose to honor him. Mamie Eisenhower, seated in the front row, stood with the others.

13

When he came alongside, Eisenhower stepped out of the line, took her hand and said, "Don't you ever stand up for me, Mamie."

* * *

Three years later, President of the United States, he came downstairs for dinner, entering the elegant family dining room on the first floor of the White House just as the gilded French clock on the mantle was striking eight. With forty years of military discipline bred into him, Ike was never a moment late or early. As an Army wife, Mamie had absorbed many of the Service's ways, but punctuality was not one of them; this evening, she was tardier than usual. Eight minutes ticked by before she left the family quarters and slid into her chair opposite him.

Ike put on a stern face. Pointing to his watch he said, "Do you realize that you have kept the President of the United States waiting?"

"Why no," Mamie replied, leaning toward him across the gleaming Sheraton-style mahogany table. "I've been busy making myself pretty for my husband."

* * *

After their retirement to Gettysburg, Ike and Mamie accepted a dinner invitation at the nearby home of friends. Having already had two heart attacks and abdominal problems, Ike was under strict medical orders to live prudently, which meant moderate exercise and plenty of rest. Soon after dinner, Mamie began urging him to leave but Ike, enjoying himself with old friends, refused to go. Finally she broke into a group and said loudly enough for everyone to hear, "Now let's go home, Ike. You know what the doctors said about your bedtime." The General's face reddened. Silently, he pushed back his chair and left.

On the way home, Ike sat as far apart from her as he could in the back seat of their black limousine, staring silently out the window. In the driveway, as they alighted, the chauffeur heard this brief but pungent exchange.

Mamie, in a small voice: "I guess I embarrassed you tonight, didn't I, Ike?"

Ike, loudly as he strode into the house ahead of her: "Mamie, you sure as hell did!"

It was that kind of marriage for fifty-three years, warm and loving, a little teasing and a little flirtatious even into its maturity, yet not without its bumps and jolts. There were times when Ike had his hands full with Mamie. Her worries about his health approached, and often went beyond, nagging. Added to her childlike insistence on having her way, this would irritate him to the point of explosion. Then the Eisenhower temper, which was almost as famous as the Eisenhower grin, would explode and he would bellow at her in a voice generals had come to fear.

"The loving relationship between Ike and Mamie was rarely smooth," their son John Eisenhower candidly admits. Julie Nixon Eisenhower says it was "sometimes tempestuous" and Mary McCaffree Monroe, Mrs. Eisenhower's social secretary during White House years, asserts that the marriage "was not without its square corners." Aksel Nielsen, a Denver investment banker who was one of Ike's closest friends, says they quarreled and even Mamie cheerfully admitted she and Ike had "spats."

And yet, for all that, it was a commitment that endured despite a gypsylike nomadism that denied them roots until the final decade, despite Army-ordered separations, despite the rumors whispered on two continents of Ike's involvement with a younger and very attractive woman while he was fighting the war in Europe. It survived, too, the demands of a public life that have caused the collapse of many marriages of famous figures, when wives sought unsuccessfully to have even a small measure of privacy for themselves and their families.

Mrs. Monroe asserts: "I was as close to them as anyone, and I knew how much they cared for each other. On their fortieth wedding anniversary, in 1956, he gave her a ruby heart on which he had engraved 'I love you better today than the day I met you.'"

The country and the world never really knew Mamie Doud Eisenhower. The face she showed was that of a smiling, easygoing, pliant, motherly, and grandmotherly woman, steadfast in her devotion to Ike but essentially moving only in his shadow. But Mamie Eisenhower was more independent than she allowed people to think, had more (and stronger) views, political and otherwise, than she let on.

She was no Rosalynn Carter, who shared actively in executive decision-making, nor an Eleanor Roosevelt, who pursued her own goals of social justice. Neither, however, was she a Jacqueline Kennedy, who despised politics and politicians, fled Washington as often as she could and infuriated her husband by refusing to attend important functions.*

Ike's First Lady had some definite opinions, though she never expressed them publicly and denied, wide-eyed, that any ever entered her mind. "She consciously developed a philosophy of always putting her husband on center stage," John says. "She could more than hold her own with him in private—her frail health belied the strength of her will—but in public she stayed in the background."

---

* During his campaign for the Presidency, J.F.K. threw up his hands in despair when he heard that Jackie had given a press conference while sprawling languidly on a carpet of their Georgetown house, clad in purple Pucci pants. "What an image for the heartland!" he fumed. Kennedy knew his opponent's wife, Pat Nixon, was traveling around the country in inexpensive dresses, talking about child-rearing and home management.

The public Mamie took great care to put her husband first in everything. Her life, she told every interviewer who asked, revolved around Ike totally. Her favorite statement, printed hundreds of times around the world over the years, was, "Ike runs the [war, country] and I turn the lamb chops." The first part was true enough but Mamie turned few chops. Ike was the cook in the family from the very beginning. And Mamie, in private, was not so self-effacing. Mrs. Arthur Nevins, widow of General Nevins and Mamie's friend for forty years, says Ike was "certainly not the boss," adding, "Who's the 'boss' in any good marriage?"

"Mamie Eisenhower was a determined woman," says Dr. Kevin McCann, a family intimate who was a Presidential aide, "as determined in her own way as her husband was." Ike himself acknowledged this. Walter Trohan, the former chief of the Washington Bureau of the *Chicago Tribune,* a close friend of Ike since 1934, recalls a talk he had with Eisenhower before World War II.

"Somehow," says Trohan in his Columbia, Maryland, home, where he is now retired, "the conversation turned to our wives. I told him that my wife had a whim of iron and, when she had her mind made up, wouldn't let me do the things I wanted. Or she would tell me what I *could* do.

"Then, I told Ike, I'd have to do it. Everybody might think I'm a son of a bitch, but I'd have to obey her order.

"Ike gave me that famous grin and said, 'What makes you think you're any different than I am!'"

Mamie was peppery and she could be demanding, even imperious as she barked orders to her staff like a first sergeant with the military crispness she had absorbed from her soldier husband and the officers—like Douglas Mac-Arthur and George S. Patton—she had met and known all her life. She could be petulant, too, griping like any GI about the Army's shortcomings. Reared as a rich man's daughter, pretty enough to attract beaux wherever she went, she was "spoiled" early in life and Ike's success as a military commander and political leader spoiled her even more.

She was never the uncomplicated Mamie she liked to pretend. In the beginning, she did not emerge as a strong personality, even to her own family. To John, Ike was the stern disciplinarian and Mamie the pliant one; to grandson David, John's son, she was the General's "soft side, always subordinate to him." It wasn't until years afterward that the family discovered somewhat to its surprise that Mamie was, in David's words, "an uninhibited, freewheeling spirit, with a strong will of her own."

But Ike knew this all along. She made it quite clear to him even before they were married. Indeed, she was probably responsible for altering the entire course of his military life.

After graduation from West Point, Eisenhower had made a study of the new and growing division of military aviation. Realizing its enormous potential, he made up his mind to get in on the beginning. There was an excitement in flying that appealed to him and the equally persuasive inducement of a fifty-percent pay raise. In 1916 he filed an application for what was then the Aviation Section of the Signal Corps and was ordered to report for a physical examination.

But there was Mamie to contend with. He had asked her to marry him but the idea of being a flier's wife did not appeal to her at all. Accounts of her early life say Mamie approved of his decision but her parents refused to give their permission on the reasonable premise at the time that a married man shouldn't be up in those new-fangled machines. But three years before she died, Mamie disclosed it was she who had given Ike an ultimatum.

"When he was thinking about going into the Aviation Service to make an extra ninety dollars a month," she said, "I told him to choose it or me. And he chose me."

He chose other things too, thereafter, because Mamie wanted them.

In May of 1960 Eisenhower returned to the United States from his final summit conference with General Charles de Gaulle, British prime minister Harold MacMillan, and Soviet premier Nikita Khrushchev. Mamie met him at Andrews Air Force Base. Back in the White House, Ike said he would like to go off to the Caribbean to rest and golf.

Mamie, however, had other ideas. She felt he would be more comfortable, and so would she, in their cottage on the grounds of the National Country Club in Augusta, Georgia. Next day, the Eisenhowers packed and left for a week-long holiday in Augusta.

That year, *Newsweek* magazine observed: "She (Mamie) has a will before which any general would retreat. The President's famous temper holds no terrors for her."

"Mamie wasn't a stuffed doll," says Kevin McCann. James C. Hagerty, Ike's press secretary, asked if Mamie ever objected to any of her husband's actions as President, replies that she had indeed. "She'd argue with him plenty of times about his policies, but upstairs, in the privacy of their living room in the White House."

Close friends of the Eisenhowers told us that Mamie pleaded Richard Nixon's cause when Ike hesitated to rename him as his running mate in 1956. She was said to have liked Nixon because he had been loyal to her husband, knew his place, never trying to upstage the President, and conducted himself ably during the crisis that followed Ike's heart attack in 1955. Ike, who had been close to dumping Nixon on the urging of his brother, Milton, and other advisers, changed his mind. It is probable that Nixon owed his job, and his subsequent rise to the Presidency, to Mamie's intervention.

During a budget conference at the White House, Ike frowned when his advisers suggested a potentially controversial proposal. "Let me try this out on Mamie," he said. "She's a pretty darn good judge of things." When it came to dealings with individuals, Ike often sought Mamie's views. "Mamie," he said, "is a very shrewd observer. She has an uncanny judgment of people."

She was critic and adviser, too, when it came to his speeches.

Once Mamie's quiet yet firm insistence that Ike change a talk sent him into a vein-popping rage. During his first Presidential campaign in 1952 Eisenhower tried out all his major talks on Mamie. In September of that year, aboard his whistle-stopping train, he read aloud the draft of a speech, written for him by Emmet J. Hughes and C. D. Jackson, for a huge rally in Detroit.

Mamie had settled down in the lounge car with Kevin McCann and Dr. Howard Snyder, Ike's personal physician. Ike, feet apart to balance himself in the swaying train, stood before them and began reading. He had spoken only a few sentences when Mamie interrupted. "Ike," she told him, "you can't say that. It's not in character." Eisenhower, irritated, looked up and went on. A moment later Mamie broke in again. "Ike," she said, "that simply isn't *you.*" For twenty minutes, she punctuated the recital with her objections.

"Finally Ike gave up," McCann recalled. "He threw the speech down and slammed his way into the bedroom of the train so hard I thought he'd throw the train off the track. But he never picked up that speech. Instead, he delivered an extemporaneous address."

When she approved of his talks, she told him so and he beamed. Even after he retired from office, Mamie never stopped monitoring his public addresses. In 1965 he was asked to speak in London's St. Paul Cathedral before heads of state and other dignitaries from 112 nations at the funeral for Winston Churchill. He read the talk he prepared before Mamie and McCann. When he finished, Ike looked up expectantly.

Mamie had been moved to tears. "Don't change a word, Ike," she said softly. And he didn't.

In her later years, Mamie no longer hid her opinions quite so carefully from people she knew. Dr. W. N. Sterrett of Arendtsville, near Gettysburg, made many calls to the Eisenhower farm as Mamie's personal physician in her later years. The doctor would spend time with her after his examination because he loved to hear her talk. And she said many things to him that she would never tell the media— tart, shrewd observations that reflected her continuing interest in current affairs and leading personalities.

These are some of her views, as related by Dr. Sterrett:

She had a low opinion of Jacqueline Kennedy Onassis, considering her "brazen and frivolous," a poor example of what a First Lady should be. The First Lady's job, she felt, was to make a home for the President in the White House, a real home to ease the pressures, not merely a center for the conduct of high-level business.

Jackie, she felt strongly, was much too concerned with her own affairs and her friends and spent too much time away from the home she ought to have managed. Mamie, who knew the value of a dollar, was appalled at how much Jackie spent on her clothes. "Why she has no respect for money at all," Mamie said.

Mamie thought Pat Nixon was "one hundred percent" because she always stood behind her husband, but she objected strongly to Rosalynn Carter's concept of the First Lady's role. Says Dr. Sterrett: "She did not approve of Mrs. Carter making independent decisions about political matters, or taking on matters concerned with the running of the Government that she was never chosen by the people to do. She did not believe that a First Lady should be a kind of Assistant President, as Rosalynn appeared to have been. She was turned off by what she called Mrs. Carter's 'grandstanding.'"

Mamie admired Bess Truman because she positioned herself firmly and immovably in the background when Harry was President, and she respected Lady Bird Johnson for her sincerity and unquestioning support of Lyndon. Both First Ladies, she felt, handled their role with grace and quiet dignity, and she liked that.

She lived long enough to see the beginnings of the 1980 campaign for the Presidency. She did not want to see Ronald Reagan head the Republican ticket that year. Her favorite candidate was George Bush because she believed he best mirrored Ike's own policies. She told Dr. Sterrett: "Ike said a long time ago that that fellow George Bush was Presidential material, and this was when Bush was low man on the totem pole. Ike had spotted him when he was a Republican Congressman from Texas. There is one thing against him, and that is he is still not very well known around the country. I hope I can do something to help him, because I think Ike would have wanted me to."

Mamie was perfectly aware of the sizable contribution she made to Ike's career. John says, "She takes full credit for smoothing the edges off the rough-and-ready Kansan and for teaching him some of the polish that later stood in good stead."

Not that Ike ate his peas with a knife, but he was, as a young man, uncomfortable in the company of anyone but equally rough-and-ready soldiers and officers. Mamie— "every bit of an aristocrat," John says—"taught him by example and, on occasion, direct instruction, the manners of the higher born." In the years to come, when Eisenhower, as wartime commander, was an honor guest of European heads of state in their palaces and mansions, he committed no gaffes and made excellent impressions that won him acceptance.

It was a marriage of hills and valleys, of good years and bad, of great glories and some defeats, a marriage of two people who had their idiosyncrasies, knew them, and

adapted to them. Ike went halfway much of the time, as we
shall see, because he knew Mamie wished it. And so did she
in matters important to him.

And it worked. It worked very well. A few days before he
died, Ike said to Mamie, "We've had a wonderful life
together." Four years earlier, as he was leaving for a
vacation in Augusta, Georgia, she had written him a note
telling him to look on his dresser, where she had left a
gardenia. It was a reminder, she said, "that I love you and
life would not mean much to me without you."

PART ONE

Early Years

1.   Rich Girl

LAFAYETTE STREET IS a quiet place. It is a broad street, with old, well-kept Victorian-style houses, each with its tended garden in front and grassy yard behind. Oaks, elms, and maples, so thick around the middle a tall man's arms cannot encircle them, line each of the sides. The trees tower high, shading the street completely from the noon sun; they have been there since the century began.

Two miles away is downtown Denver, and the contrast cannot be sharper. Downtown is a busy place, with great hotels, large modern department stores, and office towers of stainless steel which house multinational corporations hot after the oil, gas, and coal reserves of the western states. Leave downtown, head north along Colfax Avenue, and within minutes the buildings have aged noticeably and the crowds have thinned. Paint peels on the low wooden structures and missing shingles on roofs are unreplaced. Here are hamburger and fried-chicken drive-ins and, soon, a block of topless bars and stores selling "adult entertainment."

Go yet a few more blocks, turn right at Lafayette Street

25

and, between Seventh and Eighth avenues, stop at Number 750. It is a three-story brick house, once creamy beige, now silvery gray with dignified age, which sits far back from the street on a quite narrow plot only 50 feet wide and 120 feet deep. Built on a slight rise, it is reached by two series of stone steps set off from the terraced lawn by shining black wrought-iron railings and masses of wavy juniper bushes and yellow floribunda roses. The roof of the wide porch is supported by a pair of rounded pillars on each side.

It is the only house on the street unshaded by trees in front. Because of its openness, the rays of the sun glint on an etched copper plaque, placed there in 1962 by the Peace Pipe chapter of the Daughters of the American Revolution.

For this is no ordinary house. It is the girlhood home of Mamie Doud Eisenhower, where she grew into young womanhood, where she married her soldier, and where she was to return again and again through the years as First Lady with her husband, the President of the United States.

Nearly seventy years ago on Lafayette Street, John Sheldon Doud, wearing goggles and a long white duster, backed his Stanley Steamer slowly out of the garage and down the hundred-foot driveway. At the curb he waited, not too patiently, for his wife and four daughters. It was Sunday, the day for their weekly family drive, and they were already five minutes late.

Doud was a man who insisted on punctuality, but although he was always on time himself the women in his family were not. He would bellow his displeasure at their tardiness and bring them into line for a while, but since they knew much of his sternness was facade, they soon backslid with little fear of consequences.

In the days when automobiles were still called horseless carriages, John Doud had already owned several of them. In Colorado Springs, back in 1904, he had possessed a green Rambler, the first car in town. Later he had an Oldsmobile, a Winton Six, a Packard, a Pierce-Arrow, as well as the Steamer, a touring car which he kept in a condition of perpetual shine.

It was roomy enough to hold his family for its Sunday-afternoon drive, to which Doud looked forward with considerably more enthusiasm than his wife and daughters. Mamie, the second eldest, in particular would have liked to make other plans, but she knew better. The parties, the boys who said they might drop by, all had to be deferred. The family ride came first, Doud insisted, and that was that.

On this particular day, as it often was, Doud's destination was Cheesman Park, named for Walter Scott Cheesman, the architect of Denver's water supply system. His wife and one daughter beside him, three other girls in the rear black leather seat, he drove slowly down Lafayette Street, turned left at Eighth Avenue, and proceeded to the park. Once there, he headed for the marble pavilion near the reflecting pool where the girls leaped out, and, as they always did, gathered around the bronze finder to identify the high peaks of the Front Range of the Rocky Mountains just west of the city.

On other days, John Doud would vary his selection for the Sunday outings. He would go to City Park, which occupied some 460 acres on East Seventeenth Avenue, between York Street and Colorado Boulevard. Here, they would wander through the Zoological Gardens where buffalo, antelope, deer, elk, coyote, and mountain lion lived in an environment similar to their natural habitat. They would listen to the band concerts and, on summer nights, stay for the lighting of the electric fountain which sprayed water in nine color combinations.

For Mamie, the most memorable trip was to Elitch's Gardens, then one of the oldest amusement parks in the country and still a Denver attraction. Here the Doud girls would go directly to the zoo, where they could ride a live camel and then go on the merry-go-round, where Mamie had a favorite seat, the Roman chariot decorated with the figure of Columbia on the front.

There was a summer theater at Elitch's where great stars such as DeWolf Hopper would recite "Casey at the Bat" in his rolling basso, and a young girl named Antoinette Perry, after whom the Tony Awards would be named, made one of her first appearances as an actress.

Sometimes, though not too often, Doud would drive the Steamer downtown for an up-close look at the three-story granite State Capitol Building, topped by a dome covered with gold leaf from the Colorado mines, which still stands at Colfax and Sherman. Doud would make a rapid turn around the downtown area, because it was not the kind of place a family man remained long with his growing children. Still, he stared, as fascinated as the girls, at the saloons along Market and Latimer streets, where the prospectors came on their days back from the hills, and where, likely as not, drunken miners lurched in front of the automobile, alone or accompanied by fancy ladies.

These were not unusual sights in the city, because only a half-century had passed since a gold strike had brought Denver into being. The Douds themselves came to Denver in 1906 when doctors warned them that the thin air of Colorado Springs would strain the heart of their eldest daughter, Eleanor. Mr. Doud found a newly completed house going up in the Capitol Hill residential section, plunked down $6,925 cash, and moved his family to Lafayette Street.

Mamie had been born in Boone, Iowa, on November 14, 1896, in a one-story frame cottage on the edge of town. Although the family moved to Cedar Rapids when she was an infant, Boone claims her as its own. A huge sign stretched across Highway 30, at Spring Street, tells a visitor that Boone is "The Mamie Eisenhower Birthplace." The house, at 709 Carroll Street, just across from its original location, is now a museum.

Mamie's father, John Doud, was descended from English landowners who came to the American colonies in 1639 and helped found the town of Guilford, Connecticut. He was born in Rome, New York, in 1871, the son of Royal Houghton Doud, who was a partner in a large wholesale grocery firm. Royal Doud was intrigued by stories of the growing West brought to his establishment by traders. Unable to resist the lure, he sold his interest in Rome and moved his family to Chicago, founding a livestock commission business under the name of R. H. Doud Company.

He retired in 1895, a wealthy man, only to be struck by gold fever which took him to the Yukon fields in an ill-fated attempt to provide supplies for the prospectors.

Mamie's father, John, inherited this love of adventure. As a youth, he left his comfortable Chicago home several times to wander, once at the age of fourteen, serving as third cook for a Mississippi work crew. In later years he didn't like to stay put for too long and would take his family traveling whenever the opportunity presented.

John Doud studied at the University of Chicago and Northwestern University and then worked in an Omaha stockyard for practical experience. By the time he was twenty-eight he, too, headed his own meat-packing firm, the John S. Doud Co., with headquarters in Boone, Iowa.

Mamie's mother, Elivera Mathilda, was a first-generation Swedish-American. Her father, Carl Carlson, had emigrated to the United States in 1868 and had gradually worked his way West, to what is now Boone, taking odd jobs, helping out on farms and in the mills. In a year he had saved enough money to send for his wife, Johanna.

Carl became manager of the flour mill and later its owner. He and Johanna had four children, Elivera, Joel, Charles, and Eda. Only Swedish was spoken in the home and the family ate the traditional foods and kept the customs and holidays of the old country. As the town grew and the Scandinavian population increased, Carlson became its spokesman.

Elivera was only sixteen, tall and slender with deep blue eyes and golden hair, when she married Doud, seven years her senior, in 1894. He was tall, too, with gray eyes, strong features, and a sturdy physique. Eleanor, their first child, was born the following year, and Mamie the next. When Mamie was nine months old, the Douds moved to Cedar Rapids where Eda Mae was born in 1900 and Frances in 1902. The family was now complete. Doud adored his daughters. He played with them, read to them, and loved to indulge them.

One year, when she was six, Mamie asked Santa Claus for a diamond ring. "Even then," she recalled later to friends, "I loved jewelry." That evening the telephone rang—the Douds had one of the first in Cedar Rapids, testimony to his love of new gadgets—and Mamie's father called to her. "It's for you, Mamie," he said. "It's Santa Claus. He's down at the corner and wants to talk to you."

Mamie was beside herself with excitement. "I pushed a chair to the wall," she recalled, "because I was too tiny to reach the telephone, and listened to 'Santa.' He had a booming voice and he told me that he had heard what I wanted and he would have it for me. Sure enough, Santa kept his word."

Doud, who had rigged the whole thing with a friend, placed a ring for Mamie beneath the Christmas tree. A small, engraved gold band with a tiny diamond chip, it is now on display at the Eisenhower Museum in Abilene along with her other jewelry.

Mamie was eight when Doud decided to sell his business and move his family to Colorado where they finally settled in Denver. Mamie's house on Lafayette Street has changed little since that time. The driveway is gone—access to the garage is through an alleyway running back of the house from Seventh to Eighth avenues—the original brown trim is now white and the oversized front door and windows are protected against vandals by wrought-iron grillwork. A

kidney-shaped swimming pool fills the grassy yard where
the Doud girls and their friends played croquet. But there is
still an air of quiet elegance, of wealth and of comfort. It is
now occupied by Donald L. Kortz, a Denver attorney and
real estate executive, and his wife, Bonnie.

Doud had a substantial amount of money and, although
he had retired from business, he did make investments now
and then, most of which made him even more money. So
the family lived well. There were always servants, a full-
time gardener, vacations, and parties.

In the summer the Douds, hospitable and outgoing
people, entertained on their porch which was covered by a
red velvet carpet that extended down the steps. White
wicker furniture and innumerable hanging baskets and pots
of flowers provided a colorful and tranquil setting where
friends and neighbors were served tea and cookies by a
white-coated butler.

Soon after the family had settled into their home, Mamie
did what all new girls on the block will do—look for friends.
She ran down to the corner and saw Eileen Ewing, who
lived at Number 700, in front of her white house. They hit it
off just fine.

Eileen, the widow of Robert F. Archibold, Jr., now lives
on the next block in a spacious, high-ceilinged apartment
filled with polished furniture, Persian rugs, and family
heirlooms. She and Mamie had maintained their friendship
for almost three-quarters of a century. Past eighty now, she
is a dignified gracious woman with carefully coiffed white
hair, an erect carriage, and an infectious smile.

"I was two or three years younger than Mamie," she
recalls, "but we became friends immediately. Whenever she
was tired of her sisters, or wanted to get rid of them, she
would call for me. Buster and Mike stayed closer to home.
They weren't as adventurous as Mamie then."

Mamie and Eileen would rummage in their mothers'
closets and select the most colorful garments they could

find. "We played house," Mrs. Archibold says. "And we had the most wonderful tea parties, pretending we had guests and pouring for our visitors. We walked our dolls down the street and, when we tired of that, ran in for our skates and raced along the sidewalk between our houses.

"Mamie became a belle long before the other girls. When most of us were still getting kicked in the shins and having our hair pulled by the boys, Mamie was getting lots of attention. Once a boy, quite obviously smitten hard, gave her his most prized possession, a real skin of a snake!"

Mamie liked school although she was not much of a scholar. She enjoyed the social side and could skip the studying—although she was conscientious and would try to complete her assignments.

Says Jessie M. Hamilton, Mamie's eighth-grade teacher: "I remember Mamie only as one of a group of nice girls. She wasn't a troublemaker. If she had been, I would be more likely to remember that. She must have been just average as far as scholastic work was concerned, as I haven't any definite impression of her grades."

Mamie's schooling began to be somewhat sporadic, interrupted by the Douds' travels. She attended East Denver High School for a short period and Mulholland School in San Antonio. Later she went to the exclusive Wolcott School for Girls whose student body was drawn from the leading families of Denver and vicinity.

The school motto was "Noblesse Oblige" and the catalogue notes that it stressed responsibility and usefulness to others, as well as "sincerity of work and earnestness of purpose."

Mamie's adolescence was happy and privileged. She went to Miss Hayden's dancing classes dangling her black patent-leather slippers in a pink-lined black satin bag and, years later, she described the headmistress as "quite a character with her long kid gloves and ball gowns."

Mamie's first formal date was with Jimmy Cassell, whose grandfather, H. C. Brown, built the world-famous Brown Palace Hotel, still one of Denver's most exclusive hostelries. He escorted her to an evening dance, one of a series held regularly by Miss Hayden to give her pupils a chance to practice their social graces. Jimmy's younger sister, now Mrs. George Bakewell, says he and Mamie also went riding around the neighborhood in his father's battery-operated car.

On Saturday afternoons Mamie and her teen-age friends would board a trolley on Colfax Avenue to go to the variety show at the Orpheum, to be followed by ice-cream sodas or "Teddy Bears," an ice cream, chocolate sauce, and nuts concoction at Baur's, an old fashioned confectionery on Curtis Street whose white tile floors, long soda fountain, and marble-topped tables made it a favorite of Denver's young people.

At sixteen, Mamie was something of a knockout. She had wide blue eyes, a pert nose, soft brown hair worn long with a dip over a high forehead, and one of the most infectious smiles around. All this was coupled with a gaiety of personality, an honesty, and a directness which were most appealing, especially to the young men of the neighborhood, who paid her plenty of attention.

As she grew older, the attention continued. She was the prettiest of the Doud girls and drew more young men to the porch steps on Saturday afternoons and Sunday evenings, when they would gather around the piano to sing. Mamie played well by ear and there was much laughter and teasing as she banged out such favorites as "Meet Me in the Shadows" and "I Just Can't Make My Eyes Behave."

Doud's good financial position allowed him to indulge his wife and daughters with every material thing they could possibly want—or he could imagine they wanted. However, he kept an eye and a firm hand on their behavior. His decisions were final and Mrs. Doud and the girls obeyed unquestioningly.

Gregarious and neighborly he might be but his primary interest was maintaining strong family relationships. Mrs. Doud said he had many acquaintances but few close friends. "We were always at the beck and call of each other," she explained. "Looking back, I think we were too self-contained, too clannish—but Mr. Doud wanted it that way; none of us ever stood up to him, we loved him too much."

Although Mamie had to observe a curfew when she went on a date, she never objected. Years later she said, "I didn't resent my father when he made my boy friends get me home by nine o'clock."

Winters were spent in San Antonio where Mr. Doud owned a rambling white clapboard house on McCullough Street. The Douds had sought to avoid Denver's cold winters since 1910 because of Eleanor's health.

The Douds would travel South in Mr. Doud's newest car, the servants having gone ahead by train to open up the house and ready it for their arrival. Mrs. Doud's elegant electric car, a black two-ton Rauch and Lang brougham with plum-colored upholstery and cut-glass flower holders in which she always kept fresh violets, was also sent by train.

The electric, which cost $4,300 and resembled a man's top hat with windows and wheels, was a familiar sight on Lafayette Avenue. Its two-and-a-half horsepower eight-volt electric motor had a top speed of nineteen miles and could go a hundred miles before the battery needed recharging. Mrs. Doud used it for shopping and visiting expeditions all over Denver and San Antonio. Mamie thought the four-seater was "nifty" and sometimes drove it to the Wolcott School. A 1914 model, it was still in running condition almost forty years later when it was finally retired by Mrs. Doud and later presented to the Abilene Museum where it is on display.

The routine of Denver summers and San Antonio winters was interrupted in 1912 when Eleanor was too ill to leave Denver. Her health worsened and early in 1912 she died, the only tragic event to mar Mamie's girlhood. Afterward Mr. Doud's travels increased. The family visited Panama, the Great Lakes, and New York City.

By now Mamie had lost all interest in further schooling. Her social life was full: she had many things to do and her choice of beaux to do them with both in Denver and San Antonio.

2. Poor Boy

THE CONTRAST IN Ike and Mamie's backgrounds could not have been greater; she had a carefree, pleasure-filled childhood, his was disciplined and work-filled. The sons of David Jacob Eisenhower and Ida Elizabeth Stover—there were seven, one of whom died of diphtheria in infancy—knew at an early age they were responsible for helping the family survive.

They took turns rising before dawn to build a fire in the kitchen stove. They milked the cows, gathered the eggs, pruned the fruit orchards, and weeded the vegetable gardens. They helped with the dishwashing and the laundry and passed their outgrown clothes down to the next in line. Always there were after-school, weekend, and vacation jobs.

Ike picked apples for the town cider mill and applied for work with a crew of wheat harvesters. As he was too small and too young to be of much help in the fields, the foreman assigned him to guide the lead horse. At times he took jobs at the Belle Springs Creamery where his father was employed. The sons' efforts were desperately needed, for

David Eisenhower was never to earn more than $150 a month.

In the summer and early fall, the Eisenhower boys loaded produce onto a wagon and peddled it house-to-house on the "rich" side of town. Levi J. Asper, who lived five blocks away and "chummed around" with Ike, was a frequent volunteer on these trips. "They raised the stuff in the garden east of the house and hauled it around in a spring wagon pulled by an old horse," Asper said. "Two or three of them would go along, one driving and the others making the houses on each side."

Ike, good-natured even then, did not mind but his older brother Edgar did not like the experience at all. Many years later, he remembered with distaste how housewives would pick over the vegetables, strip the ears of the corn to examine them, and then bargain on the price. "They made us feel like beggars," he said.

Most observers have found a relationship between the outstanding success of all the brothers and the family's financial insecurities. Arthur, the eldest, became a successful Kansas City banker; Edgar, a prominent Seattle attorney; Roy, a pharmacist; Earl, an engineer and newspaper and public-relations man; Milton, an educator and adviser to eight American Presidents. Ike always scoffed at this.

"If we were poor—and I'm not sure that we were by the standards of the day—we were unaware of it," he said.

There can be no contesting, however, the stark difference between the childhood homes of Ike and Mamie.

The Eisenhowers lived, quite literally, on the wrong side of the tracks. Abilene is bisected by the Union Pacific Railroad, once the Kansas Pacific, whose rails formed a line separating the rich and poor. On the north lived the town's affluent citizens—its doctors, bankers, merchants, and lawyers; the working people, those employed by the railroad, the Creamery, the carpenters, and plumbers were "Southsiders." Until Dwight was eight years old, the Eisenhowers lived in a small house on a tiny plot near the tracks. Later, they were able to move to a larger house owned by an uncle.

Abilene was, and still is, a very small town. In Ike's growing-up years the streets were unpaved, dusty in summer, hard-frozen in winter, and puddled for days after rains. The sidewalks were wooden planks nailed together and raised a few feet above the street. After a heavy downpour, these boardwalks would invariably loosen from their moorings and float crazily like the wobbly walkways at an amusement park; only the reckless, or those in dire need of going somewhere, would try to maneuver across them until they dried.

The main street, as in small communities everywhere, was lined with shops: the grocer, the pharmacist, the butcher, the dry-goods store, the hardware merchant. There was even a village smithy! In values, outlook, and location, Abilene was middle America. Just twenty miles to the northeast was Fort Riley, the geographic midpoint of the United States.

Abilene was not always a decent, law-abiding, and God-fearing place. Shortly after the Civil War, the town was one of the wildest and most sinful in the entire Midwest. The end of the famed Chisholm Trail, over which a million long-horned cattle were driven north from Texas for shipment to Chicago and Kansas City, it accommodated the saloons, gambling houses, and dance halls frequented by the hard-drinking cowboys on the cattle run. By 1871, however, the townspeople had their fill of the gamblers, prostitutes, and other unsavory characters crowding the town; they hired Wild Bill Hickok, the famous "two-gun marshal" to restore law and order.

Today the only trace of those lusty times is a tourist attraction, "Old Abilene Town," a six-block reconstruction of the community during the cattle-boom days. A few of the original buildings of the period remain, some converted into shops selling food and Wild West souvenirs. Youngsters can climb aboard an authentic stagecoach driven by a ten-gallon-hatted cowboy for a ride through the town.

Abilene's streets are paved now and along Buckeye Avenue, which is Route 15, there are supermarkets, fried chicken and pizza stands, and several modern motels. There are no skyscrapers, no elegant shops, no signs of sophistication.

To an out-of-town visitor, the buildings in town that really matter are the ones that comprise the Eisenhower Center. These buff-colored structures of Kansas limestone include the Dwight D. Eisenhower Library of Presidential papers and documents, the Eisenhower Museum of war and peacetime memorabilia, the family home, a set of pylons presented by the Kansas Daughters of the American Revolution and the Soroptomists Clubs of Kansas and a peaceful little all-faiths chapel called the Place of Meditation. The buildings, which surround broad green lawns and flowered walks, seem incongruous in the middle of a small Kansas town, yet they attract some 500,000 visitors each year, including scholars and students from all over the world.

Most of them go into the Place of Meditation and admire the richly colored windows, the travertine wall panels, and the walnut woodwork. Ike and Mamie are buried side by side here, their last resting places marked by bronze plaques.

The Eisenhower family (the original spelling was Eisenhauer) came to Abilene by way of Pennsylvania. The name means iron hewer and family legends describe their ancestors as armored warriors in a medieval German army. All ties to militarism were eschewed later when they became followers of Menno Simons, founder of the Mennonite movement who preached pacifism and a belief in the Bible as the principle authority for religion. During the Thirty Years' War, the Eisenhower forbears fled the Palatinate of Bavaria for Switzerland to escape religious persecution. Later they moved to Holland for a brief period and then sailed on the *Europa* to the New World. In Philadelphia, on November 20, 1741, Hans Nicol Eisenhauer and the two oldest of three sons took an oath of allegiance to the English colony, founded sixty years before by William Penn.

These first Eisenhowers in this country—by the 1790 census the spelling had been changed—settled in Bethel Township in Lancaster County where they were often subject to attack by bands of marauding Indians, encouraged by the French who were warring with England.

Peter, the eldest son, inherited his father's property which he sold in 1779 when he moved his family to a 170-acre farm near Harrisburg. Another son, Frederick, was killed fighting the English in the War of the Revolution. Another son, who was also named Frederick after the death of his brother, was Ike's great-grandfather.

This Frederick, a skilled weaver, married Barbara Miller, five years older but also of Germanic descent and a member of the River Brethren, a Mennonite sect which derived its name from the location of its original members near the Susquehanna River. The couple used her dowry to build a three-story frame house on a hill outside of Millersburg where Barbara lived. Here Frederick installed his looms on which he wove bedspreads, table linen, and shirts, and raised his family of six children.

One of them, Jacob, became a prosperous farmer and an influential minister. He married Rebecca Matter of Elizabethville and in 1854 built a two-story, nine-room house on a hundred acres he purchased at the outskirts of the town. It was to serve him as home and as a meeting place for his congregation. Spelling bees, socials, as well as prayer meetings and church services were held in the front parlor and no one in need of food or a bed was ever turned away.

With the end of the Civil War and the push of the railroads farther west, the pioneer spirit that was developing in the East began to infect even the prosperous farmers of the lush Pennsylvania valley. Younger members of the River Brethren began to press for a mass migration and by the end of the 1870s plans were well under way.

Jacob Eisenhower sold his home, farmland, and orchards and boarded a train at Elizabethville with his wife, four children, and 84-year-old father, Frederick. At Harrisburg they were joined by his sister, Catherine, and his brother, Samuel, and their families. The destination was Abilene in Dickinson County, Kansas, a site carefully scouted by the River Brethren. They took fifteen carloads of household belongings and farm implements, including a wagon, so farming could start immediately.

Jacob purchased a 160-acre farm south of the Smoky Hill River and continued with his life exactly as he had in Pennsylvania. He worked his land weekdays; Sundays he ministered to his flock.

David, his oldest son, had little interest in the farm and persuaded his father to send him to Lane University, a small college operated by the United Brethren Church at Lecompton, Kansas, where he hoped to prepare for an engineering career. At the start of his second term he met a pretty girl named Ida Elizabeth Stover, and she changed his life-plan.

Ida, too, was descended from a family which had left Germany for Switzerland to avoid religious hatreds. In the 1730s her great-grandfather, Jacob, and his brother, Christian, emigrated to America where he settled in the Shenandoah Valley in Virginia. Ida's mother died when she was seven and she lived with an uncle until she was twenty-one, when she joined an older brother in Kansas.

In 1883, at a time when higher education for women was hardly widespread and, moreover, was frowned upon by her own sect, a determined Ida used her small inheritance to enroll at Lane University. Comely, vivacious, and outgoing, she attracted young David immediately. Before the year was out, they became engaged.

They were married on September 23, 1885, his twenty-second birthday, in the chapel of Lane University by the

Reverend E. B. Slade of the United Brethren Church of Lecompton. A framed marriage certificate, bearing their pictures, hangs on the wall of the front parlor of the home, now part of the Eisenhower Memorial.

College was abandoned. Jacob Eisenhower's wedding gift was two thousand dollars in cash and a 160-acre farm, but David, who still resisted becoming a farmer, mortgaged the property and put all the money into a general store in the nearby village of Hope, in partnership with Milton D. Good, an Abilene clerk.

For a time the picture was bright. Business was brisk and the young Eisenhowers were part of an active social set. In November 1886 Ida gave birth to their first child, a son, Arthur.

By the fall of 1888, however, it was apparent the store was in trouble. The partners had allowed their customers to run up large bills and, in turn, could not pay their own creditors. One night Good slipped out of town, taking with him the small amount of cash left in the coffers.

David Eisenhower appointed a local lawyer to sell the store's assets and pay off its creditors. Then he left for Denison, Texas, and a job in the machine shop of the Cotton Belt Railroad at a salary of about forty dollars a month. Ida, who was pregnant again, remained in Abilene until Edgar, their second child, was born. Accompanied by the two little boys, she boarded a train for Texas where her husband had rented a small frame house facing the railroad tracks on the edge of town.

David Dwight Eisenhower, their third son, was born there on October 14, 1890. Ida called him Dwight to avoid confusion with his father and the transposition of names continued throughout his life.*

*Another reason was her dislike of nicknames. She felt David would quickly become "Dave." When Ike went to school, however, his classmates thought "Ike" went well with Eisenhower, so Dwight became "Little Ike" and Edgar "Big Ike." Years later, Milton and Earl were given the same nicknames.

Ike's parents were quite unlike each other. Both were deeply religious, living by the Ten Commandments and raising their children by them, but his mother was as outgoing, cheerful and gregarious as his father was introspective, gentle, and dreamy. Despite a chronic shortage of money, Ida ran her household with a brisk optimism, allowing no long faces and no complaints. There rarely were any from the boys but Ike's father needed almost continual cheering up. Embarrassed by his business failure, worried about his inability to provide for his family, disliking Texas, and missing the life he had left back in Abilene, he was frequently melancholy. Ida spent much of her time buoying him up.

When Chris Musser, a brother-in-law who was foreman of the new Belle Springs Creamery plant in Abilene, offered him a job, David happily accepted. "The money's no better than I'm making here," he told Ida, "but at least we'll be able to go back home." Ida beamed, told the boys, and in a few days they had packed and were on their way.

For the next seven years, the Eisenhowers lived in a small house on South East Second Street, so tiny that personal privacy was almost nonexistent and with a play area so limited even the ever-cheerful Ida threw up her hands. "I spend all my time keeping the boys quiet and out of other people's yards," she said. "It's a terrible strain on them, and on me." In 1898, when Ike was eight, Abraham Lincoln Eisenhower, David's brother, decided to seek his fortune farther west and rented them his house on South East Fourth. By this time, there were two more Eisenhower boys, Roy and Earl. (A third, Paul, had died at three months.)

"For the first time," Ida told a friend, "we have a home where my children will have room to play." If Ida was happy about the increased space in the new home, Ike never noticed that he and his brothers had been especially cramped in the old one. As far as he was concerned, he said later, there had been nothing wrong with the tiny house.

It is difficult for a visitor to appreciate Ida Eisenhower's enthusiasm for the increased space. The house—the new *larger* house—was almost doll-like. How Ida Eisenhower ran a household of six boys, a husband, and a father-in-law there was something of a minor miracle. Yet Ida loved the place and lived in it until she died in her bedroom on September 11, 1946, at the age of eighty-four.

Ida and David and his father occupied the two simply furnished bedrooms on the first floor and the boys shared the upstairs rooms, with Edgar and Ike sleeping in the back bedroom. There is no door separating the front and back parlors, modestly furnished with an eclectic mix of upholstered pieces and wooden tables and chairs. A beige, blue, and gold Persian-type rug covers the floor and, near the doorway, on a small table is the family Bible where one can easily read the page, carefully preserved under glass, on which David, in a flowing script, recorded the birth of his sons.

The dining room is the largest in the house. There was no inside bathroom until 1908 when one was built in what had been the grandfather's bedroom. The present kitchen was added in 1915.

At the rear of the house was the barn, a huge affair with many stalls and an operating room where Dwight's uncle, a veterinarian, had ministered to his animal patients. The Eisenhowers kept cows and chickens which, along with the sizable amount of vegetables and fruit they raised, helped feed the family. Mrs. Eisenhower carefully rotated the chores to even each boys' load. In their free time they rode, swam, cooked out, hunted, fished, and explored the countryside for adventure and fun. It was a Tom Sawyer–Huck Finn kind of boyhood, but only after school and working hours.

"I used to help [Ike] clean out the barn and haul in the hay," Levi Asper says. "He had to milk the cow and feed the chickens and gather the eggs. I remember just before

Easter we'd snitch an egg a night and hide it some place so we'd have about a half dozen, and then we'd take them down along the river and cook them."

When spring rains swelled Mud Creek and Smoky Hill River, Ike and Levi got out their lines and went down river to fish for carp and catfish. Asper remembered one expedition which resulted in an embarrassing problem. He and Ike lost a horse.

They had packed a lunch and borrowed his family's mare which they rode to the river. They tethered the animal in a grassy spot while they waded into the water with their lines.

"When we came back from fishing he was gone," Asper recalled. "He stayed down along the river for pretty near a week before we found him. When we got home the folks didn't know what we'd done with him. They were pretty mad about it."

Playing in the flooded waters was not without some risk. Once Ike and Edgar came uncomfortably close to serious trouble. Snagging a large piece of wooden sidewalk loosened by the rains, they climbed aboard and, paddling with their hands, sailed along Buckeye Street toward the river, singing "Marching Through Georgia" at the top of their lungs. Had they remained aboard the makeshift raft when it reached the main body of the river, they might have been swept along the current and come to grief upon the submerged rocks. Luckily, a man on horseback spotted them in time, ordered them off the planking, and sent them hustling back to town.

For the first six grades, Ike attended the Lincoln School on Chestnut Street, facing the Eisenhower backyard, but when he reached seventh grade he transferred to the Garfield School where he encountered North-side–South-side hostilities.

The antagonisms between the two groups was "plenty strong," Asper said. "I remember we wouldn't let the North-side kids south of the Union Pacific tracks if we could catch them, and they wouldn't allow us north of the track.

We would go uptown, but if we got north of town, why, it meant a fight."

The year Ike turned thirteen, it meant a fight between Dwight and Wesley Merrifield, the stocky North-side champion, a fight which Asper says was "quite a tussle." Dwight, taller but slender and many pounds lighter, and Wes each seemed to have been selected to uphold the honor of his side of town.

One afternoon after school, trailed by dozens of their classmates, they went to a vacant lot on Third and Broadway for the battle. Merrifield struck the first blows, blackening both of Dwight's eyes, one after the other. Dwight fought back, searching for openings and then hitting hard.

Both boys were tiring but neither would give up. It lasted well over an hour, with each boy giving and taking hard, bruising blows. Finally, spent and battered, Merrifield admitted weakly, "Ike, I can't lick you."

And Ike replied, "Well, Wes, I haven't licked you."

His bruises kept him out of school for three days. Years afterward, Ike described the event as a case of two young boys unable to hold out against peer pressure. "Neither of us," he said, "had the courage to say, 'I won't fight.'"

In 1904 Dwight entered Abilene High, then located on the first floor of the City Hall. Although most biographers have referred to him as an "average" student, records indicate that in history and geometry, his chief enthusiasms, his grades were near-perfect and in other subjects his marks were in the high eighties and nineties.

Baseball and football were his main interests, however, and he devoted all the time he could spare from his studies and a succession of part-time jobs to practice.

An accidental fall one afternoon threatened to end his athletic career and—almost—his life. Walking home from school, he stumbled over a brick and skinned his left knee. Several mornings later, he awoke with a bad ache in that leg and a black streak running along it. Ida Eisenhower sent for Dr. Tracy R. Conklin, the family physician, who made an ominous diagnosis.

It was, Doc Conklin said, blood poisoning, against which, in those preantibiotic days, there was little medical defense. Pointing to the black streak, he said, "This is serious. If that reaches his abdomen, he'll die. The only way I can save him is to amputate."

When the doctor took Mrs. Eisenhower into the hall, Dwight told Edgar, "Don't let them operate. I'd rather die than lose my leg. I mean it. I'm counting on you to stop them."

"I promised," Edgar recalled. "Ike asked me to remain in the room and 'keep them away from me.' "

That night when Ike's fever rose he began to sink into a coma and the doctor again suggested an operation. Ike's parents were deeply worried and confused. Edgar planted himself in the doorway, feet wide apart.

"Nobody's going to touch Dwight," he told Doc fiercely. "You're not going to operate on his leg." The doctor looked at him, shook his head, and walked away.

Edgar spread blankets on the floor and slept beside the bed for two nights, guarding his brother. He permitted Doc Conklin only to change dressings and put carbolic acid on the wound. In the morning and evening, the family prayed for Ike's recovery, though Ike has denied an oft-repeated story of a two-week-long prayer vigil. "They were not faith healers," he said.

On the third day, the fever broke and the black streak lightened and began to recede. Three weeks later, Dwight was on his feet.

Ike often stopped at the Abilene office of the *Dickinson County News,* a weekly newspaper, to wait for his friend Six (John F.) McDonnell.* Six, who had an after-school job there, introduced him to Joe W. Howe, the editor and a leading figure in the local Democratic Party, who became

---

*Six acquired his nickname after his class attended an art show which included Raphael's famous Sistine Madonna. To the prankish young-sters, McDonnell sounded like Madonna, so John soon found himself being called Sistine, later shortened to Sis and finally Six.

fond of Ike and permitted him to read the exchange newspapers from other cities and to borrow history books from his personal library.

In his oral history at the Eisenhower Library, Six points out that Ike was a Democrat then and had been selected by Howe to make the student speech at a convention. "He wouldn't have made the speech if he hadn't been, because Joe was the head of the Democratic Central Committee," Six says. "He wanted a boy that had a Democratic viewpoint to make the speech and I guess he talked Ike into it. Ike made a hell of a speech. He's a good talker."

When Ike decided to run for the Presidency as the Republican candidate, Howe, then in retirement in Emporia, Kansas, was upset and said so in a letter to McDonnell.

"He wrote me about four times, I think, and I'd write him back," McDonnell recalled. "The last time I almost scolded him, telling him to quit worrying about such a thing."

McDonnell told Howe, "Even if he thought he was a Democrat when he was a boy, there's nothing wrong with him changing his viewpoint. The world differs every four, five years, you know, and if he wants to be a Republican that's his right, and don't you worry about it."

In those days, however, Ike was more interested in athletics than politics. He and Edgar played football and baseball and when the school authorities were unable to fund the teams, they founded the Abilene High School Association, with Dwight as the first president, to raise money.

As a small town boy, Ike spent at least part of his time in the local pool hall, a place of somewhat low repute, though Six McDonnell views it differently. "I ought to say something good about the pool halls in those days," he says. "They had a bad reputation, but now, take me for instance. I didn't have any home after I was seventeen years old, of any kind. The pool hall was my country club and it also was Dwight's and a lot of other guys."

The fellows would gather at the Beagle and Spader Billiard Hall on Broadway, just south of the Citizens National Bank. "Everybody would meet everybody there," Six says, "and they weren't roughnecks. Bert Beagle was a fine man, and there never was a bit of trouble."

There was, nonetheless, some hustling going on, and one afternoon after school Ike was a victim. He was taken for all the cash he had, which wasn't much but it left him broke for two weeks.

McDonnell tells the story: "Bert had a fellow name of Kindy Rogers, and he was the ball racker in there. He was a cute little old guy, and he'd act much dumber than he really was. He liked to get in an argument with you or someone else there about some fighter or something, then he'd make a bet. Well, I knew all this; I knew him better than Dwight did. We were in there one day and Dwight had a couple of bucks and I had about fifteen cents.

"So here was Kindy and he got to talking about Stanley [Ketchel] and Billy Papke, you can recall those great middleweights. Well, I knew if Kindy was leading up to a bet, that he knew what he was talking about, because the only book he ever read was the *World Almanac,* that's where he got all his information. He makes an outlandish statement, he says, 'Billy Papke whipped Stanley Ketchel, three straight times or at least two out of three.'

"And Dwight said, 'Oh, he never whipped him in his life.'

"'I betcha two dollars that he whipped him twice,' says Kindy.

"Ike says, 'You've got a bet, that's all I've got or I'd betcha a hundred.'

"I held stakes, and I kept kicking Dwight in the shins to lay off this bet, but he was so confident and just said, 'Well, now how you going to prove it? You want me to go over to the newspaper?'

"And Kindy said, 'No, I'll go right across the street there to the book store.' So he come back with the book and there was the listing, Papke beat Ketchel such and such a date and the next year he beat him again. And I had to pay off and old Dwight did too. I laughed about that a million times. Now there was a guy that wasn't very smart at all, and Dwight was very intelligent, but he got took in with this guy."

Despite the two-year difference in their ages, Edgar and Dwight were in the same graduating class at high school because the former had dropped out of school for two years. Senior-class festivities included the presentation of a play based loosely on Shakespeare's *The Merchant of Venice,* in which Dwight played the role of Launcelot Gobbo, a servant of Shylock. The school yearbook, *Helianthus,* made some interesting prophesies about the Eisenhower brothers: Edgar, it said, someday would become President of the United States. Dwight would teach history—his favorite subject—at Yale.

The boys wanted to continue their schooling, but although both parents had continually stressed the value of a college education, they could not help with the necessary funds. So Ike and Edgar made a unique pact to help each other. Each boy would work for a year and send his earnings to his brother, then switch the next year. Since Edgar knew what he wanted to do—study law at the University of Michigan—and Ike did not, it was decided that Edgar would attend school first.

That summer Ike worked first on a farm, then in a factory making steel grain bins, then at the Creamery, switching to whatever job paid the most. At one, he spent his days with his friend Abram Forney lifting three hundred pounds of ice and dumping them down a chute for $32.50 a month. Later he was promoted to the night shift and raised to $90 as an engineering technician.

At twenty young Eisenhower was a tall, good-looking young man with blond hair, broad shoulders, and an engaging grin. Though, in later years, Ike was introduced to Mamie as a "woman-hater," both Asper and McDonnell remember he dated often, mostly blond, blue-eyed Gladys Harding and redheaded Ruby Norman.

His chief concern, however, was his future. He had been out of school a year. He wanted to go to college—but where? And what should he study? His prospects seemed vague and uncertain.

He had many long discussions with Swede Hazlett, a high school friend who would drop by the Creamery in the evenings. Swede, whose full name was Everett E. Hazlett, Jr., had received a Congressional appointment to Annapolis and was cramming for the entrance examinations. With great enthusiasm he described the glories of the naval academy and Dwight listened intently.

"Being kids, more or less, we also weren't above raiding the company's refrigerating room occasionally, for ice cream, eggs, and chickens which we cooked on a well-scrubbed shovel in the boiler room," recalled Hazlett.

Mainly, however, they just talked and Hazlett, who was to rise to the rank of commander in the United States Navy, detected a more than casual interest on Ike's part.

"Why don't you try for an appointment, too?" he suggested.

"What chance have I got?" Ike asked. "You already have the only appointment available from the district."

Swede's appointment, however, came from his Congressman and he advised Ike to apply to the two Kansas Senators. Vacancies for both West Point and Annapolis existed, Senator Joseph L. Bristow wrote back, and invited Ike to take the competitive examinations for the service academies to be held in Topeka.

Ike spent the next few weeks studying with Swede every afternoon and in November took the examinations. He came out first in the competition for Annapolis and second for West Point. However, because he would be past twenty by the June entrance date, he was ineligible for Annapolis. When the man who placed first in the West Point competition failed to meet the physical standards, Senator Bristow gave the appointment to Ike. In January he took the West Point entrance examination, passed, and was ordered to report on June 14, 1911.

David and Ida Eisenhower, life-long pacifists, were deeply disturbed by their son's choice of school but they did not interfere or oppose his decision. Years later Milton told Ike he heard their mother cry for the first time in his life after Ike departed for West Point. Ike continued to work at the Creamery and play ball with his old friends until it was time to leave.

Six McDonnell says when Ike was making his farewells he asked him to look out for Gladys Harding. "Call her up once in a while, and if she's lonesome or something, go down and take her out to the picture show or something," Six quotes Ike as saying.

Gladys was a very pretty, popular girl and Six happily complied with Ike's request, until he left town to play professional baseball. When his team was scheduled to play near Abilene, he got time off to go home, intending to see Gladys.

"I hired a guy to drive me from Enterprise to Abilene," Six recalled. "I was going to say, 'Let me off here,' but you know who was sitting in the yard—Dwight Eisenhower with his West Point uniform on and Gladys were sitting on a couple of chairs out there in the nice green grass."

Six said he told the driver to just keep on going.

3. "The Girl I Run Around With"

LATE IN JUNE of 1911 Ike boarded an evening train at the Abilene station, bound for the Point. Ruby Norman was studying violin at the Chicago Conservatory of Music, so he stopped off to see her. They spent several days together, talking about his future and hers as they walked along the lakefront. There was another stopover, this one at Ann Arbor to visit Edgar at the University of Michigan.

On an unusually hot day he trudged up the hill from the railway station to the grounds of the United States Military Academy, one of 265 plebes, the largest class yet to be admitted to the Point.

Ike's experiences growing up in a large family and his ability to please many bosses along the way had prepared him well for the rigors of Beast Barracks. He raced up and down the stairs, polished his brass, cleaned his rifle, swept his room, and saluted everybody. In those first two months, which the Academy admits is the most strenuous period training cadets encounter during their entire four years, Ike

53

did almost everything in double-quick time and, in addition, underwent hazing which is the lot of all plebes. He "braced," plastering his back to the wall as he stood for hours in an exaggerated position of attention, chin pushed into his neck, stomach sucked in, every muscle constrained. He "swam to Newburgh" lying full length on a five-inch partition separating the cots in his room from the study area and rotating his arms in a swimming motion. The city of Newburgh is on the Hudson ten miles above the Academy and it takes a while to reach it. Ike "swam" until an upperclassman told him to stop. He "sat on infinity," easing himself into a chair that wasn't there, remaining "seated" until released. He took the stairs in the barracks two at a time, and "no touching the banister even with sixty pounds of equipment on your back." *

Ike later said the whole performance struck him as "funny" but admitted it was strenuous and "for some approached the unendurable." He himself endured, however, and once nonplused some upperclassmen by a too-literal obedience to an order. Told to come out after taps for some disciplining, he was instructed to "wear full-dress coat with cross belt." He showed up at the appointed time and stood stiffly at attention. The upperclassmen gaped: Eisenhower looked elegant in his full-dress coat with snow-white cross belt, but below the waist his attire was less than military. He wore no pants. Eyes straight ahead, shoulders back, Cadet Eisenhower replied innocently to the question about his incomplete attire: "Nothing was said about trousers, sir."

Still more excited by athletics than academics, Ike went out for football (he made the plebe team), baseball, track,

---

* Hazing has been ended at the Point, replaced by "corrective treatment" under which no upperclassman may do anything to a plebe which is humiliating, degrading, or demoralizing. They no longer "swim" to Newburgh. Once a retired general, unaware of the changes, visited Beast Barracks and asked the plebes, "How long does it take you fellows to get to Newburgh these days?" After a moment's silence, one young man spoke up: "About fifteen minutes, sir—by Army truck."

and boxing. During the 1912 season Army coaches, who had followed his early progress, selected him to understudy Geoffrey Keyes, a first-year man who played left halfback. When Keyes was injured in practice, Eisenhower took over, earning acclaim from the *New York Times* as "one of the most promising backs in Eastern football."

Ike twisted his knee when Army played the Carlisle Indian School team, whose mainstay was the All-American Jim Thorpe. Subsequently it was reinjured in the next game against Tufts and he was carried from the field. This time the knee was broken and he spent weeks in the hospital. When doctors released him for duty, they warned against mounting and dismounting riding exercises. However, an overzealous instructor challenged this, so Eisenhower said no more and participated in the drill for hours. He ended up back in the hospital where he was told that his football days were over.

He had more free time now but he was not inclined to spend it studying. Disinterested in grades, he studied only enough to make the top third of his class. As for conduct, he was hardly a model cadet.

He collected demerits handily and ranked 125th in conduct, out of 164 men, in his final year and 95th for his entire West Point career. However, as he later pointed out: "This to me was of small moment. I enjoyed life at the Academy, had a good time with my pals, and was far from disturbed by an additional demerit or two."

Once, while dancing with the daughter of one of the professors, he was reprimanded for rapidly whirling around the room in a manner the older, more sedate officers considered too lively.

Some weeks later, the two again met at a dance and Ike, forgetting the previous incident, spun his partner around the room even faster than before. This time he was ordered to appear before the commandant where he was punished, not only for improper dancing, but for doing it after having received a warning.

Ike had continued to correspond with Ruby, who was performing with a concert company. At one point they discussed meeting in New York during the Christmas holidays when cadets were allowed eight-day furloughs. In a short note on November 20, 1913, scrawled on West Point stationery, Ike told "dear little Ruby" that a meeting in the city might not be wise. Reading between the lines, one can assume that the young Ike did not completely trust his West Point discipline to control the situation.

"Since you sort of asked my opinion on the matter I'll tell you this," Ike wrote. "Remember this is a 'disinterested opinion'—as nearly as possible. Well then, go home on Xmas vacation. I'd sure love to see you—but, well, I believe you'd enjoy yourself in the end by going home. Anyway, nothing can happen which will prevent us being just as good friends as always—and if you'd spend your vacation in N.Y. we don't know *what* might happen. All very vague, I grant you, but meant well."

Despite his fondness for Ruby it is plain that Ike was playing the field.

A few days later, on November 24, he wrote again that he had invited "an old friend" to come down from Vassar for the Saturday-night hop at West Point. "So Ike gets out his full-dress coat and plays the devoted swain for a day or so— and me president of the roughnecks" he told Ruby.

Then, in an addition which must have confused her, he said that "my wife [West Point slang for roommate] took it on himself to remark that I might be one of those *indifferent* fellows but I certainly snagged onto Ruby's letter in an awful big hurry."

Graduation approached and Ike applied for duty in the Philippines. To his disappointment and chagrin (he had already purchased a full set of tropical uniforms) trouble on the Mexican border resulted in his being posted to the Nineteenth Infantry, stationed in Galveston, Texas. When he arrived there he found a flood had forced the transfer of his outfit to Fort Sam Houston.

The next morning Ike took the train for historic San Antonio, setting of the Battle of the Alamo, a sunny, warm, city, which many wealthy Northern families had adopted as a winter residence.

Dearest Ruby,
'Tis a long time since I've written you, n'est-ce-pas? I've really started several times—but always something happens and I get side-tracked. It's 10 o'clock now—I'm on guard—and sitting in the guard house—
I scarcely ever write a letter any more. Yes—I reckon you'll say—"well, what's the trouble"—but there isn't so much. One reason is this "you can't always hold what you have"—my life here, is, in the main uninteresting. Nothing much doing—and I get tired of the same old grind some times.
The girl I run around with is named Miss Doud, from Denver. Pretty nice—but awful strong for society—which often bores me. But we get along well together—and I'm at her house whenever I'm off duty—whether it's morning, noon, night. Her mother and sisters are fun—and we have lots of fun together.

This engaging letter, published here for the first time, was written from Fort Sam Houston on January 17, 1916. It acknowledges, though one strongly suspects with a pretended indifference, that someone important had come into his life.

By this time, any romantic attachment that might have existed between Ike and Ruby had turned into a good friendship, which was to last all their lives. (Later Ruby married Ralph Lucie and settled down in St. Louis, where she raised many children and became a strong supporter of Ike's candidacy for President. She died in 1967, having kept up a lifelong correspondence with Eisenhower.)

Ike met the girl he ran around with in October 1915 when the Douds, on their customary Sunday-afternoon drive, stopped at Fort Sam to visit friends Major and Mrs. Hunter

Harris. Ike, officer of the day, had stepped out of the red-brick Bachelor Officers' Quarters when he was hailed by Lulu Harris.

"Come here, Ike," she called. "I want to introduce you to some friends."

At first he demurred. "I have to start my inspection tour," he called out but, catching a glimpse of Mamie, whom he later described as "saucy in the look about her face," he quickly changed his mind and crossed the lawn separating the barracks from the Harris home. After chatting for a few minutes, he invited her to take a walk with him.

Mamie, handicapped by her long, Empire-waisted pink cretonne skirt, tightly laced beige shoes, and a wide-brimmed straw hat which she had to clutch against the Texas breeze, agreed, nevertheless, to accompany him.

"He was different from anyone else I knew," she explained. "I think it was probably his vitality that appealed to me."

Still, Ike did not rise all that quickly in the ranks of Mamie's suitors. Pretty, popular, and an outrageous flirt, she did not lack for escorts. Usually, her engagement calendar was booked several weekends in advance during her stays in San Antonio; so when the new second lieutenant, returning her to the house, asked for a date, he was told that, regretfully, the next three Saturdays were taken. Ike had time, and patience as well. "Then make it the fourth Saturday," he said. And she did.

Ike was plainly smitten. On off hours, he showed up regularly at the Doud home, sometimes announcing his arrival in advance but just as often coming unexpectedly. He took Mamie out for inexpensive Mexican dinners at a place called The Original and to the local movie, the Orpheum, which presented six acts of vaudeville following the picture.

Eisenhower devised a strategy to make the competition suspect that he had the inside track. When Mamie had other dates, he would go to the house and talk all evening long with Min Doud. "I'd hang around until midnight," he said, "and let the other guys see me when Mamie got back." They soon got the point and by Christmas Ike had eliminated many of his rivals.

The romance blossomed. Ike was a big hit with the Douds who invited him regularly for Sunday dinners and even family celebrations. When Ike became coach of the local military school's football team, he asked them to the games and they came to cheer him on.

Ike gave Mamie an elegant and expensive silver heart-shaped jewel box engraved with her initials, and although the Douds, in those more formal days, thought it was somewhat daring they permitted Mamie to keep it.

On Valentine's Day, 1916, they were formally engaged. Ike had sent to the Philadelphia firm of Bailey, Banks and Biddle for a duplicate of his gold and amethyst West Point ring, which he presented to Mamie.

The wedding was planned for November in Mamie's Denver home and the Douds went back to make preparations. When word got around, Eileen Archibold recalls that the neighbors on Lafayette Street were astounded at Mamie's choice.

"To begin with," Mrs. Archibold said, "everybody thought Mamie was much too young to get married. Then, the Douds were well off financially, and with all the other beaux she had, they felt Mamie could have done a good deal better. After all, he was only a soldier and a poor boy, and everybody felt he was marrying above his class."

Some of John Doud's neighbors took it upon themselves to warn him about the future. Army life, they told him, was unstable at best. "'Look,' one said," Mrs. Archibold remembers, "'if Mamie does marry that fellow, she'll never in her life have a home of her own.'" The warning was prophetic but if John Doud took it seriously he gave no sign. Min and he had developed a considerable fondness for the genial, open-faced young man and, though they harbored misgivings about their admittedly spoiled daughter's ability to cope with the stringencies of Army life, they encouraged the match.

Ike pushed for an earlier wedding date. Europe was at war and German submarines already had attacked and sunk American ships. Also, a series of punitive expeditions against Mexican bandits made it likely that he would be sent into action in some part of the world soon.

He called Mamie and explained the situation. She conferred with her parents and they agreed to a wedding as soon as he could get to Denver. When Ike's commanding officer granted a ten-day furlough, the date was advanced four months.

On July 1 Ike, his starched dress uniform sparkling white, his brass buttons gleaming, stood before the music room fireplace which had been banked with pink gladioli. A harpist, hidden on the hall landing, played softly as Mamie drifted down the staircase on her father's arm.

She smiled radiantly, a lovely and graceful bride in a floor-length dress of off-white Chantilly lace. A pale pink cummerbund circled her slender waist and in her arms was a wedding bouquet of white lily of the valley and pale pink roses.

Mamie had wanted an intimate wedding so only the family was present when Dr. William Williamson, taking the place of the regular minister who was on vacation, performed the ceremony. Later the Douds sent the following announcement to friends and relatives:

Mr. and Mrs. John Sheldon Doud
announce the marriage of their daughter
Mamie Geneva
to
Mr. Dwight D. Eisenhower
Lieutenant, United States Army
on Saturday, July the first
Nineteen hundred and sixteen
Denver, Colorado

After the ceremony, everybody moved into the dining room for a gala dinner, complete with champagne and wedding cake which Ike cut with his sword. Mamie changed into a silk dress and Ike into a gray suit and they left for an overnight stay at Eldorado Springs, a fashionable canyon resort thirty-two miles out of Denver. They knew their honeymoon would be short—but they didn't realize how short.

Noon of the following day, the newlyweds were having lunch in the hotel dining room when Ike looked up and nearly fell out of his seat. He turned to Mamie, consternation erasing his smile. "Mamie," he demanded, "what are your parents doing here?"

In the doorway was his father-in-law, his mother-in-law, and the two younger Doud girls. Doud, reasoning that his daughter and her new husband would be "more comfortable" riding back in the family Packard, had awakened everybody early so they could drive to Eldorado Springs and surprise the couple.

Nowhere in Ike's memoirs does he detail his reaction to this "surprise," but it is difficult to imagine that either he or Mamie were especially appreciative of the gesture. Nevertheless they went back with Mamie's family to Lafayette Street where Ike, ever the romantic, tried to preserve the bridal bouquet by dipping it in wax. He shaved a large candle and placed a panful of wax on the stove. When it melted, he dipped some of the flowers into the hot liquid. They shriveled instantly. He tried sprinkling a few drops of hot wax over the surviving petals, but that didn't work either. So out went the bouquet.

At midnight, they boarded the Union Pacific train East for Mamie's first meeting with her in-laws. It was a long, tiring journey, through the night and the next day and night, before they arrived at Abilene's tiny railroad station about four A.M. They were met by David Eisenhower who loaded the bags into his buggy and drove to the Eisenhower home where Ida was waiting.

Milton and Earl awakened for the introduction and by nine o'clock the family—and many of the neighbors who had been invited to meet Ike's bride—sat down to a breakfast of fried chicken, potato salad, pies, jams, and jellies.

Ike spent the next two days showing Mamie, a product of much more sophisticated Denver and San Antonio, what it had been like to grow up in a very small town. They went to his boyhood haunts, visited his schools and his various places of employment.

On the third day of their marriage came their first quarrel.

Ike decided to stroll downtown alone and look up some of his friends. He promised to be back for supper but wasn't.

After an hour, the roast shriveling in the oven, Mamie became alarmed, which turned to annoyance when Ike's mother, Ida Eisenhower, told her he had probably sat into a poker game with "the boys." When time passed and he still did not return, her mood changed quickly to exasperation, then downright anger. A few calls located Ike in the back room of a local café—in a poker game.

Mamie: "You come home *this minute!*"

Ike: "Now, now, Mamie, I'm losing money and can't quit. It won't be long . . ."

Mamie (in full fury): "If you don't come home this minute, you needn't bother to come home at all!"

Mamie crashed the earpiece of the telephone into its hook and stormed into her room. But Ike did not return home as ordered. Hours after midnight, he finally showed up. Mamie was still awake and fuming; the quarrel that followed lasted until dawn.

It was the first, but not the last, in the many years they had together.

PART TWO

Army Years

1. The Loneliness of the Army Wife

DESPITE MAMIE'S RICH-girl upbringing, a frontier outlook had been bred into her. After all, the city she grew up in had been a Pony Express stop only a few years before she was born. The women of Mamie's station in life were only a generation or two removed from forebears who had rumbled over the dusty roads into town by wagon train. Photographs of the settlers, the babies they delivered by the side of the road in their westward trek, and their overalled husbands stood prominently in living rooms, not forgotten ancestors but real presences fresh in memory.

This pioneering spirit was surely in the people of Mamie's generation. She, too, though physically frail all her life, possessed strength, resilience, and, most of all, adaptability.

She had weaknesses she could neither hide nor conquer, personality characteristics that were to cause problems between her and her husband. But, in the main, she was strong enough, and bright and cheery enough, to cope with the life she accepted.

For the next half-century, beginning at age nineteen, she was to live in thirty-seven different places around the world from a bat-infested shanty in the tropics to palaces with footmen to wait upon her and, ultimately, in the White House.* While she did not adore each of these with an equal passion, neither was she thrown by any of them. She got along, though her first home was certainly dismaying.

In midmorning on one of the hottest days of the year, Ike brought her to quarters assigned to him at Fort Sam on the second floor of Infantry Row, a long gray-painted wooden building. It had a tiny living room separated from an even smaller bedroom by sliding doors, a bath, and a kitchen, which consisted of some counter space, a cabinet, and a table-top gas cooker with two burners.

It was clean and freshly painted, though the sun glared fiercely through the curtainless windows and the place was furnished only with a sagging sofa, a few straight-backed chairs, a rectangular table, and a chest of drawers. There was no electricity, just gas jets for illumination and a gas fireplace in the living room. Missing were some essentials— a bed, for example, an ice box for food, and, disheartening for Mamie, closet space for her clothes which she had carefully packed in several large trunks due to be delivered that afternoon.

By late afternoon, a brass bed and a dressing table, purchased at Stower's furniture emporium in San Antonio, arrived by horse van. Ike's uniforms took up most of the single closet in the bedroom, but he put up rods which she curtained off with cloth for her things. In a few days, though inexperienced in sewing, she bought green poplin and made acceptable curtains for the windows. She also rented a piano—so she could continue her impromptu concerts—for five dollars a week. Ike, who sang with more gusto than tune, thought it was a good idea. The piano served another

*See Appendix A.

purpose: since there was no other storage space in the apartment, Ike tossed his knapsack, helmet, bedroll, and other field equipment behind it.

Cooking was another matter. At home, she had learned to make nothing more elaborate or nutritious than fudge, which was still her entire culinary repertoire. Ike, who loved good food, was gallant, as well as hungry. He told Mamie not to fret, they would eat their meals at the officers' mess just across the road. It would cost $2 a day, a not inconsiderable portion of his salary, which was then $161.27 a month.

After three weeks and $42 worth of this, Ike rethought the idea and told Mamie that from then on, he'd better do the cooking, which he did. Pot roast, chicken done Mexican style, and vegetable soup were his three best dishes. Later, the soup was to achieve such fame that his recipe was published all over the world. Over the next few weeks they acquired a brown wooden ice box, the old-fashioned kind with the pan at the bottom that had to be dumped each morning. Though small, they could find no room for the food chest but the bathroom, an arrangement somewhat less than aesthetic which they tried not to notice. Too often, however, they could not overlook the rivulets that flowed from under the bathroom door into the living room when Mamie, unused to such chores, neglected to empty the pan of melted ice.

In the first months of marriage she enrolled in a basic course at the local "Y" but, as she told her friends later, "I was a cooking-school dropout." All she learned was how to mix mayonnaise. Eventually, she learned how to prepare a passable meal but cooking never became one of her more prideful accomplishments.

Mamie was a little charmer. Just five feet four inches tall, she was slender-waisted with a piquant oval face, dark brown hair, and large blue eyes. She was one of those fortunate persons who, through some alchemy of nature, was gifted with a chirrupy disposition. Part of a large family, with dozens of friends of both sexes, she had always been surrounded by people and gaiety. Certainly she had never been lonely.

But now came a profound change.

The loneliness that was to be a major part of her life for the next forty years set in at Fort Sam. This was new and strange, and disconcerting. There were no jolly parties at the post, no dances for the young officers and their wives, not even a movie theater. The rented piano stood diagonally in a corner of the living room, unplayed except when Ike's friends would drop in for an occasional snack.

There were nights alone as well, when Ike had to report for duty until dawn. She had not expected this. She slept alone the first night after their arrival at Fort Sam, and too many thereafter. For a new bride very much in love with her husband, it was not a happy experience. Mamie was bewildered, then resentful. She wept a lot and, she has admitted, complained a lot.

She never adjusted to the constant separations. Toward the end of her life, she looked back and said: "It used to anger me when people would say, 'You're an Army wife, you must be used to Ike being away.' I never got used to him being gone. He was my husband. He was my whole life."

Less than a month after they had set up housekeeping at Fort Sam, Ike arrived home one day for lunch and went directly to the piano. Wordlessly, he reached for his gear. Mamie was astonished. "You're not going to leave me this soon after our wedding day, are you?" she asked. Ike turned and embraced her.

"Mamie," he said—and many years afterward she would remember every word—"there's one thing you must understand. My country comes first and always will. You come second."

At the time, however, she did not understand. "It was quite a shocker for a nineteen-year-old bride," she recalled. After Ike left, she wept in self-pity.

There was trouble along the Mexican border and Lieutenant Eisenhower had received orders to proceed to Camp Travis, many miles away, to help train a National Guard regiment for service. The United States had been infuriated when the revolutionary leader, General Francisco (Pancho) Villa, attacked American towns along the long frontier. General John J. Pershing, the Chief of Staff himself, had gone in pursuit of Villa and his band with an expeditionary force.

Ike's assignment lasted only a short time and the Mexican problem eased. But Mamie was now learning that the loneliness of an Army wife could be compounded by fear. Two incidents terrified her. One night, when Ike was leading a military police patrol in a seedy section of San Antonio, he heard a sharp crack. The sergeant walking with him along Matamoros Street grabbed his arm and yanked him backward. Ike almost fell but the sergeant's quick action saved his life. He had seen a rifle barrel and pulled his lieutenant's arm a millisecond before it fired. Another time a buck private from Chicago, roaring drunk, aimed a .45-caliber Army revolver at Ike's chest from a distance of twelve feet and fired six times. Each shot missed, but from then on Mamie was unable to sleep when Ike was on patrol.

Finally the event Mamie had been dreading came to pass. Europe had been a battlefield since 1914, riven by history's bloodiest conflict. At first Ike told Mamie the United States would never become enmeshed; it was their war and we had little or nothing to do with it. The wives of the officers consoled themselves with this view, which was accepted throughout the country. But now there were changes. America had been supplying the Allies with food and material and Germany, aware of the risks this lifeline entailed, began waging unrestricted submarine warfare against U.S. shipping. For Mamie, the dread became reality on April 6, 1917 when President Woodrow Wilson signed the declaration of war voted by Congress five days earlier.

Before the end of the month, Ike was gone again, this time to Camp Wilson, twenty-five miles away, as regimental supply officer. It was a small military outpost on a stretch of scrub land, with no quarters for officers' wives. Within weeks, the Fifty-seventh Infantry Regiment to which he had been assigned was moved to Leon Springs, thirty miles out of San Antonio but just as inhospitable. There were no buildings of any kind, nothing but rows of pup tents for the soldiers and larger ones for the headquarters and the field kitchens.

Mamie spent her days visiting the other wives, talking and wondering about who would be sent where; playing whist, writing long letters, and sitting alone in her little living room. She spent her nights missing Ike. They were, she admitted afterward, the bleakest of times for her. "She felt trapped in a pit, sealed off with her sorrow," wrote one early biographer to whom Mamie had revealed her thoughts.

Since Ike had told her that, despite the short distance, the camp could provide no transportation for men and officers to go into San Antonio in their free time, Mamie decided the obvious solution was to go to him. She did, with an ending that could have come out of a Mabel Normand silent movie.

John Doud had given his daughter and son-in-law a 1912 Pullman roadster, which Ike had parked in a lean-to near the apartment and shielded from the dust with a canvas cover. Having driven the family's electric in Denver, Mamie reasoned, she shouldn't have too much difficulty finding her way to Leon Springs. The camp lay just off Fredericksburg Road, a much-traveled highway.

There was a catch: the little Pullman had a gasoline engine with clutch and gears to shift, which she had never driven before and which did not operate like an electric at all. Nor was it the most reliable of cars: it bucked and stalled frequently and was breakdown-prone.

Mamie telephoned Ike to tell him she was coming. History does not record his reaction but it is a safe guess that he either blanched or bellowed red-faced, or did both alternately. But Mamie would not be talked out of it; she asked Ike to meet her by the roadside near the camp's entrance.

Early next morning, she removed the car's dust cover, and asked a passing soldier to turn the crank that started the motor. The engine caught and Mamie drove away. Fredericksburg Road was straight but her driving was not. A half-dozen times she ran into roadside ditches but bounced out. She weaved into the opposite lane and went into the ditches there. Wisely, she had started out at dawn to avoid traffic which in those days was almost nonexistent anyway. That morning, Mamie had the road to herself, to her good fortune and that of anyone else who might have been traveling.

At Leon Springs, Ike, waiting at the highway's edge, saw the car approaching. Their versions differ on what happened next. Years later, Ike recalled that when she drew opposite, she called out, "Ike! Get on quickly—I don't know how to stop this thing!" Ike said he leaped onto the nine-inch-wide running board, slid into the driver's seat, and stopped the car. Mamie remembered just reaching over and turning off the ignition. According to Mamie after lunch Ike got permission to drive her back to Fort Sam. But Ike says he spent part of the day teaching his wife to drive, then sent her back and fretted for two hours until she phoned and said she'd arrived safely.

In the next few years, under Ike's tutelage, Mamie tried

to learn how to drive but, like cooking, never did it well. She finally gave it up completely by the early 1930s and was driven ever since.

The separations continued. Ike would not even be present at the birth of his first child. A captain now, he had been transferred to Fort Oglethorpe in Georgia to help train "ninety-day wonders"—young soldiers who would be commissioned as second lieutenants after an intensive three-month course at officer-candidate school.

When Mamie's time drew near, her mother came down from Denver to be with her. At dawn on a Tuesday morning, as a hot early fall sun began its ascent, Mamie rode to the post hospital in a mule-drawn ambulance with Mrs. Doud beside her and, shortly before eight A.M. on September 24, 1917, gave birth to a healthy boy.

More than a thousand miles away, Ike was in a wide-open field miles from camp, instructing his men in the kind of trench and dugout warfare being waged on the European battlefields. They had been there for days, totally isolated. The telegram Mrs. Doud rushed to send him remained at post headquarters, undelivered.

Two days later, Ike returned to camp and learned he was a father.

After the baby came, Ike was sent from post to post, and not until the following year was Mamie able to join him. He had been named commander of a tank corps at Camp Colt near Gettysburg, Pennsylvania, the historic little city that was to play a major role in their lives. He sent for Mamie and she came at once, riding four days and three nights in a train with her seven-month-old son. In her haste to move, Mamie accepted some advice she would forever regret: rather than transport all the furnishings she had accumulated—antiques from home, bed, sofa, chairs, lamps, even dishes—she sold the lot for ninety dollars, a loss, she estimated later, of 800 percent of their purchase price.*

Although spring had come, the bitterest winter in years still gripped the Appalachian Highlands and the Piedmont Plateau. Bundled in an immense topcoat, Ike embraced his wife and son as they stepped off the train. Then he drove them in a Model-T Ford he had acquired to a large two-story colonial home on Springs Avenue a few blocks away. It was the recently vacated Sigma Alpha Epsilon fraternity house which still stands near the campus of Gettysburg College.

The house was roomy but uncared-for and drafty. The wind whistled through the great open space on the main floor which the students had used as a common room. And there was nothing to heat the place except a coal stove and a base burner. In a recording made a few years before she died, Mamie recalled: "I'd never seen a coal stove in my life. I didn't know what to do and how to do it." But she learned and they kept warm, after a fashion, surviving a late snowstorm that made residents liken that winter to the terrible one at Valley Forge some one hundred miles to the east 140 years before.

"It was just a summer camp," Mamie said, "and we had to go all over the countryside trying to buy up every little stove there was to keep the soldiers warm. Ike was just miserable because he was a captain in command of this thing, and he felt so badly for these boys. He bought what he could from the surrounding countryside to take care of his camp."

When summer finally came, the Eisenhowers moved into another vacant fraternity house, the former Alpha Tau

---

*She never repeated the mistake. From then on, she warehoused everything she bought and could not use in her many moves. Ultimately, every dish, ashtray, chair, and spoon would be sent to the home they were to buy.

Omega home on North Washington Street across from the campus.

Mamie: "It had the most beautiful ballroom, but no kitchen. So I could only wash dishes in the bathtub. Ike bought me a two-burner oil stove but I was frightened to death to light it. So I'd have to wait for him to come home. I was only twenty-two years old; I knew nothing about any of these things. It was really pretty rugged."

As the wife of the camp commander, Mamie had her first experience at playing hostess to visiting dignitaries. The big house, with its large ballroom, was fine for large dinners for Congressmen, Government officials, and high-ranking Army officers interested in seeing what Ike was accomplishing with his Tank Training Center. Mamie also started a bridge club with the wives of other officers, and Ike got a regular poker game going.

Ike moved up fast. In June he was promoted to the wartime temporary rank of major and four months later got his silver leaf as lieutenant colonel. The following month the orders he had impatiently sought and Mamie had dreaded finally came: proceed east to Camp Dix in New Jersey on November 19 for processing prior to embarkation for overseas service.

A second blow for Mamie came soon afterward; her second sister, Eda Mae, only seventeen years old, had died of a kidney disease. Mamie left for Denver the next day with the baby, now a sturdy thirteen months old. On the following Tuesday, the eleventh of November, Eda Mae was buried by her sorrowing family.

That evening, Lafayette Street was ablaze with lights and filled with a joyous din. The Armistice had been signed in the Forest of Compiègne at dawn that day and at eleven in the morning the war had ended.

To his chagrin, and Mamie's relief, Ike never got overseas. There were more transfers and more quick visits, with Ike coming home when he could get leave, and Mamie traveling to where he was if there was a place for her to stay.

In 1920 Ike was ordered to Camp Meade, south of Baltimore, another dusty, greenless piece of acreage like most of the others. But here there were rows of old wooden barracks, two-story boxes which were not pretty but sturdy enough to be converted into homes for officers and their families. Ike managed to obtain one and hired soldiers to help him, in their off-duty hours, transform quarters where thirty soldiers had lived into a home for a family. The large upstairs area was partitioned off into three bedrooms; downstairs, a living and dining room took shape. After the stalls were ripped out of the big communal bathroom and a kitchen of sorts installed, Mamie came down. In her bedroom were two army cots and, for a dressing table, a couple of orange crates pushed together in front of a mirror. She covered the boxes with pink cloth.

By midsummer the old barracks had become a home. It sparkled with fresh white paint and a white picket fence enclosed a sight unfamiliar enough in that barren, sandy place to stop passersby: real grass. Not for nothing had Ike been reared in Kansas country.

Mamie, young and pretty and perky, was enormously helpful to Ike's morale just by being there, though she still had a great deal to learn about how a wife can bolster her husband's reputation with the boss.

One afternoon Newton D. Baker, the Secretary of War in Woodrow Wilson's Cabinet, arrived for an inspection trip with his retinue. Ike had never seen, much less met, so high a personage. Naturally enough, he was anxious to make a good impression.

Ike was out in the field, making sure his men would pass muster if the Secretary came by; Mamie was cleaning her barracks apartment when, unhappily for Ike, Baker chose to inspect Mamie's domain, not his. He knocked on the door and Mamie, who recognized him, greeted him politely.

After a brief exchange, Secretary Baker asked Mamie,

"What does your husband do best?" Mamie hardly hesitated as she answered, "He plays an awfully good game of poker."

By the end of summer, the place was snug enough to call Eda Carlson, Mamie's aunt, in Boone, who was caring for the baby. "Bring him down," Ike said happily. "We're ready for him."

A new tragedy, from a wholly unexpected direction, was now imminent. Ike and Mamie were to call it the worst hammerblow of their lives, one that would leave emotional scars deeper and more permanent than either imagined.

2. "Icky"

IKE ADORED THE boy.

They had named him Doud Dwight but soon began calling him "Icky." The story Mamie told was that they had almost decided on "Little Ike" as a nickname but changed their minds when they realized that his father would have to be called "Big Ike." So Icky it was, though not because of its resemblance to Ike. The family secret was revealed by Dr. Kevin McCann, who served as Eisenhower's assistant from 1946 to 1951 and later on his White House staff.

"It was Ike who called him Icky, and it was because of the diapers," says Dr. McCann, later president of Defiance College, who now lives in Phoenix, Arizona. "He'd hold the boy, play with him then suddenly he'd hand him back to Mamie, telling her he was icky."

Ike always left the essentials of baby care to Mamie. Dr. McCann recalls a story of how Mamie once teased him about it. In 1948 McCann's daughter, Mrs. Marie Falcon, was helping Eisenhower with his memoir of the war, *Crusade in Europe*. The General would dictate and Marie would get it down on a typewriter. During a coffee break,

Ike began offering Marie, who had just had her first baby, advice on the raising of infants.

Mamie entered the room and asked Marie, "What is he lecturing you about?" "Oh baby-raising," Marie answered. "Some expert," Mamie said as she left. "He never changed a diaper in his life!"

Ike hated to be separated from the boy, and when they were together he played with him every moment he could spare from his duties. He would hug and kiss him until Mamie said it was enough and time for a bath and a feeding. He told the child stories about soldiers and Indians before he could comprehend a word.

Says Kevin McCann: "That boy was everything to Ike. He would put on acts for him—lying on the floor and pretending to be a kitten, growling like a bulldog, playing the clown to make him laugh."

When Mamie had to return to Denver with Icky, he would bombard her with questions over the long-distance telephone: Was Icky walking yet? Talking? What was he eating? How many teeth were there?

Icky was a bright-eyed, active child from the beginning. Even as a baby, he bore an amazing resemblance to his father from the slightly jutting ears to round face and wide mouth. He had a shock of unruly hair, yellow as Ike's had been as a young man.

Ike was already making plans for the boy's future. "His dream," says Dr. McCann, "was that the child would become one of the greatest soldiers of all time."

By the time Icky passed his second birthday, he was already fascinated by military parades. Whenever he could, Ike would gather him up and take him down to the open field between the tents and barracks to watch the troops swing by in their weekly regimental review. Icky tramped up and down in front of the apartment, making bugle sounds as he marched.

Ike showed off his son at any opportunity. "I was inclined

to display Icky and his talents at the slightest excuse, or without one," he said later. The boy won the hearts of the men too. Once a group came by with a miniature tank uniform they had bought, complete with a heavy overcoat and an overseas cap, which he wore rakishly over one eye. On days when tank drill was scheduled, the men would stop by to pick up the new recruit, deposit him inside one of the lumbering monsters, and take off.

In late summer Ike was ordered to make a cross-country tour with a convoy of Army motor vehicles to display them to an increasingly car-minded public, and at the same time publicize the acute need for a national highway system. The country's roads, built for wagons, were deplorable: few were paved, most were just deeply rutted dirt trails. Often, the convoy could travel less than six miles an hour.

The three months he spent on the assignment were one of Ike's most boring experiences, particularly since he was away from his family. He called Mamie several times a week, beginning each call with requests for news about Icky. How was he growing? What new mischief had he gotten into? Once Mamie interrupted with, "Listen here, Major* Eisenhower, how about asking how your wife is?" Ike was chastened; he chatted for a moment about Mamie, but soon turned the conversation to Icky again. Mamie gave up.

He arrived back at Meade after Thanksgiving. Icky was beside himself, Mamie scarcely less so. They made plans for a joyous Christmas.

There was so much to be done, so many errands. The Eisenhowers decided to engage a sixteen-year-old girl to look after Icky when they could not be home. She adored the child, hugged him and kissed him. Ike and Mamie felt he was in good, loving hands when they were away. One

* After World War I Ike reverted to his permanent rank of captain and was promoted to major July 2, 1920.

day, Mamie went to Baltimore and returned with an
armload of gifts. Another day, Ike came home with his
presents, including a bright red kiddie car.

A few days before Christmas, he lugged home a huge tree
and set it up in the living room. They took Icky to post
headquarters and watched with him as a great tree was
hoisted in front. There would be a party for the officers and
their wives.

Eight days after Christmas, Icky was dead.

On Thursday morning, December 23, he began vomiting.
He said his head and throat hurt. Mamie, who had a heavy
cold herself, touched his head and face; he felt hot and dry.
She called the post physician who said the boy had caught
Mamie's cold, that it would be wise to keep him in bed over
Christmas but he should be over the worst not too many
days later.

"So we'll have a celebration a few days late," Ike said,
and decorated the tree, but Icky, who could see through the
open door of his room, whimpered in his bed, disinterested.

On Christmas, the boy seemed worse. A rash, pinpoints
of red against a faintly reddish background, appeared on his
neck and chest and spread quickly over his entire body
except for his face. His temperature hit 105 degrees, and his
tongue was inflamed to a bright, almost blazing red. His
irritability and restlessness increased. Mamie, prostrated in
her room by a migraine headache, could do nothing.

The post doctor, summoned again by Ike, diagnosed the
ailment as scarlet fever, now a relatively mild disease and
easily cured, but in those preantibiotic days one of childhood's major scourges. Later, Ike told friends that the
verdict terrified him. Eighteen years before, his younger
brother Milton had contracted scarlet fever and barely
survived after a week-long horror during which he burned
with fever. The doctor, he remembered, had prepared the

family to expect Milton's death. Now Icky was taken to the post hospital with the same dread disease.

Mamie did not see her son again after he was removed to the hospital; the doctor, fearing she might have contracted the fever too, ordered her quarantined. There was nothing anyone could do for Icky. Even the specialist, rushed down from Johns Hopkins Hospital, admitted he was helpless against the acute infection.

Ike remained at the hospital constantly until the boy died at dusk on January 2, 1921.

Not long after, doctors at the post hospital told the Eisenhowers that the young girl they had hired as a baby sitter–nursemaid had recovered from scarlet fever just a short time before she went to work for them. Neither Ike nor Mamie had known her medical history. While most patients are not infectious after recovery, some may continue to be carriers of the disease for a long time, although well themselves.

Both young parents wanted to say good-bye to their son in the Denver house. An honor guard from the camp escorted them to the train station in Baltimore and a long, almost unendurably sad journey, with their child's white coffin, followed. Banked by flowers, it was placed before the very fireplace in the music room at 750 Lafayette where Ike and Mamie were married four and one-half years before.

On January 7 the child was laid to rest in Fairmount Cemetery, where Mamie's sisters, Eda Mae and Eleanor, were buried. Forty-five years later Eisenhower, by then a national hero, flew to Abilene in an unpublicized trip. Dressed in a charcoal-gray suit, his deeply lined face pale and taut, Ike stood bareheaded as the body of little Icky, taken from Fairmount Cemetery, was reburied beneath the marble floor of the little thin-spired chapel of buff-colored stone on the grounds of the Eisenhower Center. With him was Brigadier General Robert L. Schultz, his military aide. Mamie, in Walter Reed Army Hospital for treatment of shingles, had wept when doctors told her she must not attempt the journey. Ike said nothing during the brief ceremony; on the flight back to Gettysburg he sat with his legs crossed, staring silently out of the plane window.

On her forty-ninth wedding anniversary, Mamie's eyes filled with tears as her thoughts turned from the joyousness of the day to the sadness of that long ago time.

"All of Icky's Christmas toys and the tree were still in the living room when we left for Denver," she remembered. "When we returned we found that our friends had come in and taken everything away."

3. On the Edge of Breakdown

ICKY'S PASSING WAS a watershed in the lives of the Eisenhowers. It left permanent marks on their personalities and, for a time, even threatened the stability of their marriage.

Ike's grieving was profound. The fact that his military career was not going well did little to help his state of mind. Back at camp with Mamie, he was rejected for the Army's infantry training school for officers at Leavenworth, Kansas, which he hoped would be a stepping stone toward his ultimate objective, the Command and General Staff School. Now thirty-one years old, feeling himself in a rut, he gave serious thought to resigning his commission and entering civilian life.

Three decades later, he made a revealing admission to his friend, the journalist John Gunther. For months after that terrible January week, he said, he was "on the ragged edges of a breakdown."

His actions and appearance clearly showed the intense

hurt he felt. He was drifting robotlike through the lengthen-
ing days, the bounce no longer in his step, his eyes dull.

Says Professor Stephen E. Ambrose of Louisiana State
University, who helped edit Eisenhower's military papers
and had many conversations with Ike: "He found it difficult
to concentrate for a long time after Icky's death or get
interested in anything. He did his job without enthusiasm."
All are classic signs of a reactive depression. Dr. McCann
asserts: "The boy's death devastated Ike. Talking to him
about that saddest of events in later years, I got the clear
impression that he was in a very bad way emotionally for a
time.

"Neither ever forgot, not even a half-century later," says
the Reverend MacAskill of the Gettysburg Church.
"Mamie was able to speak of those heartbreaking years
while the General for the most part kept the pain to
himself."

Mamie would introduce the boy into conversations from
time to time, not bitterly nor even sadly, but as part of her
long, bittersweet life.

Always, however, she was careful not to dwell upon the
memory, aware that living with the past could harm the
present. Thus she said in Gettysburg a few years ago: "John
is the only son I have. That's the way I've thought of it after
Icky."

On rare occasions, Ike would let his sorrow surface. Ann
Whitman, who was Eisenhower's secretary during his Presidency, now living in retirement in New York City, recalls a
touching moment: "I came into the Oval Office one day and
found him staring off into space. He turned to me and said,
very simply, that he was thinking of the little boy. Upstairs,
in the family living quarters, there would always be fresh
flowers. Once he pointed to some—I can't remember what
kind it was—and said: 'Icky always liked those flowers.'
Imagine, remembering a detail like that."

Maxwell M. Rabb, who was secretary to the Eisenhower

Cabinet from 1953 to 1958 says: "Only once did Ike ever talk about his first son. 'That was a very difficult moment for us,' he said, passing over it very quickly. I think his silence on the subject was significant."

It was not until 1967, two years before his own death, that he stated publicly for the first time that Icky's passing had been the worst blow he had ever experienced—"the greatest disappointment and disaster of my life, the one I have never been able to forget completely." Years afterward, in her widowhood, Mamie told Mickey McKeogh and his wife, Perlie, who served under Eisenhower during the war and remained close friends ever since, "That sad, sad event had a lasting effect on the General."

As for Mamie, she developed fears which became almost phobic. When her second son, John, was born a year after Icky died, she was overly protective of him from the start. Coughs and sneezes caused anxiety; she would rarely let him out of her sight. In his growing-up years, John admits, he would be sent to school wrapped in layers of clothing, including a heavy coat, muffler and gloves which brought guffaws from his classmates. He was not permitted to cross a street unattended even after he was old enough to look out for himself.

Her apprehension, she knew, came close to being obsessive. "It took me many years to get over my 'smother love'," she told Dorothy Brandon, an early biographer. "It wasn't until Johnny had children of his own that I was able to stop."

Her friends are not at all sure she ever did stop. Mrs. Arthur Nevins laughs as she recalls: "Mamie kept mothering her son John even after he was fifty years old and the American Ambassador to Belgium. She kept on worrying about him. He was always like a little boy to her. She would tell him to watch what he ate and to wear the proper clothes when it rained."

Mamie's worries extended to Ike. Says Kevin McCann:

"Icky's death turned her into a worry wart. Her worries were concentrated, not upon his career and his advancement, in which she had the utmost faith, but on matters that concerned his health and safety." Even after he had been elected President, Mamie would rush out of their bedroom at times, chasing after Ike with a scarf in her hand. In the presence of maids and butlers whose lips twitched in amusement, she would wrap it around his neck. Whenever he rode bareheaded through streets in convertibles, she would shift uncomfortably and mutter: "I wish he'd wear a hat!"

Planes terrified her, not only on her own infrequent flights but whenever Ike, John and other family members were airborne. There were times when she would sit at home, literally rigid with fear, until she learned that they had landed safely. After World War II, when Ike was being increasingly mentioned as a Presidential possibility, she confided to friends that her stark dread of flying was one of her major concerns. She knew that if Ike were elected there would be many flights the Chief Executive and First Lady would have to take.

Mamie's dread of flying was eased somewhat after she went to the White House, thanks to long talks and personal demonstrations by Major William G. Draper, Eisenhower's chief pilot on the Presidential plane. Major Draper pointed out all the safety features of the *Columbine II*, Ike's name for his official aircraft, recited the technological advances in aviation, compared air and highway risks and concluded with the statement frequently told by airmen to other nonfliers: "The most dangerous part about an airplane trip is the ride to and from the airport."

Eventually, Mamie could take rides without gripping the arms of her chair in white-knuckled fear, although she preferred ground transportation all her life.

When John took up private flying after the war, Mamie was scared out of her wits. John earned a pilot's license and managed to scrape up enough money to buy a single-engine plane which he used to hop around the country. Mamie finally maneuvered to have him grounded by enlisting the help of Jacqueline Cochran, the first woman to fly faster than the speed of sound, who had become a close friend of the Eisenhowers.*

Once Mamie was in San Francisco where she was to meet John, who had flown out in his plane. Since the Odlums were there at the time, Mamie visited her and pleaded with her to talk to John about his flying. "I'm worried to death about it," Mamie confided. "He flew this little tiny airplane—a single-motor airplane!—out here all by himself!"

Cochran protested that she could not talk to an aviator about the craft he was flying unless she was asked. However, she said: "I certainly will be very happy to furnish him with my opinions which should, I think, be pretty valid. After all I've had enough experience." Seeking to reassure Mamie, she added: "If he flew it out here, you should be fairly confident."

But Mamie wasn't confident at all. "I don't think he's had enough experience," she said. "Besides, John is going to fly it all the way to Seattle, Washington, in the inland route and back into the east!"

Now that, Cochran felt, *was* risky. She knew that only highly experienced pilots should attempt to fly into the northwestern region. Along the Oregon coast heavy weather can roll in from the ocean in five minutes. "That area and certain parts of Alaska," she recalled later, "has claimed more inexperienced pilots than any other area in the United States, so treacherous is the weather." Convinced John would be in graver danger than he realized, she agreed to talk to him.

*In the years following the war, Cochran, director of the Woman's Air Force Service Pilots in wartime, and her husband Floyd Odlum, were hosts many times to Ike and Mamie at their desert home in Indio, California.

Next day she asked him: "How many flying hours have you had?" A few hundred, he replied—not a great deal. Had he had any training in the use of flight instruments? John admitted he had none and, more over, his plane was not equipped with communications equipment of any kind.

Cochran then told him his mother was anxious about his flying, adding dryly: "I think justifiably so." She pulled no punches. "Unless you have a really competent pilot with you," she told him, "I don't think you have any business going into that country."

John cancelled his trip and, not long after, gave up private flying to Mamie's relief.

"The loss of his first son changed Ike's character," Kevin McCann declares.

A new seriousness, McCann says, had been settling in after his marriage, submerging the prankishness of his nature which had bubbled to the surface during his West Point days. It seems clear that Ike had invested so much of himself emotionally in his first child and had been wounded so deeply that he could not ever again risk being so vulnerable. A parent who suffers the death of a child will inescapably develop the fear of a second hurt. Thus if Mamie reacted by becoming overly protective, Ike built emotional defenses. To his second son, he was a "good" parent but a distant one over the years. The glimpse John Eisenhower gives us into his childhood makes it apparent that Ike was not the playful, tolerant, all-embracing father to his second son that he had been to Icky. To John, Ike was strict, authoritarian, demanding adherence to rules set down. "Dad himself was a terrifying figure to a small boy," John says, a characterization that Icky probably never would have made judging by Ike's attitude toward him while he was alive. While Ike never spanked his son, his stern face, commanding voice which could (and often did) rise to a roar, scared John witless. John always lived in the shadow of his father, admiring him, respecting him, earning money by writing about him, but it is significant that in none of his accounts do we find expressions of warm feelings.

It was not until grandchildren came that Ike was able to allow the love, warmth, and playfulness that he had lavished upon Icky to emerge. He never abandoned the stern authority-figure role—the kids felt the sting of his tongue-lashings many times, as we will see—but he was at the same time affectionate and demonstrative. "He took a tremendous delight in his grandson, David," says Maxwell Rabb. "You could almost feel that when the boy was around, he would take precedence—not that Ike would ever neglect his duties; he was a soldier and he did his job. But he had a special feeling for him." As for David, to him Ike was a close and lovable person, not the awesomely important President of the United States.

Just one story underscores the point. One day, Eisenhower was delivering a major speech before a large throng in Washington. David, then about five years old, was standing to one side. A Secret Service man assigned to protect him asked, "What's your name, young fellow?"

David, emphasizing each syllable, answered, "Dwight David Eisenhower."

"I see," the Secret Service man said. Then, pointing toward the man on the platform, asked, "Then who is that?"

David looked. "Him?" he said. "That's Ike."

4. The Marriage
Totters . . .

THE MOST SERIOUS aftershock of Icky's death was the effect on the Eisenhowers' marriage, then in its fifth year.

After their return to Meade, Ike was offered a new job as executive officer to the commandant at Camp Gaillard in Panama, more than two thousand miles away. Ike and Mamie spent many nights talking about the opportunity; he also discussed it with a young major he had met, George S. Patton, even then a romantic swashbuckler but also a brilliant tactician in tank warfare. Ike and Patton had become friendly; they would talk for hours of the future of mechanized armies. Patton urged Ike to accept the Panama job, particularly since he would be serving under a man who had considerable clout in the War Department, General Fox Conner. Later, General Conner became Deputy Chief of Staff and helped advance Ike's career.

Like Ike, Mamie wanted to leave Meade and its painful memories far behind but was less than enthusiastic about living in tropical Panama. She had visited there briefly in

1914 with her parents and remembered the almost intolerable heat, high humidity, and frequent heavy rains. Despite her trepidations, she agreed they should go.

On January 7, 1922, just a year after Icky's death, they arrived in the Canal Zone. Mamie had remembered well: A fierce sun blazed down as they arrived at their "quarters," a rickety wooden structure, slightly aslant, infested with tropical insects, even bats which would swoop from the high corners, and rotting with mildew. There were gaping holes in the walls and roof through which the rains could pour; occasionally bats flapped overhead. And it stood in the midst of a jungle clearing, reached only by a steep footpath across which snakes and lizards slithered.

They did what they could to make the shack habitable but never quite succeeded. Mamie hated the place, and she hated Camp Gaillard and all of Panama for the climate, the isolation, and the almost total absence of anything to do. Her unhappiness with Panama compounded a coolness that had developed during the past year between her and Ike. The loss of Icky had caused a strain in their relationship that was not easing but, as General Fox Conner's wife was shrewdly observing, growing worse.

What had happened was predictable enough. The death of a child, experts in human behavior agree, creates a profound shock in the psyche of parents that can either bring them closer in the sharing of their grief, or force them apart because of spoken or felt accusations. Peter Lyon, one of Eisenhower's biographers, writes that in the case of the youthful Eisenhowers, "each parent shouldered a self-imposed burden of guilt. Had they taken their child too much for granted? Should they have left him with relatives in Iowa? Why had they hired a nursemaid for him? Should they have inquired about the state of her recent health? Was there nothing more they could have done for him? No gifted specialist they could have summoned to his bedside? Self-reproach is the inevitable concomitant of these sad occurrences, and unfortunately such gestures are sometimes turned from oneself toward another."

Years later, Virginia Conner recalled those difficult months in the lives of the Eisenhowers.

The General and his wife had developed a special interest in the youthful couple. Conner, handsome, slender, and cultured, had taken Eisenhower under his wing, introducing him to philosophy and literature and expanding his knowledge of military history and tactics. For her part, Virginia Conner, a motherly woman, who saw that Mamie was troubled, spent as much time with her as she could, talking to her, drawing her out, and—most importantly—advising her.

"The marriage was clearly in danger," Virginia Conner told journalist Mary Ellen Murphy years later in Washington in the fall of 1952. In her comfortable apartment in Brooklyn Heights, across the river from Manhattan, Mrs. Murphy recalls that revealing talk with the wife of the general who influenced Ike's career so profoundly. (Ike himself has said that Conner "is one more or less invisible figure to whom I owe an incalculable debt." Fox Conner, who rose to major general, lived to see his protégé become Supreme Commander; he died in 1951. Mrs. Conner died at the age of eighty-two in 1960.)

"It was evident," Virginia Conner said, "that there was a serious difficulty at the time, mainly because of the death of their child. They were two young people [Ike was thirty-two, Mamie twenty-six] who were drifting apart. It was a critical time in their relationship. It was my feeling that they had reached a turning point."*

---

*In her book, *Special People,* published in 1978, Julie Nixon Eisenhower had hinted that the marriage of her grandmother and grandfather-in-law experienced rough going, but mentioned no details. Mamie, wrote Julie, "paints no rosy, unrealistic pictures" of the union and once told her after the General died: "There were a lot of times when Ike broke my heart. . . . I wouldn't have stood it for a minute if I didn't respect him."

Mrs. Conner, married twenty years herself and the mother of three growing children, was a gentle yet knowing woman who had seen enough of Army marriages to be aware of the formidable obstacles faced by service wives. The loneliness, the long periods of separation, the frequent, unpredictable moves, the difficulty of sharing experiences had caused too many of her own friends to settle into loveless unions.

"She did not want this to happen to the young Eisenhowers," Mrs. Murphy told us. "She and her husband had grown to like them a great deal and both knew they had a very special problem, the loss of their firstborn child. And so, at this critical juncture, Virginia Conner took Mamie in hand.

The erosion that had already begun before they reached Panama could have undermined the entire foundation of the marriage, Mrs. Conner said. Ike was spending less and less time with Mamie. It was clear to Virginia Conner that a coolness had settled over them. There appeared to be little warmth; they seemed like two people moving through their days in different directions.

Mamie, in her loneliness, spent increasing amounts of time with the older woman. "I never knew exactly how Ike felt," Mrs. Conner admitted, "as he knew Mamie was wearing down a path to my front porch." But she knew quite well how Mamie felt; she was pouring out her troubles.

Mrs. Conner listened, then offered a practical suggestion on how Mamie could win back her husband. Hardly novel, it was a tactic women had employed on the advice of experts from ancient Greek philosophers to *Cosmopolitan* magazine: Use her femininity.

"You mean," Mamie asked, "that I should *vamp* him?"

"That's *just* what I mean," Virginia Conner replied. "Vamp him!"

Mamie was not long removed from her flirtation years

and she took the older woman's advice. Virginia Conner noticed the change at once. Mamie spent less time in visits to her home and more with Ike, whom she persuaded to take fewer horseback rides through the jungle paths. She took greater care with her appearance and even changed her hair style, having her long locks cut modishly short and adding a new touch for her, bangs. It was the first time those famous Mamie bangs appeared. Ike approved so enthusiastically she kept them all her life. Even when she was eighty years old, her hair was "bobbed and banged" because, she said, "that was the way he liked it." In later years, she tinted her hair a reddish brown because Ike did not like to see her graying.

Once, just after the European war ended, Mamie tired of the bangs and had her hairdresser create a different style. Ike took one look and his face fell. Next day, the bangs were back.

"Mamie did win back her husband and probably saved her marriage," Mrs. Conner said. "Had she not acted at that crucial time, the separation might well have reached the point of no return. Oh, there probably would not have been a divorce—divorces were not nearly as frequent as they are now nor so easily obtained. But a cold, lifeless marriage could have resulted."

5. . . . And Regains
its Balance

ON COURSE AGAIN, the marriage strengthened as the years passed. Ike and Mamie continued their gypsylike lives, moving many thousands of miles across the United States, Europe and the Philippines.

A new baby had arrived, making the difficult way of life even more exhausting. They had left Panama in 1924, the duty interrupted by the birth of John Sheldon Doud Eisenhower on August 3, 1922. Mamie had gone home to Denver for the event but this time Ike was granted a leave and was present at the Park Avenue Hospital when the new son arrived. He wept when he held him for the first time.

Money was a constant problem and soon became, for Mamie, a preoccupation that would last all her life. Army officers' pay was low, living allowances equally small, and perks virtually nonexistent. For most of the years before the second World War, Ike was a major, drawing down $250 a month which was raised gradually to $400. Worse, he had few prospects for promotion because Congress was holding a tight string on the Army budget and openings in the higher ranks were few.

Mamie, however, had been well-trained in money management. Despite their comfortable circumstances, the Douds had hammered home to their daughters the importance of respecting dollars and Mamie learned well. John Doud insisted she make her allowance last the full period for which it was given, and Mother Doud taught her, by example and direct sit-down instruction, the techniques of efficient, cost-cutting housekeeping. Father Doud, too, had sat with his daughter at the dining-room table in the evening and told her how to keep a household budget: write down income here, then list all expenses here, make sure you include a sum for savings and never, but never, let your spending exceed this figure—pointing to the net monthly income.

Mamie learned well, perhaps too well. Throughout her married life, she tilted toward a tight money policy that approached stinginess. She has admitted that she hated to part with cash, so she spent very carefully when she spent at all. Early in her marriage, she was compelled to open her purse by Ike as a punishment for losing her temper. She never forgot it.

She and Ike exchanged sharp words over a matter long since forgotten. Her voice rising, she slammed her hand down on a table upon which Ike's hand was resting. Her wedding band struck the heavy gold West Point graduation ring he wore, cracking the oval amethyst set in its center.

"Young lady," Ike told her, "for that fit of temper you will buy me a new amethyst with your own money." Mamie, he knew, had saved some cash from a wedding gift. Relating the story years later, Mamie ruefully said she had been hoarding the money "like a miser." But she bought Ike a new stone—"although parting with those dollars almost killed me."

Once John, when he was in elementary school, came

home without his overcoat. It could not be located despite a long search. The coat had cost ten dollars, not especially steep even for those days, but John remembers that his mother was "devastated."

When she lived in Washington, she did her food shopping at the commissary in the Army War College, later named Fort McNair, which could be reached only by taxi. Mamie figured that, even with cab fare, she could save money because food was sold at cost to Army personnel. Nonetheless, she arranged to share the taxicab each time with a friend, Mrs. Leonard T. Gerow, whose husband would command the Fifteenth Army under Ike.

Washington cabs operate on the zone system, the cost being the same in any part of a zone. However, when the cab entered a new zone, an extra charge could be imposed. Once the taxi passed Florida Avenue, five blocks downhill from where Mamie lived, another quarter could be added. Mamie wouldn't pay it. She and Mrs. Gerow would get off at Florida Avenue and trudge up the hill to their apartment building carrying their heavy bags.

Since Ike knew little about home finance and had no time for money management anyway, Mamie took over the household budget almost from the beginning. They opened a joint bank account and kept one all their lives. Mamie made the purchases, paid the bills, balanced the budget, and kept their finances in order, a task at which she spent a great deal of time.

Her care and attention paid off. "There may have been times when we had only a dollar in the bank," she once said, "but we have never owed a cent in our lives."

Three years after the new baby arrived, Mamie made one of her infrequent, yet significant, suggestions that altered the career of her husband.

After Panama, Ike was handed a series of dull assignments that bored him to the eyeballs—recreation officer of the Third Corps Area in Baltimore, recruiting officer at Fort

Logan, Colorado. Following ten months at the Command
and General Staff School in Leavenworth, they were
transferred to an infantry unit in Fort Benning, Georgia.
His career seemed at a dead end, especially when the only
offer he received was to serve as a football coach for the
ROTC on a college campus. Ike said no, but in less than a
month he received orders for a new assignment at Benning—backfield and offensive coach of the fort's gridiron
squad! "Ike practically exploded," Mamie said.

The following year, General Conner rescued him. Conner, by that time deputy chief of staff in Washington,
recommended Ike to Black Jack Pershing, who had retired
three years earlier and had been named by Congress to head
a new agency, the Battle Monuments Commission. Its task:
to design and build memorials to the American soldiers who
had fallen in France during the First World War.

Pershing wanted an official guidebook to the fields,
complete with maps, statistics, photographs, and detailed
information about each battle. "Hell," Ike burst out when
he was told about the assignment, "another dull job!" It
was nothing but a desk job, he groused, something a civilian
could do as well.

Mamie had been an Army wife long enough to be
shrewdly aware that recognition by top brass was the surest,
not to mention the fastest, route to promotion. Ike was
hardly unaware of this, but his longing for a field command
was strong and he leaned toward attempting to duck the
job, which he could have done successfully.

"I told him not to protest but to take it," Mamie disclosed
afterward. Ike accepted, went to Washington, and, working
at the War Department, within five months completed the
manuscript of a guidebook, *The American Battlefields in
France.* Pershing pronounced it a superb job and wrote a
glowing letter of commendation which praised Ike's "splendid service" and stated that "what he has done was
accomplished only by the exercise of unusual intelligence

Above: The graduation picture of the class of 1912 at Corona Street Elementary School in Denver. Mamie is #45. *Courtesy Dwight D. Eisenhower Library. Below:* The Eisenhower family in 1906. In the front row are David and his wife Ida, with Milton between them. In the back row are, left to right, Dwight, Edgar, Earl, Arthur and Roy. *Courtesy Dwight D. Eisenhower Library.*

Above: Mamie, third from left, picnics with friends in a park in Denver. *Courtesy Dwight D. Eisenhower Library.*

Right: Mamie in 1914. *Courtesy Dwight D. Eisenhower Library.*

Above: Cadet Dwight David Eisenhower at the United States Military Academy, West Point, New York, in 1915. *U.S. Army Photograph.*

Right: Mamie in 1916. *Courtesy Dwight D. Eisenhower Library.*

Far right: Lieutenant and Mrs. Eisenhower's wedding photo taken after the ceremony at Mamie's home in Denver, July 1, 1916. *Courtesy Dwight D. Eisenhower Library.*

Above: Icky, the Eisenhowers' firstborn son, at Camp Meade, Gettysburg, Pennsylvania, in 1918. *Courtesy Dwight D. Eisenhower Library.*

Right: John Eisenhower in 1925, at the age of three. *Courtesy Dwight D. Eisenhower Library.*

Left: Lieutenant Eisenhower and wife. *U.S. Army Photograph negative #SC 148569.*

Left: Mrs. Ida Eisenhower in 1945. *Courtesy Dwight D. Eisenhower Library.*

Below: General Douglas MacArthur participates in a ceremony honoring his arrival in Manila in October 1935. Colonel Dwight D. Eisenhower is third from left. *U.S. Army Photograph.*

Right: Major Dwight D. Eisenhower, Inf. American Battle Monuments Commission. *U.S. Army Photograph negative #P 1466.*

Brigadier General Dwight D. Eisenhower. *U.S. Army Photograph.*

Kay Summersby. *Courtesy Dwight D. Eisenhower Library.*

Above: General Eisenhower visits USAF Base at Mons-en-Chausée, France. Kay Summersby is at his right. *Courtesy Dwight D. Eisenhower Library. Below:* General Mark Clark, Kay Summersby and Ike in an Army jeep passing the ruins of Hitler's Berchtesgaden retreat. *Courtesy Dwight D. Eisenhower Library.*

Above: Telegraph Cottage, the small house eleven miles southwest of London which Eisenhower used as a secret retreat during his stay in England when he was Supreme Commander. Some of the reputed romantic interludes with Kay Summersby supposedly took place at the cottage. *Photograph supplied by Mrs. G. Keiller.*

Above: General Eisenhower watching machine gunners in action in Oujda, North Africa, 1943. *U.S. Army Photograph. Below:* General Eisenhower and Lieutenant General George S. Patton at the Palermo Airport in Sicily, 1943. *U.S. Army Photograph.*

Left: General Eisenhower and Kay Summersby in North Africa. *Courtesy Dwight D. Eisenhower Library.*

Above: President Franklin D. Roosevelt awards the Legion of Merit to General Eisenhower during a conference at the Russian Embassy in Teheran, Iran, 1943. *U.S. Army Photograph. Below:* General Eisenhower gives the order of the day to paratroopers in England just before the first assault in the invasion of the continent of Europe, June 6, 1944. *U.S. Army Photograph.*

and constant devotion to duty." The letter went into Eisenhower's permanent file.

Ike's work with the Pershing commission has been called by historians a major turning point in his military career.

In 1935 Mamie was called upon to make one of the toughest decisions in her life. Several years earlier Ike had been on duty in the office of the Assistant Secretary of War in Washington when he attracted the attention of General Douglas MacArthur, then Chief of Staff. MacArthur chose Ike as his aide, relying on him to prepare his reports and statements. MacArthur came to admire Ike's incisive mind and, as he told him in a letter, "your comprehensive grasp of the military profession in all its principal phases, as well as analytical thought and forceful expression."

Thus in 1935, when MacArthur relinquished his duties as Chief of Staff to become military adviser to the newly created independent Philippine Commonwealth, he asked Ike to join him there as his assistant.

Her son John was thirteen years old and entering the eighth grade at John Quincy Adams elementary school, which still stands at California and Nineteenth streets, a short distance north of the White House. John, an athlete and a top student, had just been elected president of his class and, understandably enough, wanted to graduate with his friends. (He recalls in his memoirs that his tenure as class president was jeopardized by an unwise military maneuver. He and several buddies had created a "Hindenburg Line" of massed desks at the back of the room and, when the teacher was writing on the blackboard, would let fly with a chalk volley aimed at other students. When a poorly aimed chalk bullet struck the teacher, John faced the prospect of summary removal from his post. He barely survived in school but he draws the curtain on what happened at home when his father found out, and so will we.)

"I had to decide between going with my husband or

staying with John," Mamie recalled. Ike wanted her to
come with him. Mamie hated the idea of a lengthy separation but she was clearly aware of the advantages to Ike.

"I know for absolute fact," declares Walter Trohan, the
Chicago Tribune bureau chief who was close to Ike at the
time, "that Mamie had a high opinion of MacArthur and
convinced her husband to go to the Philippines with him.
She felt it would enhance Ike's reputation. It was a hell of a
long way from home, another country, another way of life.
Even though she had had a dismal experience in Panama,
even though they couldn't be together for a year, she was all
for the move. Ike told me that and she prevailed."

"John's education seemed so important to me," Mamie
said, "that I let my husband sail away."

Ike left in September of 1935, and Mamie remained alone
with John in a three-bedroom apartment in the Wyoming
on the corner of Connecticut Avenue and Columbia Road,
near John's school. Mamie kept house, with the help of a
part-time maid—whose fifty-dollar monthly salary was paid
by her father.

Eisenhower missed Mamie and John and told them so in
long letters home.* Finally, a year after he left, Mamie put
all her furniture in storage, packed, and boarded a train
with John, bound for California. In San Francisco, the
Army transport *U.S. Grant,* on which they were to sail, had
just docked. Four weeks later, after a brief stop at Pearl
Harbor and a journey of eleven thousand miles, the *U.S.
Grant* steamed past the rocky fortress of Corregidor into
Manila Bay.

---

* His skillful handling of his job pleased MacArthur but the respect was
not mutual. Late in 1979 a segment of Ike's secret diary, a journal he
kept intermittently over the years, came to light. He had never let the
diary out of his possession nor even permitted historians to read the text.
In an entry dated January 19, 1942, Ike wrote, "In many ways,
MacArthur is as big a baby as ever." Another time Ike said that he
"studied dramatics under Douglas MacArthur" in the Philippines.

Ike, bald as an eagle, was waiting for her on the pier. Mamie screamed when she spotted his glistening head, which he had shaved because of the intense tropical heat. Only when they embraced did she notice the silver oak leaf on the collar of his short-sleeved shirt. He had been promoted to lieutenant colonel on the preceding July 1, the twentieth anniversary of their marriage, and had kept the news as a surprise.

If the climate was as bad as Panama's, and often worse, their quarters were better by far. No bat-infested shanty here, but a lavish suite in the Manila Hotel, one of the city's finest, overlooking the wide blue sweep of the bay.

But four years later, Mamie was staring dispiritedly at a drab little apartment in San Francisco, near the Presidio, the Army post where Ike was assigned to temporary duty, at the Ninth Corps Area headquarters, early in January. The years in the Philippines were over and the moving had begun anew.

They went to Fort Lewis in the state of Washington, where they were assigned quarters on the post. Lieutenant Colonel Eisenhower was Third Division headquarters chief here. Mamie sent for their furniture, which was transported nearly three thousand miles and arrived in such a deplorable state that she wept for days. Ike consoled her with promises that they would buy new things but she responded through her tears with a phrase countless wives have used before and still do: "What will we do for money?"

On their twenty-fifth wedding anniversary, they arrived at another post. Mamie was all sniffles with sentiment as Ike drove up to Fort Sam Houston in San Antonio, where they had begun their Army lives together. This time he took her to a fourteen-room house of bright red brick that had been assigned to him. It had five bedrooms, a large patio in the back, and a lawn with neatly clipped grass. Ike, promoted to full colonel, was made Chief of Staff of the Third Army here.

The summer went slowly; Ike went on war maneuvers in Louisiana, the most extensive ever conducted in peacetime, returning late in September.

On September 29 Ike got his first star. He worked harder than ever, often eighteen hours a day, but Mamie was content; he was with her. On Sunday, December 7, she was knitting in one of the bedrooms they had converted into a sitting room. The radio was turned on and she was vaguely conscious that a football game was in progress. Ike had gone into their bedroom for a nap, after working on a report offering suggestions on how to correct weaknesses detected during the Louisiana maneuvers.

Suddenly the game was interrupted by a news bulletin: the Japanese had bombed the U.S. battle fleet at Pearl Harbor. She woke Ike, who was fully dressed except for his shoes, and told him. He cried out, "Oh, my God!" At that moment the telephone rang. Headquarters was calling. Ike put on his shoes and bolted out of the house.

Wives of fellow officers, one after the other, came to the house, many entering without knocking. Mamie hugged them and they spent the day listening to reports from Hawaii. She had not known a worse day since the death of her firstborn son.

PART THREE

War Years

1. Mamie Goes to Washington

MAMIE SPENT MOST of the war years in a two-bedroom apartment on the third floor of the Wardman Towers, part of a sixteen-acre complex which included the enormous Sheraton Park Hotel. She and Ike had moved to the capital in 1941 when he was transferred to the War Plans Division. Mamie said she had finally "arrived" and indeed she had: the Towers had been home to many of the capital's movers and shakers. Herbert Hoover had lived there when he was secretary of commerce; her neighbors included Cabinet members, Senators and Congressmen, and the famed hostess Perle Mesta.*

Mamie grappled with her customary problems of packing, storage, shipping, and apartment-hunting in relocating

---

*Later, Lyndon Johnson and Spiro Agnew took apartments there when they were Vice-President. So did Secretaries of State John Foster Dulles and Dean Rusk, and two Chief Justices of the U.S. Supreme Court, Frederick M. Vinson and Earl Warren.

East. Remarkably enough, nothing went astray or terribly wrong, except for one incident that upset her and terrified a young soldier. She lost Ike's orderly, who had been instructed to accompany her and help her with her considerable quantity of baggage, on the train.

Mickey McKeogh tells the story in his stone-and-clapboard ranch home in a hilly residential development in Bowie, Maryland. Mickey has earned a measure of fame himself through his association with the Eisenhowers. He was close to the General for four and a half years—"I put him to bed nearly every night and was at his bedside when he awoke in the morning practically through the entire war." Mickey's wife, Pearlie, a small attractive woman, was also attached to Eisenhower's headquarters as a Woman's Army Corps driver. Mickey retired in 1980 from the Office of War Information, where he was a section chief.

Former Master Sergeant McKeogh, seated on a couch in front of autographed photographs of Ike and Mamie, recalls that December day, a few weeks after the Pearl Harbor attack.

"The General was working night and day at War Plans. He had gotten a phone call to rush East and work directly with the Chief of Staff himself, General Marshall. Back at Fort Sam, Mamie and I got her stuff together and, just after Christmas, took off. Tex Lee—that was Captain Ernest Lee, the General's aide-de-camp—had made the arrangements. Mrs. Eisenhower was heading first to New York, because she wanted to visit her son, John, in his final year at West Point. Then she was going on to Washington.

"Tex had gotten a first-class compartment for Mrs. Eisenhower, while I was forward in coach. None of us knew that, at Chicago, the train would split into two separate sections, one going to Pennsylvania Station, the other to Grand Central. After we left Chicago, I went back to see if Mrs. Eisenhower was okay or if she wanted anything.

"But after the last coach, there was no more train! The first-class part was off by itself."

Mickey worried through the next twenty hours, visions of courts-martial in his head. Who loses the wife of a general? When his section reached Penn Station he rushed to Grand Central and found Mamie on the platform, surrounded by baggage. She glared at him. "Where were you?" she demanded. Mickey explained as best he could. He was forgiven and for the next forty years the story of how he mislaid his boss's wife was a running joke between them.

Mickey had joined the Eisenhower "family" five months earlier at Fort Sam. Then twenty-five years old, he had been a bellhop at the Hotel Plaza in New York before his induction. He recalls the day he was "hired" by Ike:

"At Fort Sam my master sergeant told me, 'Mickey, I got a good job for you. Some new colonel wants a dog-robber.* Go over and see him.' Well, I had been in the Army only about four months and expected to be discharged in a year—we all did in those prewar days—and figured that would be an easy way to pass the time.

"Next morning at eight sharp, I showed up at his house. The Colonel and Mrs. Eisenhower were having breakfast. He got up, stuck out his hand, and smiled. I was standing stiff as a ramrod but relaxed and shook it. That great smile put me at ease. I had no way of knowing, but that grin was going to light up the whole world.

"'What's your name?' he asked.

"'Private Michael James McKeogh.' A pause, then I added quickly, 'sir.'

"'What do they call you?'

"'Mickey. Er, sir.'

"'Okay, it'll be Mickey from here on out. Mrs. Eisenhower will acquaint you with my field equipment. In a couple of days we'll be going on maneuvers in Louisiana.'

"He stuck out that big hand, smiled, and we shook again. From that moment, I became part of his personal staff."

The boy who thought he'd be in civvies before the year

* An orderly, or striker.

was out was soon to go to Europe with the Supreme Commander of the Allied armies.

Mickey worked from nine to five in Eisenhower's home, before and after maneuvers.

"Mrs. Eisenhower was an easy person to get along with, as long as you did things right," he says. "If you didn't she would let you know, and fast. She'd bawl me out in a motherly way. One day I skipped two chores out of a half dozen she'd asked me to do. Another time I went shopping for her at the post store with a grocery list she'd given me, and forgot a couple of items.

"'You're just like John,' she said in exasperation. 'You have to be told to do things more often than you should be told.'"

Mamie never told Mickey but, he learned later, she wrote frequent letters to his mother telling her he was well and not to worry.

"She was a stickler for neatness," Mickey recalls, "not only with me but with the General. She'd pick up newspapers he'd left scattered and didn't like it one bit when he'd toss his cigarette butts into the clean fireplace. He'd always get a stern: 'Now Ike, can't you stop being so messy!' but he never learned, not even when they lived in places that had artificial fireplaces."

Off duty, the Eisenhowers lived simply. Ike was home every night when he wasn't on maneuvers or at meetings. Occasionally they would invite another couple for bridge. Stories about Ike's addiction to Western tales have become part of the Eisenhower lore. Mickey was assigned to corral magazines; he scoured the shops for them and stacked them on Ike's bedside for his sleepless nights. He could tell when Ike had had a bad one by the number he read and tossed aside. Later they even provided him with a barometer of how the war was shaping up: none scattered around, all was well; a load at the bedside, the Allies were in trouble.

Before Pearl Harbor, when officers and men were permitted to wear civilian clothes off hours, Ike bought inexpensive suits off the racks, mostly in conservative-cut blues and grays. Mamie went along to pass judgment on the fit.

She would, now and then, try to talk him into something with an up-to-date flair but Ike balked at anything more jazzy than double-breasted outfits that, Mickey said, made him look like a "staid lawyer or accountant." Once Mamie had him try on a suit with a jacket that extended far below his fingertips and buttoned low. "Jesus, Mamie," he burst out, "I look like a goddamned zoot-suiter!" He didn't buy it. Despite Mamie's urging, he never succumbed to anything more flashy in ties than solid colors or small patterns and narrow blue-and-red stripes.

Even his uniforms were ready-made, except for his riding breeches, which he had custom-tailored. "He was the best-dressed soldier in the world in that riding outfit," Mickey says. In pink breeches, gleaming boots, and pink officer's shirt, pressed with sharp, regulation creases down the front and back, he looked like the very model of a modern brigadier general, straight out of Central Casting. "He was a Clark Gable in that," Mickey declares.

Ike's culinary tastes governed their daily fare. He loved food but scorned what he called "hifalutin gourmet stuff." Dinner consisted of Ike's favorites: steak, fried chicken, pork chops, lamb chops, roast beef, broiled fish, and, as often as he could persuade Mamie to persuade their cook to prepare it, a special baked-bean dish. It was prepared without the customary tomato sauce but with salt pork, molasses, and onions. Ingredients had to be measured exactly and combined properly, and, most important, it had to be baked slowly! Mamie knew the secret and, though she was too kitchen-clumsy to make it herself, could supervise its preparation by the Eisenhower cook.

Ike loved the beans so much that, as Supreme Commander, he taught his mess sergeant, Marty Snyder, how to prepare them at all of his European headquarters. Marty often had trouble finding molasses and substituted sorghum syrup which Ike thought equally good. One day, when Winston Churchill came to lunch in England, Eisenhower asked Snyder to prepare a typical American dish—"franks and those beans." Churchill personally congratulated the mess sergeant as Ike beamed. As for the hot dogs, the British prime minister pronounced them "a delicacy fit for a king, which is why His Majesty enjoyed them so much himself." Before the war, President Roosevelt had served hot dogs to King George VI and Queen Elizabeth at a garden party in Hyde Park.

The General was also fond of Chinese food, but preferred the take-out kind to a sit-down Oriental dinner in a restaurant. Even in the White House the First Family would, from time to time, send out for containers of egg rolls, chicken chow mein, egg foo yung, and roast pork with Chinese vegetables. (Later, Richard Nixon dined occasionally on Mexican dishes brought to the Executive Mansion in containers by Julie and David.)

Soups, too, were high on Ike's list. He had a special fondness for a dried noodle-soup mix that came in a packet. It was unavailable overseas, so Mamie would regularly send him quantities in the official War Department pouch that was flown from Washington to the Supreme Commander every morning. Nestling beside top-secret documents and official communications from President Roosevelt, General Marshall, and others would be a neatly wrapped bundle from Mamie, containing the soup mix.

When he could find time, Ike would put on an apron and cook himself at Fort Sam and even in Washington, though not as frequently as before. (In both homes, the Eisenhowers employed a part-time cook.) It was at Fort Sam that Ike perfected his home-style chicken-vegetable soup, which took two days to prepare. When Ike yielded to persuasion and published his recipe in a Columbia University cookbook, he observed ruefully that it received as much press coverage as any announcement he made as president of the institution. The soup's ingredients included turnips, raw cabbage, and nasturtium stems; the latter, he knew from his farm-boy days, had a spicy juice. Since nasturtium stems are not generally found in supermarkets Ike was inundated with letters asking where they could be obtained.

Ike's real specialty and greatest pride was a steak, charcoal broiled, which he did to perfection. He tried a number of techniques, finally settling on an unorthodox method that surprised cooking experts: for part of the time, remove the meat from the grill and toss it squarely into the glowing coals.*

Overseas, Ike paid regular visits to his kitchens, not to inspect but to see what was for dinner. Once in England he had invited a large number of high-ranking British officers for a major conference on the progress of the war. Boiling on the stove was a pot emitting a tantalizing aroma. Ike lifted the lid, inserted a spoon, and tasted.

"Boy, that's great," he said. "Absolutely great! But is there enough for all the company?"

"No, General," he was told. "That's slumgullion, just for the staff. The company is having chicken." Chicken was fine but Ike looked longingly at the pot as he left. The mess sergeant had spiced up leftovers for a kind of GI pot-au-feu.

Soon after his arrival in London, the General had executed a tactical maneuver that got him better chow.

One morning, when Mickey was arranging his office, Ike turned to his orderly and asked, "By the way, how's your food?"

"Fine, just fine," Mickey replied. "We get eggs every morning."

Ike turned in his chair. "Eggs?" he asked. "You guys get eggs?"

---

*See Appendix B for Ike's method of grilling the "perfect steak" and other favorite Eisenhower recipes.

"Sure," said Mickey, who was having his meals at the GI mess on Green Street, just off Hyde Park. "We have them scrambled, and with bacon."

Ike, who was having his meals at the British officers' mess, was wide-eyed. "Bacon and eggs?" he said. "We don't get anything like that. We get kippers, cold oatmeal, that sort of thing. And the coffee . . ." His voice trailed off.

"Why don't you come over and chow down with us some day, sir?" Mickey said expansively. Ike accepted at once. He'd be there the next day for lunch.

And he was. Mickey alerted the mess sergeant, who prepared roast pork and sauerkraut, which Ike loved. After that, the Commanding General was at the Green Street mess each day until he moved to the posh Dorchester Hotel, where his meals were prepared by the kitchen staff and served in his room. Even then, Mickey managed to liberate some eggs regularly from the GI mess and give them to the chef who cooked them for Ike.

Ike instructed his staff in matters other than military. At breakfast time one morning, Sergeant Snyder was preparing flapjacks in the kitchen when Ike walked in. Nudging them with a spatula, he noted that some were adhering to the griddle. The Commanding General said that the problem could be avoided by adding melted butter to the batter. Snyder explained that he had greased the griddle. Ike replied that his way was not only more efficient but would make the flapjacks taste better. From then on, flapjacks were done Ike's way.

On another occasion, when the Allies had established a beachhead in France and were moving inland, a delegation of joyous civilians arrived at Ike's headquarters leading a cow. "So the General could have some fresh milk," their leader explained. The General had given strict orders not to accept food from the liberated population, but this was different. The staff took the cow and a stool for milking her.

The trouble was that nobody on the staff knew how. Marty Snyder reached underneath, yanked but produced nothing. Others tried but got nowhere. While they were circling the animal, trying to unfathom the secret of her milk production, Eisenhower came out of his trailer head-quarters and wanted to know what was happening. Snyder, who relates the story, said, "We can't get this thing to work."

Ike, the one-time farm boy, could, and did. "I'll show you how to do this," he said. He squatted on the stool and squeezed the right places in the right way, quickly filling the bucket.

Along with most Army men, Eisenhower had a rich vocabulary of profanity, and used it when the occasion warranted, which occurred with a fair degree of frequency. Nor was he apt to clean up his language for Mamie. At first she was shocked, but as the years went on she barely noticed the words, though she never used them herself.

Once Mickey thought she did. He was driving her home late in the afternoon when he heard her exclaim in the back seat, "Oh, shoot!" Startled, Mickey half-turned his head and said incredulously, "What did you say, Mrs. Eisenhower?"

"I said, 'Oh, shoot. I forgot an errand.' Why, what did you think I said?"

Mickey blurted, "I thought you said something else."

"Oh, Mickey!"

While Mamie never tried to sanitize Ike's language, she sought to protect those who she felt should not be overex-posed to it. One day, shortly before he went overseas, Eisenhower asked George Patton, by then a brigadier general commanding the Second Armored Division, to the Wardman Park for a discussion of the war.* Mickey had parked the Eisenhowers' car in the basement garage and had come upstairs to give them the keys.

"The General is having a visitor over this evening,"

---

*Patton impressed Mickey. While visiting Ike at his headquarters in Algiers the General would rise at five A.M. and shave by flashlight in cold water.

Mamie told Mickey. "Why don't you just put out some ice and drinks and then you'd better leave, because if you hang around you're going to hear some language that, at your age, you ought not to listen to."

Says Mickey: "There I was, twenty-six years old, in the Army, a big boy. And she was afraid I'd hear naughty language."

Later, Mickey and the others of Ike's staff heard paint-blistering language from the boss when things went wrong, as they often did. One of Ike's worst tirades occurred on the February afternoon in 1943 when Eisenhower received his fourth star making him a full general. The trouble was that almost everyone knew about the promotion before he did.

A submarine mother ship captain named Barney Fawkes telephoned Tex Lee to tender his congratulations. Lee told it to Butch, who called Fawkes and asked how he found out. "Hell," the captain said, "it's on the BBC!" Butch there-upon congratulated Ike, who was stunned, but only for a moment. His face reddened and he burst out, "Why the hell doesn't somebody tell me these things!" It was accompanied by language which, in these days, would be labeled fit for mature audiences only. In the midst of Ike's frustrated tirade against the way things were done in the military, a Signal Corpsman called from the message center. There was a teletype from Mamie: "Congratulations on your fourth star." He still hadn't been told officially.

Ike's swearing earned him rebukes from some people throughout the country. When one woman wrote just after the war ended that America's great soldier hero should be "praying instead of cursing," Ike was hurt and a little bewildered. "Goddammit!" he burst out, "I don't curse. I just use some words as adjectives."

2. On Two Continents

"I'M WORRIED SICK about him," she told Walter Trohan, and looked it.

After Ike left for London in mid-June, 1942, as Commanding General of the entire European Theater, Mamie suffered intensely. Before there had been loneliness when he left, but this was a different kind of going-away; now he was in a shooting war. The harrowing radio news and the photographs of the relentless bombings of London in the Battle of Britain had badly frightened her. The newspapers were filled with ominous reports of new victories by the Germans, who were swallowing up Europe and North Africa and sinking American troopships in the Atlantic as well.

Mamie's anxiety over Ike's safety became severe. She was unable to eat solid food without retching. Never a good sleeper, she began suffering long bouts of insomnia. She had frequent sick headaches, each lasting hours.

She would wander around the rooms, looking at the seven framed photographs of him, in uniforms and civvies. She refused to go to the movies because there would always be newsreels of the war, which she did not want to see because inevitably Ike would appear on the screen, and that would make her cry. At home, she would cut out newspaper and magazine articles about him and paste them in a scrapbook. "My husband has become a pin-up boy," she told a visitor.

She kept one of his old tweed suits hanging in a closet; the rest were put away in storage. When she had a particularly bad day, missing him too much, she would touch it. "I wanted to handle it," she told Mrs. Robert H. Guggenheim, whose husband later became Ambassador to Portugal, "and luxuriate in that wonderful tobacco smell."

Her friends became alarmed at the way she looked because her health had never been robust.

A heart valve had been slightly scarred, aftermath of an undiagnosed attack of rheumatic fever in early adolescence. Since the valve did not shut properly, some blood continuously leaked back into a heart chamber, causing her to tire easily. Doctors told her the condition was not serious, but as the years went on she spent increasing amounts of time in bed. She had a chronic stomach ailment which baffled even the specialists at the Walter Reed Medical Center in Washington; it had been aggravated by her years in the tropics.

In the Philippines, she had given Ike a big scare. One day, she traveled to Baguio atop Mt. Santo Tomas in Luzon to visit John, who was enrolled in a school there.

Shortly after her arrival, she suffered intense stomach pains; within an hour she fainted in her hotel room. Rushed back to the post hospital, doctors found she was hemorrhaging. She was in a coma for days and barely survived. The stomach problem plagued her all her life.

"I feel fine," she told everyone during those times she later called "my three years without Eisenhower," * but

---

* A wry pun on the memoirs of Captain Harry C. Butcher, Ike's naval aide, *My Three Years with Eisenhower.*

there were many times when she did not. There would be a variety of ailments as time passed, among them severe colds, influenza, pneumonia, and shingles.

When Eisenhower's body was borne into the great rotunda of the United States Capitol to lie in state, Mamie did not follow the casket with the other dignitaries. She was unable to climb the long, steep steps.

In addition to her physical illnesses, Mamie had a claustrophobia in moderately severe form, one of the two reasons she hated to fly in planes; the other was, quite simply, fear. Her hospital doors would be kept slightly ajar to avoid the feeling of being enclosed. Even in the movies, she would look for seats with nobody on either side. "When I went with her," Mickey says, "she would ask me to sit behind her because she couldn't stand anybody that close. It made her feel hemmed in." In the White House movie theater, Ike's chair would be placed slightly apart from Mamie's.

The first year Ike was away, Mamie lost thirty pounds, her weight dropping to just above 105. She looked emaciated, knew it, and avoided photographers.

Ruth Butcher, who lived across the hall, came in each day, comforting her, trying to make her eat. Ruth was the wife of Captain Harry C. Butcher, who was Ike's naval aide in Europe and another close member of his Army "family." The Eisenhowers and Butchers had met in Washington in 1926, when Ike was a major, and had become good friends.* After Eisenhower was named to head the European Theater, he made an unprecedented request to have Butcher, a Naval Reserve officer on active duty, assigned to his headquarters as an aide and personal public-relations

---

* At that first meeting, Ike impressed "Butch" with a quite remarkable parlor stunt. Standing at rigid attention, hands at sides, Ike would fall forward like a wooden soldier. An instant before it looked to worried eyes as though his face would be smashed against the floor, his hands would flash forward to cushion the fall. In his war diary, Butch wrote in 1945 that Ike "can still do the trick and does on appropriate occasions."

man. It was granted and Butcher, a vice-president of the Columbia Broadcasting System when he enlisted in 1942, joined Ike in London.

Ruth had Mamie drinking several glasses of milk daily to help her keep solid food down, and to add poundage. After a year, she began to eat and sleep better but was never completely at ease all during the war.

"I finally told myself I couldn't carry on that way," she said. "I came to feel that God was not going to let anything happen to Ike until he had done what he was intended to."

(The faith, however, did not quite extend to cover her son, John, who went overseas following his graduation from West Point in 1944. In an observation that was pure Mamie, she admitted: "I wasn't quite so sure about Johnny. He was just a second lieutenant.")

Mamie had a small circle of friends, all Service wives whose husbands and sons were overseas. They pooled ration coupons and spent most afternoons playing mah-jongg in each other's homes and talking. One observer called it history's longest mah-jongg game—running three years without interruption. Often the games would lapse and there would be gloomy silences. "Mamie would always sense when somebody was worried," recalls Mrs. Henry J. Matchett, wife of a brigadier general. Then, though scarcely cheerful herself, she would attempt to snap the gloom. Mrs. Matchett, in retirement at Port Hueneme, California, recalls: "She'd say, 'What have you got in your icebox? Come up to the house tonight and we'll have potluck at Wardman Park.' We'd go up and Mamie would play the piano or organ and we'd sing together."

But they fooled nobody, least of all themselves. The worries were never far from the surface.

Other Army wives whose husbands were serving under Ike came to Mamie and poured out their troubles. Though lonely and fearful herself, Mamie became a kind of mother confessor to the younger women. "She was so responsive," declares Ruth Butcher, "that everyone felt comfortable with her."

Much of Mamie's time was spent solving home, child, and other problems brought on by the lengthy separations. Sometimes the misfortunes involved other women, a problem Mamie and Ruth were to come face to face with before too long.

Some days Mamie was a hostess at the Stage Door Canteen in Washington and waited on tables at the Soldiers, Sailors and Marine Club. Once she spilled gravy on a young soldier's uniform and got a: "Hey, lady, watch what you're doing!" She mopped up the stain, told him to wash it quickly in cold water, and assured him it would come out. He never knew he was spattered by the Commanding General's wife.

Other days she did Red Cross work, read mystery books, and for a brief time joined a small group of Senate and Service wives who had decided they wanted to learn Spanish. No brilliant linguistic performances resulted from the class. Mamie said later all they did was have lunch and talk.

For the most part, she was ignored by Washington's political leaders. Few seemed to know she existed, fewer invited her to cocktail and dinner parties which, though less elaborate than in prewar days, had not ceased to be a major part of the capital life style. The invitations that did arrive were politely declined; Mamie disapproved of wives who partied while the war was on.

She wrote letters to Ike regularly but was careful to include only amusing news about home, never items that might cause him concern. She would read them over carefully and if she felt they weren't upbeat enough she would tear them up and start over. Many evenings were spent answering the hundreds of letters she received from mothers and wives of servicemen Ike commanded. Frequently women enclosed clippings from hometown newspapers containing stories and pictures of her husband they thought she might not have seen.

Ike wrote as often as he could but often only had time to dash off a few paragraphs. Some letters were just a couple of short sentences, such as: "Loads of love. I miss you terribly and what a heap of good it would do me to have a long talk with you." The notes, rarely newsy, told of the enormous pressures of his work ("I'm swamped. I'm simply swamped"), of his loneliness for her and his family, and of the endless disappointments and difficulties that created severe nervous strains.

In the midst of the hectic preparations for the invasion of Sicily, Ike did not forget his wedding anniversary. On July 1, 1943, he sent Mamie one of his briefest yet most tender messages by cable from Algiers: "After twenty-seven years my only regret is that we cannot begin once more and live them all over again. Much love always." * Nine days later he led the force of a half-million men across the Mediterranean and secured the island on August 27.

Mamie waited eagerly for the letters, no matter how brief. Once, when nothing arrived for two weeks, she wrote to ask why. Ike answered quickly:

> You'll get others, dated between, because I never, no matter how rushed, let that much time intervene.
>
> I miss you terribly. The war wouldn't be nearly so tough on me if you could be here. It's been very lonesome and I'd love to see you home when I get there every day.

Sometimes, though she never knew when, there would be a telephone call, made and received with the greatest secrecy. Esther Thomas, the chief operator at the Wardman

---

* This touching message, not included in John Eisenhower's collection of *Letters to Mamie,* was published in *The Papers of Dwight D. Eisenhower*, vol. 2, Johns Hopkins Press, Baltimore and London, 1970.

Park, instructed her staff that all overseas messages must go through her. Miss Thomas knew that when a call came informing her that an unidentified person wished to talk to Mamie, that Ike was on the phone. Occasionally, Mamie, lonesome for his voice, would put a call through from her end but, Miss Thomas recalled, there were many others, high-ranking and celebrated, who also wanted to make overseas calls. "Miss Mamie always waited her turn," Miss Thomas recalls. "She never used rank to get service."

But Mamie was still spoiled enough to bug Ike about items of clothing and other products unobtainable in the States because of wartime shortages. She asked for warm woolen socks which she heard could still be purchased in Italy. Ike managed to acquire a couple of pairs and sent them to her for a birthday present. When Mamie wrote that stories were circulating in the United States that other merchandise, unavailable in the U.S., could still be had in Italy, Ike explained with little-concealed impatience that he had been hearing the same tales. However, Mamie had to understand that the Commanding General could not go off on shopping expeditions to check out products on sale in the stores. In all the time he had been in Europe and Africa, he told her, he had found time to visit a shop only once—when he bought her a scarf.

Nonetheless, Ike kept sending Mamie gifts he thought she would like: a small rug, though he had to pay four times its peacetime price; a silver bracelet made by a North African craftsman; another bracelet with gold ID tags; a pair of silk socks; white leather gloves.

To fill in the gaps, Mickey McKeogh wrote to Mamie faithfully every two weeks, his letters coming by official Army pouch.

Mickey: "I told her how he was doing, how he felt, how he looked—all personal stuff. If he had a cold, I told her not to worry, we're taking good care of him. If he needed anything from home, like underwear, shirts, pajamas or whatever, I'd let her know. The General never would bother; he'd wear pajamas that were torn or had all the buttons ripped off.

"Since the letters did not go through the official Army censors, I could tell Mrs. Eisenhower where we were, mention places we've been, the important persons he met. I'd tell her if he had a rough day, or describe a birthday party his staff gave him—who was there, what we had to eat, even if he blew out all the candles.

"Since I couldn't scrounge for Western magazines, and paperbacks where I was, I turned that job over to Mrs. Eisenhower. When the General ran out of them, I'd tell her and she'd send fresh batches."

Ike liked to pad around off hours in dime-store grass slippers which wore out quickly. Mamie sent new ones. He asked for, and got, a recording by Frank Crumit, a well-known popular singer, of a marathon-type song called "Abdul, the Bulbul Ameer." Ike knew at least fifty verses, and would sing them all at parties with very little urging. She sent him candy, jars of special foods, and, with regularity, the noodle-soup packets, as well as presents at Christmas, on his birthday, and their anniversary.

On the following New Year's in 1944, Mamie got her finest gift—and biggest surprise—since her husband left.

She had spent most of that Sunday in bed, reading and writing letters. Late in the afternoon, the doorbell rang. "Who is there?" she called out and a voice boomed from outside, "It's me!" Ike had come home on a twelve-day visit which was to remain a closely guarded secret until the war ended. Not even the doorman at the Wardman Park knew he was there that first day; Ike was taken around to a side entrance and rode to his floor on the freight elevator.

The week before, in Algiers, Eisenhower and his staff were sitting down to a Christmas Eve dinner before a tiny

TRAVEL TALK

With Your Warsaw Travel Specialists

Mary Robinson-ABS Supervisor

CRUISES FOR SENIORS

A cruise can be an ideal vacation for many seniors. Retirees can do as much or as little as they prefer each day. They will have the comfort and convenience of familiar surroundings to come back to after an excursion ashore. They will be secure in the knowledge that there will be no last minute surprises to destroy carefully planned budgets. There are staff personnel aboard ship who quickly learn passenger needs and preferences concerning cabin and table service. There is generally a medical facility with doctor, clinic and pharmacy to cope with basic health care. On many cruise lines, the purchase of an air/sea package also means escorted travel and assistance with baggage, customs and transportation in foreign ports.

If you are thinking of taking a vacation this winter, whether a warm cruise or a ski vacation, call the WARSAW TRAVEL SPECIALISTS (269-6771 or 1-800-342-5221) now. Get a jump on the people who wait until the last minute and then can't get what they would like. We are a full service agency with a friendly, knowledgeable staff waiting to cater to your every travel need. We are located at 1301 N. Detroit Street, Monday thru Friday 9 to 5:30 and Saturday 9-1. Most major credit cards are accepted.

<u>*SPECIAL ESCORTED GROUP:</u> Hawaii-$695.00 from Warsaw. Nov. 5-13. Space Limited!

At Wit's End

By Erma Bombeck

Remember the good old days when a sign would flash across the TV screen, "IT'S 11 O'CLOCK. DO YOU KNOW WHERE YOUR CHILDREN ARE?" And you wouldn't have a clue?

Now we know where they are. They're sprawled all over the living room in front of the TV set with a stack of rental video cassettes, eating and drinking their way through the house like a plague of locusts.

The VCR and the baby boomers have found one another, and the combination is revolutionizing the American family as we know it.

The other night as our kids were watching "Flashdance" again, my husband and I tiptoed through the room to the door.

"Where are you going?" aske my son.

"Out," we said.

"Out where?"

"Just out."

"Do you know what time it is?" he asked.

"Ten or so, why?"

"It's time when most people are going to bed. The only thing you can get into at this hour i trouble."

"Look," we said, "we don't tel you what to do. Besides, we're jus going to bum around."

My daughter said, "I don't know why you can't just spend a night a home once in a while and watch television with us. Would it kil you? We could pop a little corr and be a family."

VCR And The Baby Boomers

"It's boring," we said. "Besides, how many times can we watch 'Flashdance' and 'Romancing the Stone'? You never watch our shows."

"We'd watch them if you didn't watch trashy things. The only things you want to see are people with English accents."

"Well, we'd like to know where you get all this money to run around," said my son.

"That's our problem," said my husband.

"So, what time are you coming home?" asked our daughter.

"I don't know," I said. "Whenever we get here."

"That's not good enough, mom. You know you have to go to work tomorrow. Let's make it no later than midnight."

"Give me a break," I said. "I'm 57 years old."

"No, you give me a break. I lose another night's sleep and I'll look like an unpaved road."

Later, my husband and I returned to see them slumped in their chairs and the VCR playing "Raiders of the Lost Ark."

My daughter stirred, "It's about time. You know I can't go to bed until I hear the motor turn off and you're home. Lock up before you go to bed and turn off the VCR."

Kids can be so cruel. She knows I don't know how to turn it off. I'll be glad when we get our own apartment!

- Donnie R. Adams, 35, Rt. 1, Claypool, was charged with driving a motor vehicle while intoxicated. He was released on his own recognizance.
- Gordon Lee Yeager, 33, Rt. 1, Topeka, was charged with driving a motor vehicle while intoxicated. He was released on his own recognizance.
- Kevin Pennell, 19, Rt. 7, Rochester, was charged with illegal consumption.

Personal Injury Accident

County police investigated the following personal injury accident:
- 4 a.m. Sunday, County Rd. 900 North, one-mile east of County Rd. 450 West. One-car collision. Driver: Joseph R. Fortner, 22, Elkhart. Injury: Fortner, treated and released from Kosciusko Community Hospital. No damage estimates available.

Property Damage Accidents

Area police investigated the following property damage accidents:

supermarkets advertise "limited quantity" specials, as long as it is clear in the ad that supplies of the product might not meet demand.

IN A SEPARATE action, the commission voted 4-1 to drop proposed regulations for the hearing aid industry.

That rule sought to require that hearing aid sellers offer a 30-day trial period on their products.

The FTC staff reported last month that most hearing aid companies already offer trial periods, and a survey found that in general customers are satisfied with the devices. Thus, the staff said, it is unnecessary to impose a new rule that would cost time and money to enforce.

Finally, the agency was considering a proposal to drop a plan to set up industrywide regulations to prevent organizations that set standards from engaging in activities that might restrain trade. Instead, the commission staff said, any problems in this area should be handled tree strung with canned popcorn sent from home by Harry Butcher's mother. Wind whistled through the windows, broken by bomb blasts and inadequately stuffed with paper and covered with cardboard. They were celebrating Ike's Christmas present that year, a new job as the Pershing of World War II.

The Axis forces in North Africa had yielded and the drive up the Italian boot was well underway. The Allies were now projecting a victory and the time had come to plan and execute the invasion into Europe from the West. Ike would lead the leap across the channel as Supreme Commander of the entire Allied Expeditionary Force.

But first, there would be a fast trip to America.

Mickey began packing Ike's gear to be ready for the order to move the General out on the first leg of his journey. They would be heading to England where, Mickey thought, he would get Ike settled in his new quarters and await his return from the States.

On the morning of December 31, Mickey received his own belated Christmas gift. From the bathtub, Ike called out to his orderly, "Mickey, how long will it take you to get ready to come home with me?" Mickey, rarely speechless, admits that this time it took several seconds to find words. "Well?" Ike bellowed from the bath.

"Less than ten minutes!" Mickey finally hollered back, and he was, although the General, Harry Butcher, and Mickey did not leave until the next morning, flying first for Marrakech in Morocco, six hundred miles to the southwest. That evening, Mickey got hold of a bottle of champagne and brought it to Ike with three glasses, for Ike, Butch, and another officer flying with them. "Get yourself a glass" Ike told Mickey—and the four toasted the New Year in.

They reached Washington at one A.M. on January 2. Ike headed for the Wardman Park and told Mickey to go home until he received orders to rejoin him for the trip back.

When he reached home on 35th Avenue in the Corona section of Queens, Mickey's mother, Mary, a tiny gray-haired woman, almost fainted with surprise.

At the Wardman Park, the wives of Ike and Butch were no less astounded and happy, though they accorded a somewhat less joyous reception to three pets Ike and Butch had brought home. Ike had been given a black scottie named Telek for a birthday present the year before to whom he had become quite attached and the affection was strongly reciprocated. Telek had sired two puppies six months earlier. Ike, disliking the thought of leaving the little family behind, took the three with him, and promptly regretted it. Less than a minute after they entered his apartment, the two puppies, Junior and Rubev, disgraced themselves on Mamie's Oriental rug. "Oh, Lord," Ike groaned, as Mamie stared bleakly. Ike picked them up and brought them, with their sire, to the Butchers' apartment where, this time to Ruth's dismay, the performance was repeated. The dogs were banished to the kitchen. Later, one of the puppies was presented to Milton Eisenhower's son, Buddy, and the other to the daughter of a close friend.

Next day, Ike and Mamie were driven to a railroad siding in a desolate part of Maryland where, in total secrecy, they boarded a special car bound for West Point. It stopped just short of the Academy, and young John joined them for a happy reunion, the first since Ike's departure.

The next ten days were a whirlwind of travel. It included a trip to Manhattan, Kansas, where Ike's brother Milton was president of Kansas State College. The General's mother and other members of his family joined them there. Ike and Mamie managed to have several private days together at a secluded cottage on the grounds of the Greenbrier Hotel in White Sulphur Springs, West Virginia, which had been taken over by an Army hospital as a convalescent home.

Time had to be made for leading Democratic and

Republican leaders to meet the Supreme Commander, for briefings on new weapons-development systems by military experts, for talks on the problems the Allies would face in their cross-Channel bound.

And then it was over.

"I said good-bye to him and thought my heart would break," Mamie said.

Early on the morning of January 14 the Supreme Commander flew back to the war. At Prestwick, Scotland, a private train took him to London.

The entire trip, all eleven days of it, was managed with military precision. Ike saw his family, met with leaders, and even got in an evening of poker with generals and admirals at the Alibi Club in Washington. And the country never knew he was there, thanks to perfect arrangements and total cooperation of the press.

There was only one "unfortunate incident," Ike wrote to Mamie on his return. Somebody stole the bag of pecans and vitamin chocolates Mamie had given him when he left.

3. Mamie's D-Day

JUNE 6, 1944, was Mamie's longest day too.

Summer comes early to the nation's capital. On the morning of June 5, with the mercury already beginning its climb, Mamie, Ruth Butcher, and Mr. and Mrs. Doud took a taxi to Union Station and boarded a train for Jersey City. A corporal approached them on the platform, identified himself, and led them to a waiting Army automobile. He drove them fifty miles along the Hudson Highlands to the expanse of massive granite buildings and broad green lawns of the United States Military Academy.

Near the gate, a mile from the gray cadet barracks where Grant, Stonewall Jackson, Pershing—and Eisenhower— studied, they entered the cool lobby of the gray-stone Hotel Thayer, operated by the Academy. Mamie and Ruth shared a twin-bedded double room (for which they paid six dollars), next door to the Douds, who had arrived in Washington from Denver the day before.

The four had dinner at the hotel, then Mamie pleaded she was tired from the journey and went to bed early. But she was too keyed up to sleep. John Eisenhower was graduating

122

from the Point next morning and she was excited at the prospect of watching him toss his white hat into the air with the other new lieutenants in the traditional gesture of farewell. There was another reason why her nerves were more taut than usual. Rumors had been rising in intensity since spring that the war in Europe was approaching a climactic phase.

She had brought along a portable radio to hear the newscasts. There was little to report. Few on the home front knew that Plan Overlord, involving the greatest invasion force ever assembled on earth, was about to be launched.

Shortly after midnight, Mamie fell asleep but she had a restless night. "At seven or seven-thirty," she said, "the telephone rang. Most of my calls were screened to protect me, and I didn't know what to expect. It was a reporter asking, 'What do you think of the invasion?'"

Mamie bolted from bed, the phone still in her hand. "What invasion?" she demanded.

"They just made the landings in France," the reporter told her.

Half stunned, Mamie cradled the phone, then lifted it again to call her parents next door. She woke them with the news, then switched on her radio.

"Breakfast was a blur," she remembered. "The reality of the news was a shock. I had two of them—my husband and my son, all I had in the world. Ike was in it; Johnny was heading right toward it."

The next few hours had a dreamlike quality. She remembered trying to watch the cadets' parade on the green plain and the graduation ceremonies that followed, but it was as though she was peering through gauze. She could barely make out the words of the message her husband had sent from Europe, which was read to the more than eight hundred members of the graduating class, among them her son.

Ike had said: "Clearly and soberly recognizing the sternness of the tasks still ahead of us in this war, we face them calmly and with confidence, because of our trust in divine Providence and our faith in her young leaders, upon whose shoulders the heaviest battle burdens habitually fall. We know that by the soldierly qualities of devotion to duty, character, and skill, you will measure up to the high standards and examples daily being set by your contemporaries from all walks of life, who are carrying on the work in which you will soon be engaged."

Mamie, whose womanly wisdom had always been underestimated, was profoundly moving in her recollections of that day. What she said, and what she felt, was a measure of her growth as a person in the quarter-century that had passed since the death of little Icky. For she knew on D-day, as she had failed to realize as a young mother, that in a time of crisis neither a wife nor a husband can truly know the thoughts and the emotions experienced by the other.

Many years afterward, she and Ike were to talk about their thoughts, feelings, and experiences that crucial day after he had given the order to launch the immense force of ships, men, and planes despite miserable weather conditions that could doom the entire operation.*

Even later however, it was hard for Mamie to put her thoughts into words. To Perle Mesta she confided that she and Ike underwent a private anguish that could not really be shared. "Neither of us," Mamie said, "really knew what the other went through. I think, I felt most strongly the awesome responsibility he held—to have to send all those men into action. It's something that's hard to grasp. I know that when we went back to those Normandy beaches, I marveled at how they did what they did. If I had known

---

* Ike, unsure of the outcome, had prepared two messages to his troops. One congratulated them on their great victory for having secured the beaches; the other expressed regret that the attack had failed, and that "if any blame or fault attaches to the attempt it is mine alone."

then what they were up against on D-Day, it would have been much worse for me."

After lunch at West Point, John Eisenhower, still in starched white trousers and full-dress coat with cross belt, came to the Thayer Hotel. Mamie saw an envelope in his hand and, as a long-time Army wife, recognized it at once. She felt giddy and closed her eyes for a moment. John, she knew, was holding sealed orders that could only mean combat duty and, the most likely of possibilities, in the European Theater where the fiercest fighting in history was even then bloodying the beaches and countryside.

She was right. In a few hours she was standing at the hotel window waving as he entered a car for the drive to New York where he boarded the *Queen Mary,* on duty as a troopship, heading for the war zone.

Mamie's concerns were not confined to the physical safety of her husband and son. Rumors began to circulate around Washington that Ike had become involved romantically with an attractive young Irishwoman from County Cork who had been a fashion model and a movie bit player before the war. She had enlisted in the British Women's Auxiliary Corps in 1942, a volunteer group, and had been assigned to drive General Eisenhower on his arrival in London. Shortly afterward, she was attached to his personal staff.

Her name was Kathleen McCarthy-Morrogh Summersby, separated from her husband Gordon Summersby, an Englishman then serving with the British Army in India. In 1942 she was thirty-two years old. Mamie was forty-seven.

As the months passed, the reports intensified. Men returning from Europe for brief leaves told their wives, who told Mamie's friends who, in turn, tried to shield Mamie, though unsuccessfully. A veiled reference to "Eisenhower's pretty Irish driver" found its way into print; no gossip columnist ever wrote the story but here and there innuendos that could not be mistaken by those who were hearing the rumors were published.

The new worry, coming on top of Mamie's loneliness and fears, increased her agitation and undermined still more her fragile emotional stability.

She began drinking too much.

4. Kay—The Myth of the Letters

THE GOSSIP ABOUT Eisenhower and Kay Summersby was more widespread than Mamie realized. Correspondents covering the European Theater were among the first to hear the stories. In London they flew through Fleet Street and, after the invasion, livened the talk at the bar of the Hotel Scribe near the Place de l'Opéra, where most of the war reporters stayed. In London, Paris, Nice, Strasbourg, and Rome the staff of *The Stars and Stripes,* the Army newspaper, swapped Ike-and-Kay stories and jokes, taking it for granted that the General had found what many GIs serving under him were seeking, and often finding, too.

"Ike," commented one *Stripes* staffer in the Rue de Berri offices in Paris, "has a better deal than the rest of us. He can get as many packs of gum as he wants." It was a cynical reference to the fact that many girls overseas were bedding down with soldiers in exchange for gum, chocolates, and other unobtainable items.

As managing editor of the *Stripes* Paris edition, Lester

David heard the gossip almost as soon as he joined the staff in September 1944. One correspondent returned to the office from the front with the story that Ike and Kay had spent the weekend in a walled-in country chateau forty kilometers southwest of Paris as guests of a wealthy Frenchman. Another confided that the General and Kay were even then less than a few blocks away, overnight guests of the Duke and Duchess of Windsor at their rented home just off the Avenue des Champs-Élysées. Several of us walked over after dinner to catch a glimpse, but the mission was a failure.

Eisenhower's case is hardly unique in our history. The historian Fawn M. Brodie of UCLA wrote, "Eventually the idea would become a part of the folklore of the American Presidency that there must surely be a mistress, if not in the White House then in some dark closet of the President's past." Some of these scandals had some basis in truth, others just a little, still others none at all. Few Chief Executives have escaped.

The tradition began with George Washington himself, who, historians have established, had an ungovernable passion in his youth for one Sally Fairfax, unhappily for him already wed. Washington wrote her many ardent letters, in one of which he rhapsodized about "those happy moments, the happiest of my life, which I have enjoyed in your company." After Sally left for England, her belongings were auctioned off. As keepsakes, perhaps as reminders, for all one knows today, Washington purchased the pillows and bolster she had in her bedroom.

The story that Thomas Jefferson had a long-time liaison with Sally Hemings, a slave woman, had been rumored, and disputed, for almost 175 years. In her biography of the third President, Dr. Brodie offers evidence that the relationship was not debasing exploitation of a slave on Jefferson's part as many claimed, but a "serious passion" that gave to both "much private happiness" for thirty-eight years.

Grover Cleveland admitted fathering an illegitimate child, a confession that allowed Republican opponents to parade down city streets shouting in derision, "Ma, Ma, where's my pa? Gone to the White House, ha, ha, ha!" President Warren Harding actually used a closet in the Executive Mansion for a tryst, his biographers disclosed after his death. F.D.R.'s long relationship with Lucy Mercer Rutherford has been amply documented. John F. Kennedy had apparently borne out Norman Mailer's prediction that his thousand days might one day be equally famous for its nights. Lyndon Johnson has been reported to have had numerous liaisons in a little room off the Oval Office with a "woman around town."

If the gossip about these Presidents has been found to have some substance, talk about the others has not, yet it persisted nonetheless. Even straitlaced Richard Nixon was a victim. Just before he resigned his office following the Watergate scandal, newspersons got wind of a report that he was having a relationship with a beautiful Far Eastern woman. Another time, Nixon was alleged to have written almost two dozen love letters to the wife of a member of the diplomatic corps. Both stories were fakes and soon faded.

What, now, about the Eisenhower-Summersby story? Added to the lengthy list of Presidential scandals, it has become one of the most widely publicized illicit romances of modern times.

Did it all happen as described? Was it partly true, or not true at all?

When the war ended the rumors quickly became old gossip and faded fast until suddenly, in 1973, they exploded into world headlines.

According to a published account that year, former President Harry Truman revealed that after peace had been restored in Europe, Ike and Chief of Staff George Marshall exchanged letters. Truman was quoted as saying that

Eisenhower asked to be relieved from duty because he
wanted to divorce Mamie and marry Kay Summersby with
whom he planned to return to the United States. To this,
Truman said, Marshall sent a blistering reply in which he
denied Ike's request and warned that if he "even came
close" to putting such a plan into action he [Marshall] would
"not only bust him out of the Army, he'd see to it that never
for the rest of his life would he be able to draw a peaceful
breath." In or out of the service, and wherever he was,
wrote Marshall, "if he ever mentioned a thing like that
again, he'd see to it that the rest of his life was a living hell."

As one of the final acts of his administration, Truman said
he "got" the two letters from General Eisenhower's official
file, stored in the Pentagon, and destroyed them.

Truman's sensational remarks were published post-
humously late in 1973 in *Plain Speaking,* a series of
conversations Merle Miller, the author and journalist, had
with the late President in 1961 and 1962. The Truman
account blew the dust off the rumor by then almost three
decades old. Ike himself had been dead since 1969, Mamie
was nearing her seventy-seventh birthday, and Kay, close to
her middle sixties, was dying of cancer in New York.

Three years later Summersby's memoirs, also post-
humous, were published. In this, her second book, she
wrote about the "intimacy" that had grown between her
and the General during the three years she served as his
driver and later his secretary. The book, called *Past
Forgetting,* bore the subtitle *My Love Affair with Dwight D.
Eisenhower.* In May of 1979 the American Broadcasting
Company televised a six-hour mini-series called "Ike" in
which the story of the relationship (considerably watered
down from the version told by Kay and charged by Truman)
was an integral part. Published simultaneously with the
telecast was a paperback book, also titled *Ike,* a "noveliza-
tion based on fact" which purported to tell about "the
human being who found tenderness and compassion in the

British [sic] girl he made the first female Five Star Aide in the annals of warfare."

Despite the headlines, only two pieces of hard evidence could have confirmed the existence of a romance—the letters reportedly exchanged between Eisenhower and Marshall. But investigation leads to the conclusion that these letters were never written. Kay's memoirs, while rich in detail, including conversations, places visited, vows of love, and even such descriptions as "his kisses absolutely unraveled me," offer no documentary proof. A number of eminent historians, including Dr. Forrest C. Pogue, who has spent thirty-five years studying the lives of Marshall and Eisenhower, told us: "Almost everything there is slippery. There is nothing that can be impartially checked by scholars."

The letters and story amazed and infuriated close associates of Eisenhower. James C. Hagerty, Ike's former White House press secretary, was living in retirement in Scarsdale, New York, when the story broke. When his wife asked him about them, Jim replied with a flash of his famous temper, "That's a lot of bull!"

In Washington, General Gruenther, Ike's Chief of Staff during the war before becoming NATO Commander, was irate. Now in retirement (the General was eighty-one years old in 1980) Gruenther told us, "I knew Ike, and the story is absolutely false." Gabriel Hauge, former chairman of the board of Manufacturers Hanover Corporation, who served on Ike's White House staff, said in New York, "It was not the Ike I knew."

These and other strong comments from Eisenhower's associates—including the angry outburst from his son John that it was all "hogwash"—could, of course, be dismissed as attempts to defend Ike's reputation. But there is other evidence that Ike's relationship with Kay was less than rumored.

Begin with General Marshall and the way he treated similar kinds of behavior on the part of his officers.

As noted earlier, sexual interludes by the brass, including generals and admirals, were commonplace during the war. The U.S. high command spent little time worrying about these incidents, generally adopting the view that a man's dalliances with women should properly be of no concern to anyone but his wife, if he had one—that is, unless the involvements became serious enough to affect his work.

Then George Marshall would step in. The Chief of Staff, though based in Washington, knew more about his officers' personal lives than they suspected. It was not easy to hide a heavy relationship with a woman; other officers would almost inevitably know and, for the good of the service or perhaps their own careers, would manage to let Marshall know. When Marshall heard, he investigated, and he acted.

How he acted is central to the mystery of the Eisenhower-Marshall correspondence.

We talked at length about the purported letters with Dr. Pogue, a military historian who was, for eighteen years, director of the Marshall Research Center and later the Marshall Library in Lexington, Virginia. In 1956 he was commissioned by the George C. Marshall Foundation, with the General's approval, to compile the official biography and spent two decades at the task, examining thousands of Marshall documents, including all of his letters. He also interviewed hundreds of his associates in this country, Britain, and France, and in addition was given access to all of the Marshall files in the Pentagon.*

During the war, Dr. Pogue told us, a number of stories came to Marshall's attention about officers who were seriously involved with women. To these, he wrote letters of reprimand.

In one note, the Chief of Staff declared that he was not a

---

*Three volumes of Dr. Pogue's massive four-volume biography have been published: vol. 1, *Education of a General* (1963); vol. 2, *Ordeal and Hope* (1966); vol. 3, *Organizer of Victory* (1973). New York: Viking Press.

"prudish person" and, moreover, the officer's private life was actually none of the General's business—that is, unless it becomes "Army business." In the present instance, Marshall said, the officer's affair was adversely affecting the reputation of the Army in the area where he was stationed. He added that if the officer could not end his relationship, he [Marshall] would reluctantly have to shift him to another post.

In another case, stories had reached Marshall that a general had developed a serious alcohol problem. The Chief of Staff wrote that the General's drinking was affecting his ability to command. In his letter Marshall said he had intended to give the officer a higher post but, under the circumstances, could only conclude that it was inadvisable. (Later, when word came that the General had taken the warning letter to heart and straightened out, Marshall showed compassion and did approve another, important command for him.)

"In his letters of reprimand," Dr. Pogue said, "General Marshall always concluded with these words: 'There are only two copies of this letter. You have one. I have the other. It is not going into your 201 file.'" (An officer's 201 file is the permanent record of his Army career in which all transfers and promotions are recorded, and commendations and reprimands, if any, are placed. It is kept at the headquarters of the command to which he is attached and follows the officer to whatever post he is sent.)

Copies of these reprimands were placed in a special sealed file in the Pentagon, Dr. Pogue said, files which he opened, studied, and resealed.

"Marshall did not rave or rant in any of them," Dr. Pogue told us. "The tone was not harsh or threatening, as the Truman account says of the letter purportedly written to Eisenhower. There were no caustic warnings of 'I'm going to bust you' or that he would make an officer's life a 'living hell' if he did not straighten up. That was not Marshall's style at all. Instead of verbally pounding the table, his attitude was that of a favorite uncle, somewhat sadly, yet necessarily, chastising an errant nephew.

"If this was his pattern of dealing with others of his staff, why then should Marshall have reversed it completely for Ike, of whom he was genuinely fond?"

Was there, or was there not, a letter in General Eisenhower's file?

Dr. Pogue found none, but of course he examined the reprimand file in 1956, four years after Harry Truman said he had destroyed it.

"If it existed at all," Dr. Pogue says, "that letter would have to have been in that special file which I know *General Marshall never allowed to be taken from the Pentagon.* That is crucial to understand. From the time Marshall left the job of Chief of Staff in November 1945 until the day he died in October 1959, Marshall had an office in the Pentagon. All five-star generals after their retirement are given a small Pentagon suite and are assigned an aide-de-camp, a secretary, and an orderly.

"Truman said he destroyed the letters as one of the last acts of his Presidency. Since he left office on January 19, 1953, that would be in late 1952 or even early 1953. During this time frame, a Colonel C. S. George was Marshall's aide-de-camp. He was stationed in Marshall's Pentagon office and was in sole charge of that special file."

We tracked down the Colonel, now retired and living on Woodhaven Lane in Bowie, Maryland.

"I started my service with General Marshall," Colonel George says, "on January 21, 1947, and remained with him until his death in 1959. General Marshall's files were kept in Room 2E664, a small two-room suite consisting of a main office and the anteroom, or secretary's office. It is on the first floor as one comes into the building through the mall entrance.

"The cabinet in which the file was kept was a brown metal

safe-type, which could only be opened by one who had the combination. I was the only one who knew it. The letters of reprimand were kept in one of the drawers in a slender manila envelope and were sealed with scotch tape."

We asked Colonel George, "Did you ever get a request from President Truman or any of his aides to destroy a letter written to General Eisenhower?"

"None whatsoever."

"Did President Truman himself ever come down to see the file, open it, and destroy any letter inside?"

"He did not."

"If the President had sent anyone with orders to destroy any letter, would you have obeyed that order?"

"Not without checking with my boss first."

"With General Marshall?

"Yes."

"Could that metal cabinet have been tampered with without your knowledge? Could someone have entered the office in your absence and, in some way, opened the safe?"

"There was a sign on the cabinet which read that, in case of violation of security, notify Colonel George. My telephone number was given. Therefore if a secretary or anyone else had noticed any evidence of tampering, I'd be called, but I never was and I personally never noticed any evidence that the cabinet had been forced open."

Further, Dr. Pogue had many interviews with General Marshall while he was preparing his definitive four-volume biography. Marshall talked of many things, including the lives and behavior of his officers, but never once did he make any mention of any correspondence he had with Eisenhower about Kay Summersby.

Another item that stretches credulity is that Summersby admits in her memoirs that she had no idea that Ike planned to make her his wife. She said she learned it for the first time when the Truman account was shown to her. The question must be asked: if a man is seeking to divorce his wife to marry someone else, would he keep his intention a total secret from the woman he wishes to wed?

The letters story also surfaced briefly during the 1952 Presidential campaign when Adlai Stevenson ran against Eisenhower. Somehow the Democratic National Committee reportedly obtained what it claimed was a copy of the letter.

At the time, Senator Joseph R. McCarthy was scheduled to deliver a vicious speech in Chicago attacking "pinks and pansies," an unveiled reference to charges that Stevenson was soft on Communism with innuendoes of homosexuality. The Democrats, through an agent planted in the opposition's hierarchy, got hold of the talk and sent word to the Republicans that unless the venom was removed, they would make the Marshall letter public. When the speech was delivered, the tale continues, the offending remarks had been omitted.

While there was no scarcity of persons who had heard the story, we could find nobody who actually saw a copy of the letter. In a book of memoirs, the political correspondent Marquis Childs offers a version of the letter that differs from the Truman account. In this, Eisenhower actually came to the United States during the war for the purpose of divorcing Mamie to marry Kay. Childs writes, "In blunt military language, Marshall informed him [Eisenhower] that he was aware of the reasons for his return, that he was absent without leave, and that if he did not resume his post immediately he would be relieved of his command." Alistair Cooke also reports that Marshall, in his letter, commanded Ike "to stay with his command, and his wife, and forget a young Englishwoman, who had been his wartime chauffeuse and, apparently, his mistress."

One has only to search the record to affirm that Eisenhower did not come back to this country on his own initiative. *He was ordered to return by Marshall himself.* Planning for the invasion of Europe was getting underway;

Ike would soon be under considerable tension. Marshall, aware of this, sent him the following, dated December 29, 1943:

> You will be under terrific strain from now on. I am interested that you are fully prepared to bear the strain and I am not interested in the usual rejoinder that you can take it. It is of vast importance that you be fresh mentally and you certainly will not be if you go straight from one great problem to another. Now come on home and see your wife and trust somebody else for twenty minutes in England.

Among the documents in the Marshall Library is a memorandum written by Marshall which states that, on January 4, 1944, the Chief of Staff informed President Roosevelt about the order. "I had brought him home over his strenuous objections," he told the President, "to force him to take a brief rest before he undertakes his heavy obligations in England."

His eleven days in the United States have been fully documented. Moreover, it was the only time he returned to America from the time he left until his triumphant welcome in June 1945. Historians have raked over Eisenhower's military career thoroughly, Dr. Pogue asserts, "and nowhere is there the slightest evidence that he came back to the States more than that one time." Moreover, Marshall would hardly have ordered Ike home for a rest prior to D-Day only to state that he was AWOL.

Still another fact that raises doubts about the existence of the Marshall letter lies in Harry Truman's private diary, in which during his Presidency he recorded, in his own handwriting, his thoughts and observations. After he died the diary was placed in the Truman Library at Independence, Missouri, where it was discovered in the summer of 1980 by Dr. Francis L. Loewenheim, professor of history at Rice University in Houston.

Dr. Loewenheim, a diplomatic and political historian, went through all of the entries in the hundreds of pages. "There are biting references to Ike," he told us, "many of them highly critical. But there is nothing in any of the entries that refers even remotely to Kay Summersby and the reported letters. This was a sealed, highly personal document. If the letters did exist, surely there would have been some reference to them there."

It is quite likely, in view of the evidence—or lack of it— that Truman's story about Ike, Marshall, and Kay Summersby came from a dimming memory and his own feelings about Eisenhower.

Harry Truman did not let a grudge die easily. His bitterness toward Ike is well known. It began in 1952 when Ike refused Truman's offer to step down if Ike ran for the Presidency as a Democrat. What followed was nasty. Truman launched into a vicious assault on Ike. At one point he went so far as to charge that the General had not only shirked his Army duties but believed the very "master race" theories of the Nazis he had defeated! Another time Truman said Ike was "showing the nation—he has certainly shown me—that he's not the man we thought him. He doesn't measure up."

Then there was the story of Bess Truman's breakfast which Ike spurned.

After Eisenhower's election, Truman invited Ike and Mamie to the White House for breakfast on Inauguration Day. Bess had ordered a special meal prepared for the incoming President but Ike, parked outside in a limousine, sent word that he preferred to go directly to the Capitol steps for the ceremony. Truman was incensed. Eleven years later, says Robert Sherrod who interviewed him on his eightieth birthday, he recalled the incident and clearly showed that the snub still rankled. "The madam had this lovely breakfast all ready," Truman said. "I told her what

Ike said and she said, 'Well, if he doesn't want to come in and that's his kind of courtesy, go ahead.'" Leaving the breakfast untouched, Truman, still seething, went to the Inauguration.

For his part, Ike was angry because his son, John, had been ordered home from Korea in a manner that had bypassed usual Army channels. Ike, a stickler for military discipline, was puzzled and annoyed. En route to the Inauguration he asked Truman who had summoned John home. Truman replied: "Ike, you're looking at the Commander in Chief and he ordered him here. What the hell are you going to do about it?" It was a generous gesture on Truman's part but Eisenhower felt it should not have been done because it smacked of special privilege.

After that, Truman and Eisenhower hardly communicated with one another. Several times, Ike invited the former President to the White House but Truman never accepted. John says that his father just wrote off Harry Truman because he did not "particularly admire" his abilities. Truman felt the same way toward Eisenhower.

There was never any reconciliation.

It is a curious coincidence that another tale Truman told about a historical military figure has been labeled "cockeyed" by a reporter who witnessed the incident in question. It involved General Douglas MacArthur and, like the Ike-Kay divorce account, has been widely accepted as fact.

The story centers around the historic Truman-MacArthur meeting on Wake Island in the west-central Pacific in October 1950, shortly after the invasion of South Korea. MacArthur, then Supreme Commander of the Allied occupation army in Japan, had also been named to head the United Nations defending force.The General, flying in from the East, was to meet the President coming from the West.

Truman's account of the meeting, the heart of which is a sharp putdown of the General by the President, differs markedly from that of observers. The President's recollection: a game of one-upmanship began when their planes approached Wake; each sought to land first so that the other would be waiting on the field. Ultimately, the MacArthur plane landed first but the General remained in his Quonset hut, in no hurry to greet his chief. Finally, he emerged and Truman came down the ramp. Later, at a private meeting, the General kept Truman waiting forty-five minutes before showing up, whereupon he told MacArthur, "I don't give a good goddamn what you do or think about Harry Truman, but don't you ever keep your Commander in Chief waiting. Is that clear?"

Robert Sherrod, then a reporter for *Time* magazine, who was there, points out that the planes could not have vied to be last to land because MacArthur was already on Wake, having arrived *about twelve hours earlier.* Secondly, while MacArthur did remain in his hut until after the President's plane landed, at six-thirty A.M., he rode out to the aircraft in an old Chevrolet just as the ladder was being put in place and in time to greet him.

Sherrod, writing in *The New York Times,* on December 8, 1973, reports that a "grinning President" descended the ramp and said to MacArthur, "I've been a long time meeting you, General." To this MacArthur answered, "I hope it won't be so long next time, Mr. President." Sherrod in his dispatch to *Time* magazine cabled that "all was geniality," and adds, "As for what the President said to the General in their one-hour tête-à-tête, the evidence is overwhelmingly against any hostility." MacArthur had just successfully completed the landing at Inchon which had earned him great acclaim. Truman had told Sherrod how much he admired MacArthur "whom he wanted to decorate."

Sherrod believes Truman did not become disenchanted with MacArthur until after the meeting, when the General's views on the conduct of the war continued to clash with those of his administration. Six months after Wake, on April 11, 1951, Truman fired MacArthur.

"At age seventy-eight," Sherrod says, "the late President had come to confuse the wish with the deed—something I noticed in a series of interviews with him in 1964. Historians are painfully aware of the fallibility of old men's memories."

In his monumental biography of MacArthur, *American Caesar,* William Manchester also refutes the Truman version of the meeting. Manchester examined the flight log of the General's plane and talked with General Omar Bradley, Army Secretary Frank Pace, and Dean Rusk who flew with the President. He confirms that MacArthur arrived hours before Truman. Rusk, then Assistant Secretary of State for Far Eastern Affairs, told Manchester, "The account given by President Truman in his interview with Merle Miller simply represented a very old man's faulty memory and Merle Miller's willingness to exploit it."

And finally, Truman himself in his memoirs, published in 1956 when memory was fresher, wrote: "General MacArthur was at the ramp of the plane as I came down. His shirt was unbuttoned, and he was wearing a cap that had seen a great deal of use. We greeted each other cordially and after the photographers had finished their usual picture orgy we got into an old two-door sedan and drove to the office of the airline manager on the island."

A mysterious flickering light, likened by some to a pale flame, is sometimes observed in marshy grounds and in churchyards. Scientists studying the phenomenon call it *ignis fatuus,* Latin for foolish fire. Popularly, it is known as will-'o-the-wisp. Whenever anyone searches for this strange light, it vanishes. On close examination it would seem that Eisenhower's request to Marshall and the latter's "warning" are little more than foolish fire.

5.   Kay — The "Romance"

"THE GREAT LOVE in Kay Summersby's life during the war was not Dwight Eisenhower but Dick Arnold, a tall and very good-looking West Pointer from Florida. He was a captain in the Corps of Engineers when she met him in London before Ike came over and she remained in love with him until he was killed in North Africa.

"To the very end of her life, more than thirty years later, she never forgot Dick. To the day she died she kept all the letters he ever wrote, all his pictures, everything.

"As for Ike, she had nothing but nice things to say about him. He was kind and helpful and wonderful to her. He, of course, found her very attractive. Who wouldn't? As for Mamie, Kay never would say anything against her."

We were talking with Anthea Saxe, an attractive former Englishwoman who now lives in Westport, Connecticut. Mrs. Saxe was revealing some truths about Ike and Kay that have never been told before.

It has been said that, with both principals gone, nobody can know the full story, yet there are aspects of the

142

relationship that, if they cannot be cleared up entirely, can be clarified by persons who were in day-by-day contact with them during the time of the reported "affair."

Few were closer to Kay than Anthea Saxe. Anthea and Kay Summersby met in London shortly after Pearl Harbor. Anthea served in the same division of the Motor Transport Corps with Kay and they remained friends all through the war and for many years afterward until Kay's death in 1975. Kay was godmother to Anthea's eldest son, Chris, and both were with her the day she was taken to the hospital where she died. Anthea was the executor of Kay Summersby's will.

Kay and Anthea met for the first time in Grosvenor Square, the posh area in the heart of the Mayfair section which became the headquarters of the U.S. Commanding Officer and his staff. Today, the gardens are well-kept and the square, one of London's largest, is a quiet oasis in rush hour.

In wartime, the elegant private homes and expensive flats on all four sides were occupied by the Americans, whose jeeps and command cars darted in day and night from Duke Street to the north and up from Carlos Place to the south. Major General Eisenhower's office was on the second floor at Number 20, an apartment building across the square from the white granite American Embassy.*

There was even a mess hall in the basement from which the smells of cabbage boiling and bacon frying drifted into his small suite. Dozens of persons, British and American officers as well as high-ranking civilians from the Allied nations, bustled through it hourly to see Ike, crowding past Butcher and Tex Lee, who were jammed into a ten-by-twelve-foot office that had once been a dressing room.

---

*The old embassy building at Number 1 has since been taken over by the Canadian Trade Commission. A new embassy has been built on the west side of the square. Designed by Eliel Saarinen, it is a showplace with its huge eagle and massive gilded front.

A group of young, attractive women would arrive early each morning and wait in the large room on the main floor, smoking, drinking coffee, and chatting until summoned to duty. These were the drivers of the British Women's Motor Transport Corps, all volunteers, all civilians though they wore dress uniforms of British Army officers. The corps had been created in 1939 shortly after the general call-up to free men for active service.

One of this group of about two dozen drivers was young Anthea Gordon, eighteen years old and recently arrived in London from her home in Dorset near the Channel coast some one hundred miles to the southwest.* Under the British conscription laws, all persons, male and female, eighteen and over, had to work in the war effort. In 1941, just after the attack on Pearl Harbor, Anthea chose the elite Motor Corps and was assigned to the Americans. At first, the Corps drivers were stationed at the U.S. Embassy; a few months later they were moved to 20 Grosvenor when the American Army took over the building.

"When I joined the drivers, there was Kay," Anthea recalls, "already a veteran of the group. She was tall, five feet ten inches, very thin, but incredibly glamorous in her uniforms. She was tremendously energetic and she knew everybody. She also knew her way around London like a cab driver, no, better than a cab driver. She got all the calls from the top generals. The rest of us drove for the captains, majors and colonels, the lesser lights.

"The first time Kay got the assignment to drive Ike—it was May of 1942—she came into the room where the pool of drivers gathered and made a face. 'I just drew a general with a funny name,' she told me. 'I think they called him Oozenhower, or something.' We all laughed."

In November of that year, Ike was named Commander in Chief of the Allied forces and moved his headquarters to

* In 1946 Anthea married Edward Saxe, an Army major, and returned with him to the United States.

Algiers when the drive to sweep the German Afrika Korps and the Italian Army from North Africa was gaining momentum. The Axis forces had been routed at El Alamein under Montgomery and the British were pushing toward Tripoli. Kay, who had been assigned to headquarters, followed the rest of Ike's official Army "family" a month after the others had left.

She was assigned to the *Strathallen,* a barely seaworthy old vessel which had been stripped and reconverted into a troopship. Steaming in convoy toward North Africa, the *Strathallen* and three other ships were struck by German torpedoes shortly after midnight, a few hundred miles from the coastal city of Oran. Kay escaped from the badly listing ship into a lifeboat and drifted until dawn.

Her spirits were remarkable. Margaret Bourke-White, the famed photographer, was aboard the *Strathallen* and assigned to the same lifeboat. Kay, Bourke-White wrote in her account of the experience, in *Life* magazine, was buoyant, brave, and "irrepressible." As the lifeboat bobbed away from the mother ship, Kay called out her "breakfast order" for the morning: "I want eggs," she said, "sunnyside up and no yolks broken." A GI, catching her mood, called out that he'd like his brandy with a splash of hot milk. Soon the men and women in the lifeboat were trading quips but the only food they had was a single orange which had been saved from the ship by a nurse. Each of the passengers got a section.

After eight hours, a destroyer was seen dimly in the gathering dawn. As it neared, a soldier stood up in the lifeboat and, still in the jocular mood with which Kay had infected her fellow passengers, waved his arm and bawled, "Hey, taxi!" The survivors were picked up, swathed in blankets, and given hot Ovaltine to drink. Kay—"the beauteous Kay," Bourke-White called her in her dispatch— had saved her lipstick. She refused to be rescued, she said, looking like a wreck.

A joyous reunion followed with Dick Arnold, who had

been assigned to North Africa two months earlier. Arnold's wife had agreed to a divorce, erasing one of the two major obstacles to their marriage. Kay's own divorce would become final by spring, and they were planning a June wedding. "She was madly in love with him," Anthea says, a fact Kay does not conceal in her two books.

But she did not disclose the depths of her despair late in May when Eisenhower had to tell her that Dick Arnold was killed when an antipersonnel mine exploded inches from his feet. Arnold, by then a full colonel, and a captain had been inspecting a field in Tunisia that had been strewn with mines by the Allied forces after the Nazis had been cleared out of the area. The location of the mines had been clearly marked by white tape but the captain had missed his footing and tripped a wire. He survived the blast but Arnold was blown to bits.

Anthea, in England, heard from friends about Kay. Later, when the two met again in England, Kay told her about the emotional ordeal she had undergone.

"After Dick died," Anthea says, "Kay went into a deep depression. She felt dreadful. Everything was bleak and black, though she tried not to show it. Outwardly, there was not much evidence of her feelings. She carried on her work but inwardly she had changed from a happy person into a very sad one. She would not have her hair done, very unlike Kay; she even stopped writing to her mother.

"General Eisenhower did notice the change, and tried to help by keeping her busy so that she would have as little time to brood as possible. He gave her extra work to do, letters to write, filing, other secretarial duties.

"And this helped. Gradually, Kay emerged from her depression and, eventually, she became her old self again, but Richard Arnold remained forever in her memory.

"To the end of her life," Anthea says, "Kay remained loyal to Ike. She never boasted about the relationship, whatever it may have been; indeed, she said very little about her wartime experiences at all."

Anthea: "The one thing she did talk about was how wonderful he had been to her after Dick died, how much he extended himself, despite all the burdens he was carrying, to help her get over the tremendous shock she had suffered. She remained forever grateful to him for that.

"As her executor, I have everything she ever possessed. There were no letters, no notes, nothing whatever from him [Eisenhower]. If there had been any, she destroyed them.

"From time to time, Kay did let a few things drop, perhaps inadvertently, about how she felt about Eisenhower, and how he had felt about her. From this, and from my own friendship with Kay, I would surely have to conclude that this was scarcely the greatest romance since Romeo and Juliet!

"It is evident that Kay did play a part in his life, but I'll tell you what that part was. She was invaluable to the General, not as a lover, not as an object of romance, but because she was right there. She was the one person he could talk to in his rare moments of free time.

"He said to her—and she told me this: 'Kay, there's nobody I can discuss things with, nobody I can talk to freely. They all ask to be promoted, or if I talk to the wrong person, what I say is reported all over the world. I know that I can let my thoughts flow with you.' And that's precisely what he did. He would use her as a sounding board for ideas, perhaps for gripes he might have, to let off steam. He knew that Kay was completely trustworthy, that what he said would end with her. And she was comforting as well. This played a large part in their relationship. As soon as the war ended, that aspect of the relationship ended too, and he went on to other things.

"Kay played another role. Even though Eisenhower was Supreme Commander and surely no longer the farm boy from Kansas, he still was not completely prepared to deal with the British aristocracy. Kay, though Irish born, knew her way around British society and helped him bridge what could have been a serious communications gap.

"Finally," Anthea points out, "in this whole Ike-Kay matter, we seem to have lost sight of one rather important matter.

"And this is time. How much time did Dwight Eisenhower really have when he was leading the Allied armies in the war against Germany? If he had moments with Kay, there were probably five minutes, certainly not much more, at the end of a very busy day, and perhaps a few other minutes in between. Every other hour was filled with his incredible responsibilities—the planning that went into all phases of the military operations, the reports he had to read and to write, and the countless other details. How much time, really, did a man with those duties on his shoulders have for romance?"

One day in North Africa a young WAC named Pearlie Hargrave was driving General Eisenhower from his headquarters to lunch. Along the way Pearlie coughed heavily several times.

Ike leaned forward and asked, "Is that cigarettes, Pearlie, or do you have a cold?"

"I think it's probably a combination of both, General," she replied.

"Well," Ike said, "you slow down on the cigarettes and get right up to the medics and get something for that cold."

It does not require any special alertness on the reader's part to note that a WAC named Pearlie and not Kay Summersby was at the wheel of an automobile, chauffeuring the Supreme Commander. Nor, indeed, was the driving job assigned exclusively to these two women.

This was one of the interesting facts that came to light when we tracked down and interviewed surviving members of Ike's headquarters staff, the men and women who served with him throughout the war and who knew and worked with Kay. Some of the women were Kay's roommates during the war, several knew her closer in postwar years too. All tell a story that differs markedly from her own.

Actually, Eisenhower's chief chaffeur in wartime was not any of the women on his staff but a sergeant named Leonard D. Dry, who was assigned to GHQ in late October of 1942. He served Ike all through the African campaign and later in England and on the Continent. Dry remained with Eisenhower for many years after the war ended. As a master sergeant, he was Mamie's official driver during the Eisenhower Administration and, on his retirement, drove for the couple at Gettysburg.

Kay was one of three women who drove the General. The others were Pearlie Hargrave and Inez Scott, both WACS, and Elsbeth Duncan, an Englishwoman. Mickey would also drive him at times, though not as frequently as the others.

Dry, now retired and living on the eastern shore of Maryland, says: "I guess Summersby was the one who got all the publicity, but it wasn't that way at all. Oh, sure, she drove the General at times, but so did the other girls too. They did the driving in and around Algiers, but when Ike wanted to go to the front, he would call me."

Pearlie Hargrave arrived in North Africa in February, just before Field Marshal Erwin Rommel's victory at Kasserine Pass. A small young blonde—she was twenty-five, no stripes yet on her sleeve—she joined Ike's staff and was assigned to the motor pool at the venerable St. George Hotel in Algiers.

Later, Pearlie married Mickey McKeogh in the Marie Antoinette Chapel at Versailles. Mickey said, "She had a face I had been looking for all my life . . . the prettiest girl I had seen in a long time, with the bluest eyes." Pearlie, too, is now retired and works busily in community activities in Bowie, where she recalls the wartime years, and Kay's role in the Eisenhower "family."

The wedding of Pearlie and Mickey was something of a military event. Her wedding dress was created by a Paris designer and General Eisenhower headed the list of honored guests who included Lieutenant General Walter Bedell (Beetle) Smith, Ike's Chief of Staff; Major General Everett Hughes and Brigadier General Thomas Jefferson Davis of his staff, and assorted other brass. After the ceremony, Ike gave the bride and groom a reception, a one-hundred-dollar war bond as a wedding gift, and a week's leave for a honeymoon in Paris. Pearlie's stunning white wedding gown, Army-owned, became a WAC hand-me-down, worn thereafter by dozens of women who were married in the ETO until it literally fell apart.

Pearlie: "There was a room in the St. George Hotel in Algiers where Kay, Elsbeth, Inez, and I reported each day to wait for our calls. Generals, high-ranking officers, and civilian officials flew in all the time and we'd hop out to the airport, take them to headquarters, and then drive for them while they were visiting General Eisenhower. Generals Patton and Omar Bradley came frequently; so did Bernard Montgomery, British Air Marshall Sir Arthur Tedder, and so many others. We got them in rotation. I drew General Eisenhower just about as often, I suppose, as anyone else in the pool.

"I was astounded to read, and later to see on television, that Kay Summersby was his only driver."

Dry, too, is surprised and amused at the portrayal of Kay as the General's secretary. "She wasn't," Dry says bluntly. This fiction was created more by the television mini-series, "Ike," which highlighted the romance, than by Kay herself. The actress Lee Remick, portraying Summersby, is seen at a desk typing furiously, at sight of which Pearlie burst into laughter. "Kay couldn't type at all!" she says. Eisenhower himself, in his memoirs of the war, *Crusade in Europe,* says Kay was "corresponding secretary and doubled as driver."

Actually, General Eisenhower had three personal and office secretaries, Nana Rae, Margaret Chick, and Sue Sarafian, all WAC sergeants. A WAC officer, Mattie Pinette, was his confidential secretary.

Pinette, who rose to lieutenant colonel before she was discharged, now lives in Arlington, Virginia. A member of Ike's headquarters staff from the time he left Algiers to several months after D-Day, Pinette knew Kay well, rooming with her at their various billets. After the war, she worked for the Atomic Energy Commission; at her retirement in 1964 she was chief of the employee development branch.

"I handled all the official correspondence for the General," Pinette said. "Kay was the receptionist, greeting visitors, and also was given the job of answering letters from high-school kids who wrote the General, parents of soldiers, that kind of thing. She didn't type, she just dictated answers to the letters to another headquarters staff member."

Surviving veterans of Eisenhower's staff are agreed that if a torrid romance existed, it was one of the best-kept secrets of the war.

Harry Butcher, seventy-eight years old in 1980, lives in retirement in a suburb of Santa Barbara, California, tending his citrus orchard.

"If there had been any romance going on, of course I would have known," Butcher says. "I lived with Ike in the same house, the same houses, all through the war. I would not deny that he was fond of Kay, but he was fond of all of us. He considered us his family. But there was no sign whatever of a romance. We were a close family, united by wartime camaraderie. If a romance had been brewing between Ike and Kay, I could hardly have missed it."

At least some of the romantic interludes supposedly took place in and around Telegraph Cottage, a small house Eisenhower used as a secret retreat during his stay in England. Harry Butcher searched the London suburbs the summer Ike arrived and discovered the tan-stucco two-story home eleven miles southwest of the city in Kingston-upon-Thames. Ike used it on weekends at first but liked the place so much he began spending more and more time there,

commuting to 20 Grosvenor, only a half-hour's drive. No
public announcement was ever made that the General was
occupying the house; it was only after the war ended that
the story was made public.* Except for the months in
Africa, Eisenhower used the house from midsummer of
1942 until after D-day, when the GHQ were moved to
France.

As a hideaway, the house was perfect: it sat on ten
wooded acres which were ringed by hedges, and was
accessible only by a private road. The staff was quartered
near by. Three of the GIs occupied a former maid's room
behind the garage; others, including the women, were
billeted in British homes several hundred yards away. For a
few weeks, Mickey set up house in the General's own trailer
on the grounds which contained a bath with a hot shower
and, for a change, a real bed. Mickey gloried in the
unaccustomed luxury of his "private bungalow" and was
saddened when it was taken to Portsmouth on the coast as a
command post for an advanced General Headquarters for
the cross-Channel thrust.

Mickey then moved into the cottage, which had a large
living room with an ample fireplace, a dining room, a
kitchen with a range that had to be stoked with coal, and
five small bedrooms.

"My room was at the head of the stairs," Mickey told us.
"Butch was in the room directly opposite, while Ike
occupied the bedroom down the short hall. The fourth
bedroom was reserved for overnight guests, important
generals, and civilian officials who came frequently.

"I woke the General in the morning and I never went to
bed until the boss was in bed at night. There was never
anyone in the General's bed but the General. Never, at any
time all during the war, wherever we were quartered.

*Telegraph Cottage, now a historical site, has been restored to its
original appearance when Ike lived in it and is open to the public. Many
photographs of the General and his staff adorn the walls.

"I was the General's orderly, and nobody in that Army was closer to him personally than I was. The General insisted that I be there when he wanted me. He didn't want me traipsing off, so I made sure I stayed around. And I can tell you I saw and heard nothing that could be interpreted as hanky-panky.

"Remember, too, that I had been a bellhop at a swank New York hotel for eight years before I entered the Army. In that job you learn to spot men and women who are playing around, and I spotted plenty. So I wasn't naive.

"Kay and the General played bridge occasionally in the evenings at the cottage after work was finished. She was good at it and there were always two others for a foursome. It was great relaxation for the General, bridge and those Western magazines. But as for hand-holding or private whisperings—well, if there was any it had to be done awfully fast because they were almost never alone.

"Not only that, but we had guards outside the house all the time, stationed everywhere. After all, you don't leave the Supreme Commander unprotected. All those long walks they were supposed to take together just had to be observed by some of them. If there had been any romantic little strolls in the evening, the two would have been seen and believe me, we would have heard. Look, that would have been some gossip, wouldn't it? The boss and the pretty lady? We never heard a word, though."

The story Kay tells of the General's unsuccessful attempt to make love to her astounds Mickey. He points out that one encounter was supposed to have taken place in the house in London that had been rented for Ike when he returned from the States on his leave. It was a three-story home in the West End and, as usual, Mickey slept there.

He had the run of the place. For example, whenever he wished he could come down to the kitchen on the main floor for a glass of milk or a snack. Yet it was in the living room, right off the kitchen, where the General, according to Kay's book, ripped off his clothes and tried to take Kay to bed. *"I was living there, for heaven's sake!"* Mickey says. "I was right upstairs! I had come back from the States with him and had gone to my room after making sure he was O.K. Could you, could anyone, imagine that General Eisenhower would ever. . . ?"

Harry Butcher: "Kay has said that one of their episodes of attempted lovemaking occurred in the living room of Telegraph Cottage. Would Dwight Eisenhower have been stupid enough to have done anything like that in the living room, knowing that Sergeant McKeogh and I were quartered there and could walk in at any time?"

We asked Butch: "Kay says that you understood what she calls their special relationship but you had never said a word. Any comment on that?"

"Yes. It's just not true."

Mattie Pinette is another who, Kay has intimated, knew about the romance but was discreet. We asked Pinette for her views.

"I think the General was very fond of Kay," she says, "and he had every reason to be. She was an excellent driver, always on time. If she had the assignment and the General had to go out early in the morning, she set her alarm, and she was never late. He was very grateful to her for these services she rendered, which were important in wartime.

"Then he felt sorry for her when she lost her fiancé, and he tried to give her something to do. Most drivers, if they are assigned to a general, just sit there in the room with the other drivers and they wait, and wait and wait, which is pretty dull stuff. So the General gave her the correspondence to handle.

"Kay had Dick Arnold's picture around all the time. Later, when she came to the United States, she visited his mother in Florida. And General Eisenhower had Mrs. Eisenhower's picture in his office wherever the headquarters were.

"The General was a family man who liked small groups of people around him in a home. He decided when he went overseas that he would not accept a lot of invitations from Lady This and Lady That because his social life would become impossibly active. Instead, several of us would be invited to his home after dinner to play bridge, or to see a movie that Tex Lee would get for him. Kay would be there with us. We were always told to go home by ten o'clock because the General liked to go to bed early and read a little. He was a very early riser.

"As for the romance—the story, I am afraid, has been grossly exaggerated."

That Eisenhower had a "special relationship" with Kay Summersby is undeniable, but his headquarters staff defines it differently. "The General," says Pearlie McKeogh, "took a personal interest in the welfare of every woman in the office." Mickey adds, "And every officer and man too."

Mickey recalls one of his own experiences. Just before the invasion of Europe, he went to the hospital for an operation to correct a nasal problem. Despite his overwhelming burdens, Ike found time to visit his orderly in the hospital.

Kevin McCann, who was not with Eisenhower during the war but knew the man well, makes this assessment: "Kay was a tragic figure, and for tragic women everywhere Dwight Eisenhower had a heart of pure mush. Any woman who suffered a hurt of any kind could make his heart bleed. He suffered with Kay, and he helped her in all the ways he could. It is unfortunate that what he did was misinterpreted by so many people, including the woman herself."

Harry Butcher: "The crucial fact you've got to underscore heavily is that he was fond of all of us personally. She was a pleasant, charming woman, very helpful to the General.

"Why, hell, even his son John was fond of her!"

John, who was stationed in England, visited his father a number of times at Telegraph Cottage and, on occasion, joined in the bridge games with Kay in the party. Once, during a particularly heavy buzz-bomb raid, he, the General, Kay, and others of the GHQ staff spent the night in the air-raid shelter outside the house. On July 1, 1944, John was sent back to the States by Ike, who also granted Kay and two others of his staff a short leave. Kay flew back to the U.S. with John aboard Eisenhower's personal B-17. "When Ike sent her back," says Dr. Pogue, the military historian, he instructed John, " 'See to it that she meets people.' "

John did as his father requested. Kay was introduced to Mamie in Washington and then was shown around New York by John, who took her to see *Oklahoma!* It is extremely unlikely that Eisenhower, or any man in his senses, would have deliberately asked his son to bring his mistress and wife together.

More than thirty years later John Eisenhower told Steve Neal of the *Philadelphia Inquirer:* "He [his father] was on my back to come and live with him. If he had been having an affair, I don't think he would have wanted his son around."

If an affair had existed, one would have to assume that a general conspiracy of silence existed among all of the many hundreds of newspersons who covered the greatest war in history and, later, the President of the United States—a dubious proposition considering, among many things, the fierce competitiveness of the media.

In Abilene we discussed this point with Henry B. Jameson, editor of the *Reflector-Chronicle,* Ike's hometown newspaper. Jameson, an Abilene native, was a war correspondent for the Associated Press in Europe and was the first newsperson wounded on D-Day.

"Sure, we all heard the story," Jameson says. "Everyone heard it—Edward R. Murrow, Walter Cronkite, Quentin Reynolds, all the major reporters. No one wrote that story, not because they wanted to protect Ike, but because they all knew that it didn't amount to peanuts."

Another point in Summersby's account of the romance arouses suspicion. Kay states that in their two attempts at lovemaking Eisenhower was impotent. Yet he is described as wanting to marry her. Writing in *The New York Times Book Review,* Tom Buckley asks, "Why would Eisenhower, still in the prime of life, have been so eager to marry a woman, whatever her amiable qualities, with whom he was sexually incompatible?" (Ike was then in his early fifties.)

The evidence strongly suggests that there was no romance of any duration or intensity between the General and the lady. Which is not to say, of course, that in some place, at some time, some intimacy did not take place. Even John Eisenhower would not rule that out. "Nobody can bear witness," he says, "that an incident did not happen." One can argue persuasively that, since Ike was a healthy, vigorous, active male it would have been surprising if he had not engaged in some sexual activity overseas. But, as the historian Stephen Ambrose, who compiled his official papers, told us, "Ike put in a killing day, slept only a few hours and had very little time for fun and games."

The notion that he was involved in a continuing affair is a titillating one. Perhaps, as Dr. Fawn Brodie says in the case of the other Presidents similarly accused, we may actually desire these evidences of virility in those we select to lead us. In this particular case, however, the evidence is still lacking.

6. Kay—How Mamie Reacted

MAMIE, A CONTINENT away, took it hard.

"She didn't know what to believe," says Walter Trohan. As an Army wife, she knew all too well that a husband, far away for long periods of time, can meet and fall in love with another woman; it had happened before. She knew Ike, trusted Ike, and of course was devoted to Ike.

"Yet the stories persisted. She was terribly upset."

Once she told an Army chaplain whom she had met at West Point and knew Eisenhower well: "Of course, I don't believe it. I know Ike." It was the only time during war years that her reaction to the purported romance was published.

John is not so sure. "Mother was under a lot of strain," he says. "I don't know if she believed the rumors, but she thought enough of them to bring it up in her letters."

As early as August of 1942, just three months after Ike had left for England, Mamie was writing worried notes to him. On file in the Eisenhower Library at Abilene is the following reply the General wrote on the twenty-fourth of the month. (The text was not included in John Eisenhower's book, a collection of some of the General's wartime correspondence with his wife, published to blunt the impact of the projected ABC television mini-series about the alleged affair.*

Darling [Ike wrote] Stop worrying about me. The few women I've met are nothing—absolutely nothing compared to you, and besides I've neither the time nor the youth to worry about them. I love you—always.

Yours, Ike

Apparently, her questions about Kay continued, for on December 3, 1944, Ike wrote: "I assure you again—you are my only girl. I love you and I can say no more than that." On September 1, 1945, after the surrender of Germany, he asked her to come over to Europe if arrangements could be made. Her reply has not been made public, but on the twenty-ninth, Ike wrote again: "I'm not even going to argue about the coming over business; apparently you don't choose to believe anything I say so that's that. But I'm not trying to be noble."

He had been overseas only a little more than two months when he wrote to his brother Milton the extent to which he missed his family. He led, he said, a lonely life, his every move under observation. Because of such an existence, he said, an overlay of strain was created that was totally separate from the burdens of the task itself. If he were back

---

*The original draft of the series hit more heavily on the purported affair than the version that was finally shown. "I had treated the whole thing broadly," said Mel Shavelson, the Hollywood writer and producer of the series. "It was a first draft so I threw in the kitchen sink. There was no intent to sensationalize. No thought of hurting a wonderful woman [Mrs. Mamie Eisenhower]." But John Eisenhower saw that draft, without Shavelson's knowledge, blew a gasket, and published his father's letters to his mother in an effort to prove that the rumors were untrue.

in the United States, he felt that strain would be eased because then he could go home at the close of day and leave the burdens for a brief time.

This feeling grew more intense as the war dragged on. Almost three years later, after the surrender of the German Army, he told Milton that the final six weeks of the conflict had been the hardest of the entire war for him, and only partly because political problems still existed that could not be neatly solved. The other reason was stronger: "I just plain miss my family."

But Mamie, across the ocean, was confused. They were anxious times for her, and in those times Mamie Eisenhower slipped close to being a problem drinker.

She had, from early times, enjoyed an afternoon or predinner cocktail. Her favorite was an old-fashioned—which she insisted be made "light and with plenty of fruit." In the more than two decades she had been married to Ike, she had almost never had more than a single drink.

After Ike left for Europe, this pattern changed. During those mah-jongg games with the other lonely and anxious Army wives, the hostesses would serve drinks. Mamie, at first, would have her customary one. But as time passed and her fears increased, she would accept another, and then a third.

In Abilene, editor Henry Jameson revealed Mamie's wartime battle with alcohol. *

On one of the hottest days of the year, with the mercury

---

* Jameson has been an Eisenhower supporter and a family friend for many years. During the war, when Ike heard that a man from Abilene was covering the conflict, he asked to see the correspondent. "I wanted to meet you," the General said. "I didn't think our hometown newspaper could afford to send a reporter here." Jameson said he was there for the AP.

In 1960 Jameson returned to Abilene to become editor and eventually own the newspaper. During Ike's Presidency, reporters covering him on his visits to Abilene would often ask Jameson to obtain inside tidbits of news on what the President was doing. Because of his family connections, Jameson was generally able to oblige.

hitting 114, we visited Henry Jameson in his modern red-brick office on North Broadway, a few blocks from the Eisenhower Center. "It was an old, old story," he told us, "one that happened many times during the war. It was tied to a whirl which led many officers' wives during that period of stress and loneliness, to drink too much.

"For a year or even two, Mamie was part of that whirl, worrying too much, drinking a little too much. There is not much doubt that the Summersby story was a significant factor.

"It reached a point where members of the family became seriously concerned about her, afraid that she might be approaching an alcohol problem. I must emphasize that it had not reached that point. Still, one close family member talked seriously to her and Mamie quickly understood what was happening and where she would be drifting.

"She stopped at once. And after that, she took only a single drink." *

---

*Nevertheless, stories about Mamie and alcohol followed her all through her life.

7. Kay—
The After-years

KAY SUMMERSBY'S STAR faded after the war ended.

In 1944 Eisenhower helped her obtain a commission in the American Women's Army Corps and after VE day she was put in charge of a special residence for distinguished visitors to the U.S. sector of occupied Berlin. She remained for a year, then, a captain by this time, decided to come to the United States for a new life.

There was a brief round of parties and reunions in Washington. Once again she met many of the officers she had known overseas, recalled war days, joked with them, drank with them. She spent a year in California as a WAC public-relations officer, became an American citizen, then resigned her commission and moved to New York. In 1948 she published her wartime memoirs, *Eisenhower Was My Boss*. This first book made no mention of any romantic entanglement with the General but it sold well and Kay was in demand for a while on the lecture circuit.

When calls for appearances ended, and the money she

had earned for the book's sale began to run out, she looked for a job. After a long search, she was hired as a saleslady at an exclusive women's specialty store on Fifth Avenue, a dull job she hated. Finally she landed one that appealed to her, where she could utilize her fashion training: in the costume department of the Columbia Broadcasting System.

On November 20, 1952, she was married to Reginald E. Morgan of New Canaan, Connecticut, a Wall Street broker, at the home of a friend on East Seventy-seventh Street in Manhattan. Kay was then forty-three and Morgan forty-seven. The couple lived for a while in Antigua in the British West Indies. They were divorced in 1958 and Kay resumed her star-dressing jobs on a free-lance basis for CBS and for motion-picture companies producing films in the New York area. She made several trips to the West Coast on assignments, and in between fashion jobs supplemented her income by working as a script girl.

She never made much money but managed reasonably well on her earnings and an alimony check. She lived at a smart address on upper Park Avenue but her tiny living room, bedroom, bath, and small kitchen had once been the servants' quarters of a much larger apartment which had been renovated and sold as a cooperative. She bought it in the 1950s for only five thousand dollars and lived there for the rest of her life.

In the 1960s she discovered the Hamptons on the eastern end of Long Island and would spent her vacations there and as many weekends as she could afford. Still attractive, still vivacious, she made many friends, among them Dr. Carver Livingston, a surgeon, and his wife, Carol, who remember her with affection.

In their stunningly beautiful Southampton home, with its two-story living room, Dr. and Mrs. Livingston talked about the Kay they knew.

Dr. Livingston: "She was an avid golfer, and was pretty good at it. Her sense of humor made her immensely popular; she was just fun to be with. Kay, my wife, and I became very close friends. She stayed at our home many times when she came out here.

"But as long as I knew her, and I guess that goes back about twenty years, I never heard her mention anything about Eisenhower other than the fact that he gave her a dog.* She never spoke about the war years at all. Because of his position, I suppose she felt that anything she would say wasn't going to be good for him, so she never opened her mouth, one way or the other, not even the day we ran into someone who served for a while on Eisenhower's staff. He talked a lot about Ike, but Kay didn't say a word.

"Once she showed me her photograph album. It was nothing remarkable. There were pictures of Kay standing in her uniform by her car, with the General getting in. There were no intimate photos."

Carol Livingston: "We loved having her here. She was like one of the family. Whenever she called and said she would be out, we would never make any special preparations. Whatever we had to eat, she would have. She would swim in the pool, fuss around the garden, play golf and bridge. We had great times together."

Kay would drive out to the Hamptons in an ancient red Volkswagen which, Dr. Livingston recalls with a chuckle, was always breaking down. "Kay never had much money," he said. "If she had, she'd never have been driving that

---

*The Scottie became quite famous at headquarters. The General had named him Telek, for Telegraph Cottage, and kept him throughout the war. Telek resisted being housebroken but was so loved nobody wanted to discipline him for his lapses, one of which occurred the day General Marshall visited the cottage.

Ike had given orders to put the Chief of Staff in the bedroom he occupied. When Marshall arrived, Telek leaped on the bed and soiled its red satin cover before Mickey could grab him. It was not one of Mickey's, nor Telek's finest hours, but Marshall thought it was a huge joke. The Chief of Staff, ever analytical, theorized it was Telek's way of objecting to having his master put out of his bedroom. After the war, Ike gave the dog to Kay, who kept him until his death in 1958.

thing. Each time she came, it would barely make it up the driveway, but it got her here, and she was perfectly satisfied with it."

Even when she was past sixty, Carol says, Kay was extraordinarily attractive. "Her hair," she asserts, "was then a dark red, her skin was clear, and her eyes very blue. She wore clothes beautifully and when she was dressed for the evening she was a stunner. You'd turn around and take a look."

As the 1970s opened, Kay, finding herself caught more tightly in a money bind, decided to return to England where, she thought, living costs were lower. In London she found a job as saleslady in one of the exclusive Jaeger International shops but soon discovered that, with galloping inflation, it was even harder to make ends meet than in New York. In less than a year, she was back at her old jobs in the United States.

By 1973 the cancer, which had begun in the rectum, had spread and there was no longer hope. After recovering from surgery in New York Hospital in the summer of that year, she kept coming out to Southampton in her battered old car as often as she could, loving the still-unspoiled beauty of the dunes. Kay had never been frightened under fire, and she was not frightened now. Certainly she never said anything about her illness to her friends.

By the fall of 1974 jaundice set in as the malignant tumor cells spread to her liver. Her skin turned sallow, then increasingly yellow. Dr. Livingston, who was not treating her, could tell she was seriously ill, but Kay remained silent. In the winter he and his wife went to California to visit their children. They asked Kay if she would house-sit for them while they were gone and she agreed.

On their return, Kay rented a tiny house, with almost doll-size rooms, on Herrick Road and moved in. The jaundice worsened, but her spirits remained undimmed. She would still joke and even play a few rounds of golf with

Carol Livingston. "By January," Carol recalls, "Kay looked terrible. Her entire body looked golden, her eyes, her face, her skin, everything. Even so, she played bridge at our house, sick as she was, and never complained."

On Sunday morning, January 19, Kay stumbled and fell in her house, striking her head on a coffee table. For almost two hours she lay unconscious, then struggled to a telephone and called Carol. "I don't know what's the matter with me," Kay said. "I just seem to be falling most of the time."

Carol and another friend drove to Kay's house and found her dazed and unable to get up from the floor. Carol quickly called her husband, who arrived in a few moments.

By this time, Anthea Saxe, her friend from London, had arrived at the house with her son Chris. The day before Kay had called Anthea and said, "Come see my house," adding "but don't wait too long." The words sounded ominous to Anthea, who drove to Southampton in a driving rainstorm.

Dr. Livingston called for an ambulance but Kay, overhearing, resisted. "I'm not going to a hospital," she said. "If I go, I'm never coming out." In minutes, two attendants arrived, policemen working in their off-duty time. Recognizing them, Kay called out, "Get those flatfeet out of here!"

Finally, Dr. Livingston persuaded Kay to go. She asked Anthea to fetch her a comb from her dressing table. Her hair hadn't been done in days. "I don't want to arrive at the hospital looking like a fright," she said. Anthea handed her a comb. When she was satisfied, she allowed herself to be taken to the ambulance.

That evening, in Southampton Hospital on Herrick Road, a few blocks from her little house, Kay slipped into a hepatic coma. The Livingstons were at her bedside that evening and the next day. With her, too, were Anthea and Chris.

She died the next afternoon, never emerging from the

coma. Her body was cremated and the ashes flown across the Atlantic to be strewn over the coast of County Cork.

It was during her last illness that Kay began her second book.

"Kay was hurting for money," Dr. Livingston says. "She was hoping to get her book finished so that she could get the royalties from its sale to help her in her financial difficulties." Anthea Saxe adds, "Kay had all these doctor bills coming in, and she was getting quite paranoid about them."

Ironically, Kay did earn money from the book when it was too late to help. Her estate amounted to about $100,000, but much of it went to pay bills and back taxes.

The final piece to the puzzle, answering the question of why she said what she did, may lie in this desperate need for money to pay her rapidly mounting medical expenses in the final months of her life, a need that, understandably enough, might have clouded the good judgment she had exercised most of her life.

PART FOUR

White House Years

1. "She's Worth 50 Electoral Votes"

FOR SEVEN YEARS after the shooting stopped and Ike came home, Mamie enjoyed a measure of tranquillity. Best of these were the eighteen months in New York, while Ike was president of Columbia University. There she lived in a kind of splendid isolation from mid-1948 until the end of 1950. Ike was home for dinner, and often lunch, almost every day.

And, unlike Mrs. Nicholas Murray Butler, her predecessor as the university president's wife, she did little entertaining. Mrs. Butler had often held receptions for hundreds of guests and given multicourse banquets, accompanied by vintage wines and brandies. Before Ike accepted, he asked if such parties were essential to the job and was assured that they were not, that the trustees, each independently wealthy, would do most of the entertaining and that the president would only be called upon to receive some special VIP.

With his $25,000 Columbia salary and $15,000 annually

authorized for a General of the Army, Ike was well-fixed for those days. But it was the first time in his life. A few months before his appointment, he had purchased a car in Washington. When it was delivered, he studied it for a while and turned to Mamie. "That's the entire result of thirty-seven years' work since I caught the train out of Abilene." (He wasn't poor for long. Following publication of *Crusade in Europe,* his account of World War II, a special ruling by the Internal Revenue Service allowed him to declare the $625,000 he earned as capital gains instead of regular income. Thus Ike netted $476,250 from the book instead of considerably less.)

Mamie was content with her life at Columbia, and comfortable in her new residence at 60 Morningside Drive, the third floor of which had been remodeled into a private family apartment containing a large bedroom and sitting room with its own kitchenette. "She was not projected into public view," says Anne Wheaton, "except when she wanted it." Which was practically never. She saw her old friends for lunch, though she made few new ones, and went to the theater and movies. She preferred musicals, light comedies, and romantic films, shunned war and gangster pictures, and adored Clark Gable.

Before she moved to New York, Mamie was concerned that she might not find players who used the Army-wives system of mah-jongg, the Point 20 method which originated at the Wright-Patterson Air Force Base near Dayton, Ohio, and called for different rules from that of the international method. It was no small matter, considering Mamie's devotion to the game.

She need not have worried: she did find Army wives who knew it. She hoped, too, that she might persuade her husband to substitute mah-jongg for bridge, at least once in a while. "You don't need to concentrate so hard," she explained. "You can still talk and have a good time while you're playing." But, while she herself once more spent hours at it, she never got Ike near a mah-jongg table.

The Columbia assignment appealed to her, too, because she was now a grandmother and, like most, an affectionate one who wanted to see the children as often as she could.

John had married a beautiful girl, dark-haired Barbara Jean Thompson, whom he had met while he was overseas. She, too, was an Army brat, daughter of Colonel Percy Thompson. On June 10, 1947, Ike and Mamie had gone down to Fortress Monroe, Virginia, where John was stationed, for the military ceremony. Now John, a captain, was at West Point where he was teaching English. They were the parents of two children, Dwight David II, whom they called David, born on March 31, 1948, and Barbara Anne, fourteen months younger. A third child, Susan, would come along on the last day of 1951.

John, Barbara, and the children could, and did, drive down frequently and there were many happy family gatherings during the Columbia days. Later, David was to resent some of Ike's Army-bred ideas of discipline, but not when he was two-going-on-three. These years, they doted on each other. One day, while he was upstairs with Mamie, David slipped out the door, raced down the stairs, and entered the library where the General was conferring with a quartet of distinguished professors. With a broad Eisenhower grin on his round face, he bawled out, "Hiya, Ike!", then dashed back upstairs. Ike had difficulty resuming the discussion of academic affairs.

After so many years apart, Mamie was hoping for some stability in her life but Ike, a national hero, was not left alone. Nor, in fact, did he want to be. He was in Washington frequently, consulting on defense and security and testifying before Congressional committees. He accepted invitations to speak at civic and college groups and attended private dinners and meetings. While the "Draft

Eisenhower" movement for 1952 was heating up Ike was not going after the prize, but neither was he doing much if anything to avoid it. Mamie rarely went along on these trips, which often kept him away a week or even longer at a time, preferring the peace and privacy of her home and her friends. To some Columbia faculty members she seemed "sad and frail" during these years.

But not so frail that she would not insist, and stoutly, that unless his duties were so overwhelming or business urgently kept him out of the city, Ike must spend his Sundays with her. "It is the only day," she told him, "that you do not belong to Columbia." Ike could understand a command when he heard one, and for the most part he obeyed.

And not only on Sundays. Once a friend telephoned Mamie on the morning of the Army-Navy football classic and said, "I suppose you'll be going with the General." Mamie replied happily: "Oh, no. John and Barbara are going. The General and I will watch it over television. We're baby-sitting." Ike missed one of the most exciting games in years. He was on the edge of his chair all afternoon as the contest see-sawed, finally ending in a 21–21 tie.

The Columbia experience did not work out especially well for Ike. Many faculty members resented the presence of a nonacademician; and Eisenhower's chain-of-command methods made him virtually inaccessible. While he made it a point to visit classrooms and often watched football scrimmages at Baker Field uptown, he angered students by some of his speeches. Once, at the Waldorf, he assailed the then-current stress on material security at the cost, he felt, of America's freedoms, adding, "Maybe we like caviar and champagne when we ought to be out working on beer and hot dogs." The editors of the student newspaper, *The Spectator,* observed tartly that "we are willing to bet beer and hot dogs weren't on the menu at the Waldorf-Astoria last night." Ike was so enraged that, for a time, he privately threatened to stay away from the graduation ceremonies that June, the first time in the school's history that a president would not attend. Later, he cooled down and went.

Nevertheless, having settled in, neither Ike nor Mamie was especially eager to be uprooted again, but another summons came and they were off once more.

On December 6, 1950, he got his old uniforms out of mothballs and had to have them altered; he had gained a few pounds since retiring from active duty. He had been on his way to Denver with Mamie to spend Christmas at the Lafayette Street house and the train had stopped at Bucyrus, on the way to Tiffin in northwestern Ohio, where he was scheduled to make a speech at Heidelberg College. There was a telephone call from President Truman. Truman asked him to assume the Supreme Command of the twelve-nation North Atlantic Treaty Organization forces in Europe.

It was a summons Ike had expected. Two months before, at a meeting in the Oval Office, Truman had alerted him to the assignment and Ike, in principle, had accepted it if it came. Truman's call came after the NATO Council of Ministers approved the choice of Ike by a unanimous vote.

When he emerged from the stationmaster's office, he told Mamie, "We're going back to Europe." All she said was, "When?"

In the middle of February the following year, Ike and Mamie boarded the *Queen Elizabeth* and sailed across the heaving North Atlantic for Cherbourg. At a quarter to six in the morning of a bitterly cold day, they were met at the pier by a delegation of Frenchmen bearing a magnum of champagne, which had to be drunk with the obligatory toasts despite the hour and the fact that neither had had time for breakfast. Mamie captivated the welcoming party, one of whom exclaimed to a friend after the brief ceremony: "Her smile anticipated the sunrise by almost an hour. She was radiant, monsieur, absolutely radiant."

Radiant she may have been, but after a flight to Paris, then a motor trip to Versailles to the Trianon Palace Hotel, she was wilted. They ordered dinner sent to their rooms. It had been a long and tiring day, which was to end unhappily.

Ike had opened a western-story magazine and Mamie was twisting the dials of a portable radio. They both heard Ike's name mentioned and looked up to listen. A play was in progress. Ike's French was reasonably good and he could follow the dialogue; Mamie, too, had studied French at the Wolcott School. A Communist organization had purchased radio time and was dramatizing what purported to be Ike's arrival that morning in Paris. An actor portraying Ike was repeating the comments he had made to the press and radio.

Then it got nasty. The scene shifted to a hotel room and another member of the cast, identified as the "secretary to the General," was pretending to be drunk. In slurred tones, she said the French equivalent of "lesh have 'nother li'l drink, General."

Mamie, silent all the while, the Kay Summersby gossip still fresh in her mind, now began to weep softly. Ike went to her, sat on the arm of her chair, and silently stretched his arm around her shoulders. Bob Considine, who reported the story, said Mamie told Ike: "Let's go home. Do we have to take this?"

Two days later, Mamie was in hot water with the French people. Offered a magnificent fourteen-room villa in Versailles as a residence during Ike's stay in Europe, she turned it down. The mansion, called the Villa Trianon, was once the home of Marie Antoinette; more recently, it had been the mecca for the international social set when it was occupied by the late Lady Mendl, the former Elsie De-

Wolfe, who had been the acknowledged queen of society in her day.

Mamie had no complaint with the house, which was magnificent, and certainly not with the grounds. It stood at the rim of the fabulous gardens, with their flowing fountains, geometrical floral beds, walks lined with statues, and broad lawns.

She didn't care for the furniture. Louis XIV had built things for show and that wasn't Mamie's taste. The house was filled with heavy and formal pieces; the upholstery was rich damask, velvet, and tapestry; most of the chairs were high with straight backs. Mamie's "no thanks" shocked the French, who are as sensitive about their fine buildings and furnishings as they are about their wines.

The fact that Ike had approved the choice earlier made matters even worse. A headline on page one of the Paris edition of the *New York Herald Tribune,* "MRS. EISEN-HOWER VETOES GENERAL'S CHOICE—14-ROOM VILLA OF LADY MENDL—BECAUSE OF FURNITURE," was instantly picked up by the French press and sent Mamie into seclusion. A tea to introduce her to the press was cancelled. She would give no interviews on the subject but an announcement was made that she thought the Lady Mendl house "charming" but unsuitable for the General, who needed a place more accessible to his staff.

Another home was quickly found, this one in the tiny village of Marne-la-Coquette, a few miles closer to Rocquencourt near Paris, where Ike took over as Commander of Supreme Allied Headquarters, Allied Powers, Europe (SHAPE). The two-story Villa St. Pierre sat on six landscaped acres, hidden behind tall hedges, and looked very much like the home some well-to-do businessman might occupy with his father in Denver, which is precisely why Mamie liked it. Moreover, the privacy was unmatched. Villa St. Pierre and eighteen other homes like it were surrounded by a twelve-foot-high iron fence. Only residents or approved visitors could enter.

Despite the Villa Trianon incident, Mamie stuck to her guns about what she wanted in her house. Vacant for about seven years, the villa needed reconstructing; she ordered the U.S. Army Engineers to rebuild along the lines she had in mind. She thought the fireplace was too large and too ugly. It was changed. She wanted the dining room enlarged, a small kitchen installed downstairs where Ike could putter.

Then, no fewer than fourteen of France's leading interior designers came down to decorate. Mamie instructed them on how she wanted the house to look: comfortable and homey. She was not averse to graceful and beautiful period pieces in some of the rooms, but there had to be comfortable chairs and sofas.

Her bedroom, yellow and green with a floral-patterned rug and strewn with family pictures, was so middle-America that she once told a visitor: "I know what you're thinking. We might as well be sitting in the States." But that was how she wanted it. And she wanted, too, the corn fields she had planted outside her kitchen. When it was all finished, she added a surprise for Ike: a putting green on the lawn.

The earlier brouhaha was soon forgotten, but Mamie was Mamie and she soon had another minor incident on her hands.

Careful about spending, she was not about to pay large sums for the creations of the great couturiers in Paris. When she discovered the prices charged at the salons, she gasped and said to a friend, "Can you see my paying seven hundred dollars for a dress?"

She didn't; she bought her clothes off the racks in the less-expensive department stores. Once a guest at a party asked her where she purchased a stunning-looking hat she was wearing. If the questioner thought she would hear the name of a major house she was disappointed. Mamie told her: "I got it by mail order from home. It cost me $9.95."

The French were miffed but Mamie's unpretentiousness won them over. She strolled the wide boulevards, lunched in the restaurants, greeting people affably, American-style, like neighbors, discovering little inexpensive snack bars the location of which she told her visiting friends. As for Ike's staff, she was someone from back home, as American as the apple pie, hog jowls, and black-eyed peas she served them for New Year's Eve dinner.

But she also met world leaders. In London she was the dinner partner of Prime Minister Clement R. Attlee and had a chat with Winston Churchill. At The Hague she had a long lunch with Queen Juliana of The Netherlands, with whom she talked about home, children, and the fine points of canasta. In Oslo she met King Haakon VII, the once-exiled king of Norway who had regained his throne. In England she also had several meetings with King George VI, Queen Elizabeth, and other members of the Royal Family.

It was good schooling for what was to come.

The day Ike defeated the formidable Senator Robert A. Taft for the nomination, Mamie was in bed with a blinding headache. With his four brothers, Eisenhower had watched the tense convention balloting on television in the living room of his suite at the Hotel Blackstone in Chicago. When the leader of the Taft forces moved to make the choice unanimous, Ike's eyes filled with tears. He slipped quietly into the bedroom.

In the darkness, he sat on the bed. Mamie snapped on the bed lamp. Noting the tears, she put her hand on his. "By golly, Mamie," Ike said, "this is a terrible big thing we've got ourselves into."

Mamie smiled. "We've been through big things before," she told him. "This one won't let us down."

The campaign that followed was the last of the whistle-stoppers, closing a century-old tradition in American politi-

cal history. No candidate for the Presidency would ever
again board a train, as Ike and Mamie did, and travel tens
of thousands of miles through forty-five states, stopping at
railroad crossings to speak to the people.

At four o'clock in the afternoon of September 14, 1952, a
fleet of sleek black limousines moved in convoy off the
mezzanine ramp of the old Hotel Commodore in Manhattan, GOP campaign headquarters, and drove crosstown to
Pennsylvania Station, where the nineteen-car Eisenhower
Special waited.* On the front of the locomotive, the first
thing spectators would see as the train neared, was a
circular sign, "Look Ahead, Neighbor." In all, 163 persons,
including the Eisenhowers, boarded the cars and, at six
P.M., the train slid out of the station.

Wherever they campaigned, at railroad crossings, in small
towns, or at huge rallies, the cry went up: "Where's
Mamie?" She would appear on the rear platform of a
whistle-stopping train beside the grinning candidate, from
behind a curtain on some stage, or on a hastily built
speaker's stand and call out in her small throaty voice,
"Here I am!"

Then the crowd would go wild. Sometimes the volume
was so great that the reporters could actually feel their notes
quiver. "Between the instant when the crowd first sees Mrs.
Eisenhower and the instant of explosion," wrote Robert
Wallace in *Life* magazine, "there is a brilliant flash of
communication, an exchange of emotion between the
woman on the platform and the people below."

She was, in short, an enormous asset in Eisenhower's
campaign for the Presidency. James Reston of *The New
York Times* appraised her value at the ballot box after
traveling with the pair. "Mamie," he wrote, "must be worth

---

*The campaign train did not make one continuous journey but a series
of trips of varying durations. It would return to New York, then move
out again for another swing to a different area after only two or three
days.

at least 50 electoral votes." In 1952 that was slightly under ten percent of the total; Presidential elections have been won by far smaller margins.

Mamie had never wanted to be on the campaign trail, yet there she was. When the war ended she longed for an end to her rootless life. "I've put in my time, too," she told a friend. "I think that's plenty, don't you?" She wanted to settle down somewhere with her husband.

At the same time she knew it was a vain hope. By the time the war ended there was no doubt in Mamie's mind that Ike eventually would be asked to run for the Presidency and that he would be elected.

"Mamie Eisenhower took it for granted," says Kevin McCann, "that sooner or later there would be such strong pressure on him that he would not be able to resist. She didn't want it to come but she knew it would and that he would heed the call." Walter Trohan adds, "If Mamie was certain of anything at that stage of her life, it was that Ike would be President."

Her conviction was a fusion of intuition, faith, and, a fact that was not being overlooked by politicians, his vast popularity. She did not have to read the polls to be aware of how people felt about him. When someone called to her attention that he had been voted the greatest living American in a large sampling published in the *Saturday Review,* she replied: "They didn't have to go to all that trouble. I could have told them."

"And," says McCann, "Mamie knew her history. She knew that victorious commanders very often are elvated to the highest position by a grateful country." Mamie would talk to her friends about this strong tradition, calling the roll of mililtary heroes who, since George Washington, became Presidents. She would talk about the other great generals such as Andrew Jackson, the hero of the War of 1812; of William Henry Harrison, the rugged Westerner who swept into the White House on the strength of Tippecanoe; of

Zachary Taylor who became a national hero after his brilliant successes during the Mexican War; of Ulysses S. Grant, who led the Union armies at the close of the Civil War.

For all that, Mamie had strong misgivings about the prospect of becoming First Lady, McCann asserts. "While she was an outgoing person who loved people and made friends easily," he says, "there was a shyness and a timidity too about her. She was not quite certain what would be involved for her, but she was sure of one thing, that she would be in the center of a very bright spotlight and she did not look forward to that at all."

Ike and Mamie rode in the "headquarters car," a special Pullman at the rear of the train. It had a private parlor, furnished with easy chairs and a sofa, a tiny dining room which doubled as Mamie's sitting room between mealtimes, a bathroom, galley, and six sleeping compartments. These were occupied by Ike, Mamie, Min Doud, General Howard Snyder, the candidate's personal physician, Ike's valet, and Mamie's maid. The rear door opened onto a small railed-in platform.

Ahead of the HQ car rode the chief aides who formed Ike's staff, arranged the schedule, wrote speeches, guided his public relations, mollified him when he was irritable, which was often, and gave him advice, most of which he didn't take. Former Senator Fred A. Seaton of Nebraska, a tough-minded newspaper publisher and owner of radio stations, managed the timetable. James C. Hagerty, the trigger-tempered, politically astute press secretary for Governor Thomas E. Dewey of New York, had been recruited for the same job with Ike. Gabriel Hauge was there, and Sherman Adams, the Governor of New Hampshire, with his wife Rachel, and Representative Leonard Hall of New York, Dewey's campaign manager in 1948 who was a liaison man with the GOP National Committee.

Forward of the staff car was the VIP Lounge where local dignitaries would be received and, if they were candidates themselves, would ride with Ike to greet the public. Stretching backward were sixteen more cars filled with newspeople and their equipment.

The schedule was rigorous as any battlefield campaign, if not as risky. Ike and Mamie rose shortly after six A.M. and were dressed and ready for the first speech usually before eight. Even at that hour, the crowds were enormous. Ike would make his set speech, always ending with, "And now meet my Mamie." She would emerge, smile, and wave to cheers and applause. At this point, a staff member would start a record-player which would blare out over a loudspeaker "The Sunshine of Your Smile" as the train pulled away to louder cheers and more applause.

There were times during the trip when Ike and Mamie had spats. Mamie confided to Katherine G. Howard, who had been secretary of the Republican National Committee and was on the train as a staff member, how to tell if Ike was miffed at her. Instead of introducing her as "Mamie," he would tell the audience, "And now here is Mrs. Eisenhower." In her memoirs, *With My Shoes Off*, Mrs. Howard gallantly says she never heard Ike call her anything but Mamie.

Campaigning aboard a whistle-stopper was scarcely a restful experience. For thirteen hours each day, often longer, Ike and Mamie were on call—swaying and rattling from town to crossing to city, popping in and out of the train onto the platform or, in larger cities, into cars that would take them to places where off-the-train addresses had been scheduled. Some of these stops involved enormous rallies. At the University of Notre Dame they spoke to 35,000 supporters. In St. Paul the crowd was estimated at 100,000 and in Minneapolis there were twice as many as that! The next day, Ike and Mamie appeared before 60 people in a Wisconsin hamlet, where a dozen boys climbed trees to watch the famous General.

Everywhere the train halted, there were presents. Everything from flowers to fruit, vegetables to toilet soap, and, of course, bottles of something to warm the chill nights. The lounge and sitting room were filled with gifts which the Eisenhowers would send to hospitals along the route, give to visitors, or send to the other cars.

Life's little amenities became luxuries. Baths, for instance. There was nothing in any of the cars that could provide a decent wash for the staff, Katherine Howard recalls. The train's sole shower was in the Eisenhower car. Ironically, at almost every stop Mamie would receive dozens of bars of scented soap as gifts, which she would pass along to the staff members who considered them about as useful as gold-plated drinking cups on a raft in mid-Atlantic.

Some lyricist, whose identity has been lost, wrote this parody, to the tune of "I'm Looking Over a Four-Leaf Clover":

As Ike's train keeps moving
Its passengers are proving
A bath is needed every day;
Sometimes it's three days,
Other times it's four;
Mum's the word, they're saying,
When it's a week or more.

There's no use complaining,
It needs no explaining,
We're doing it for a dear friend Ike;
'T would take atomic power
To scrape off the spot each night.
Without a shower,
We've all seen the U.S.A.!

At the close of each long day, a small group, usually Sherman Adams, Dr. Snyder, and Katherine Howard, would join Ike and Mamie in their car after dinner for a brief chat and a drink. Ike would have a scotch and soda, Mamie either a soft drink or a half-ounce or so of Canadian Club and water.

Mamie was acutely conscious all through the trip of rumors circulating since the war that she drank too much. One day, at a large reception in the ballroom of the Copley Plaza in Boston, she stood on a receiving line with Pat Nixon, shaking hands with many hundreds of guests. After an hour she left the stage for a short break and asked for water. As she lifted the glass to her lips she noted a flash; a photographer had taken a picture. Mamie called out sharply that she wanted the film destroyed, Mrs. Howard recalls, and it was. "She never permitted a picture with a glass in her hand," Mrs. Howard says. "There were too many people ready to misinterpret the contents of the glass."

The second day out, Mamie had the unique experience of meeting Ike's high-school girlfriend.

In Warsaw, Indiana, Ruby Norman, by then Mrs. Ralph Lucier and active in Republican politics, boarded the train. Ike introduced the two women. That same day, Mamie wrote Ruby a note in which she described the encounter and her reaction:

> What a delightful surprise to meet my husband's old girl friend! But I do think our meeting was ever so much more pleasant than what the movies have led us to expect from this classic situation. I am so glad you were able to board the train. And wasn't Ike funny when he said: "Does she admit it!" Seriously, though, it was wonderful meeting you, one of our strong supporters.

As time went on, Ike became impatient with the routine.

Unused to campaigning, he became bored with the sameness of the days: the same speeches; the same local politicians; the same interviews. He would be sitting in his easy chair, reading, as the train lurched to a stop and a staff member knocked on the door. "Here I go again," he would grouse as he walked to the rear platform. The day's schedule was so tight that once, during a rare lull, he said to Fred Seaton: "You're slipping, Fred. You almost left me enough time to shave." Says Anne Wheaton, Mamie's press secretary: "Ike was not too crazy about it. I always questioned his love of campaigning."

Mamie was good at it. She listened carefully on being introduced to a local politico or industrialist, and always got the name right afterward. To special people she gave special attention because, having known troubles and tragedy herself, she could understand theirs. Many times she talked quietly with a woman who, she learned, had lost sons in the war. She filled her pockets and handbags with Ike buttons and passed them out from the platform. She told everyone, "I've been working on the railroad."

She was one of those rare women who could create a magnetic field between herself and the public without seeming to try. She said little, often only a "thank you very much," and "you are very kind," but there was a warmth and friendliness about her that caught an audience. People understood at once that her smile while Ike was speaking was real and they responded to it.

So they wanted more of Mamie than her strength could permit her to give. Regretfully, yet firmly, she demurred when she felt that another appearance would be overtaxing. "I do all I can," she said, "but I can't do any more than I can do, because if I do I'll get sick, and if I get sick I'll be a burden to Ike, and I can't be a burden to Ike."

Only once did she lose her affability. In San Francisco they spent the night at the St. Francis Hotel after a long day of motorcades and speeches. She discovered that she was assigned to a room on one floor, Ike on another. Mamie said no, and she said it loudly and furiously. She would not be separated from her husband. In moments, they had found her a room on the same floor as Ike.

Even though Ike could easily contain his enthusiasm for the trip, he did all he was asked and more. Once the train halted before six A.M. at a tiny hamlet. The entire town's population was outside, having waited for hours in the chill night. "We've got to speak to them," Ike said to an aide.

Ike and Mamie put on robes, Mamie tied a ribbon around her hair, and out they went onto the rear platform.

Aboard the train at that point were three photographers whose instincts had been finely honed: each time the train stopped they automatically grabbed their cameras and raced to the rear car. One ran over and got the unusual shot of the candidate and his wife, in bathrobes, waving from the platform, but the others missed it. Since there was no pooling of photographs, the two who were scooped feared for their jobs.

When the train started again, word of this reached Jim Hagerty, who told Ike. "Let's do it again," Eisenhower said. So after breakfast, Ike and Mamie donned their robes again, Mamie tied the same ribbon in her hair, and the engineer was instructed to stop the train. They stepped onto the platform and, waving to an imaginary crowd, posed for the same picture that the other alert cameraman had taken hours before.

Mrs. Howard and Mamie shared many personal moments, one of which occurred almost as soon as they met. After Ike's nomination, Howard, who had been asked by Sherman Adams to join the campaign staff, flew to New York with Ike and Mamie to help set up headquarters at the Commodore. Barbara Eisenhower and her three children were also on board.

Susan, the baby, was eight months old. Mamie, wearing a black-and-rose-print taffeta dress, held Susan on her lap in the plane's forward section. A short time after takeoff, Mrs. Howard saw Mamie approaching her in the aisle, holding her pleated skirt away from her and smiling ruefully.

"The baby's diaper wasn't waterproof," Mamie explained.

The major crisis of the trip occurred only four days after the train had chugged out of Penn Station. Ike's running mate, Richard Nixon, and his pretty wife Pat, who was then forty years old, were whistle-stopping themselves when the *New York Post* headlined the story of a "secret Nixon fund." A group of one hundred wealthy Californians were chipping in five hundred dollars each annually to help support the young Senator.

The events of the next week are now political history; less well known, however, was the rapport between Pat Nixon and Mamie Eisenhower.

Although they never became close friends, Mamie liked the tall, slender woman with the red hair and quiet manner. She had met Pat for the first time on the speaker's stand at the International Amphitheater in Chicago after the nominations. Her first words of greeting were, "My, you're the prettiest thing." Later, the two wives had only the briefest time to chat, but Mamie was convinced of Pat's intense loyalty to her husband. It was something she understood and admired.

On September 22 Nixon made his "Checkers" speech from the El Capitan Theatre in Hollywood. Eisenhower was watching it on television in the manager's office of the Cleveland Public Auditorium where seventeen thousand persons had come to hear a major address. Mamie was at his side as Nixon defended himself against the charges that he was living high on the hog. He was broke, he said, and had accepted no gifts but a spotted black-and-white cocker spaniel his daughters had named Checkers.

Throughout the speech, Pat sat like a waxen figure, eyes fixed on her husband. Watching her, Mamie knew at once what was going through her mind. "She is praying," she told friends. Pat said Mamie hit it dead center. "She had long experience when her husband was under fire," Pat explained later, "and she recognized another woman's prayers when she saw them."

Even before the campaign started, rumors kept cropping up that both Eisenhower and Stevenson were in poor health. One newsletter, sent to subscribers, claimed the General was so sick he dreaded facing audiences for fear he might collapse in the midst of a speech. The whispers grew so loud that on May 1 reporters put the question to President Truman at a press conference in the White House. Truman ridiculed any intimation that Eisenhower was ailing; nonetheless, the rumors would not stop.

In early August, Lester David, after consulting physicians at a state medical society and a major life-insurance company, drew up a list of thirty-six questions designed to reveal the complete physical conditions of a patient and presented them to General Snyder and to Dr. Emmet F. Pearson, Stevenson's doctor. Within two weeks, replies were sent back. Thus Eisenhower and Stevenson became the first Presidential candidates in American history to disclose medical facts about their health.

Both physicians reported their patients in excellent health. Neither had any chronic or disabling illness. Heart, lungs, blood pressure, and pulse were normal. Each had a tendency to become overweight and had to guard against it. Both had minor ailments which had since been cured.

Ike's blood pressure ranged between 120 and 140 systolic, and 80 and 90 diastolic, though on a few occasions it had been noted as high as $156/96$, lowered by periods of relaxation and rest. Stevenson's pressure was "within normal range." Ike's pulse rate averaged 72 resting, 92 to 96 after exercise, returning to 72 or 74 within two minutes' rest. Stevenson's pulse at rest was 80; after 20 brisk steps on an 18-inch stool it rose to 110, returning to 84 in two minutes.

Eisenhower's vision was corrected to 20-20 by plus lenses for farsightedness and Stevenson wore glasses for reading due to a slight "accommodation" loss. Both had good hearing, color sense, and teeth.

Neither had any allergies or chronic illnesses, and blood chemistry and urinalysis have revealed no deviations from the normal.

The General liked eight hours of sleep but frequently got only six or seven because of work pressure, while the Governor was usually in bed by midnight and up at seven-thirty A.M. Stevenson had trained himself to relax easily while traveling and both he and Eisenhower were rated good sleepers.

Eisenhower "drinks only a dilute highball of scotch whisky and plain water," declared his doctor, "rarely more than two glasses before dinner. He almost never touches alcoholic beverages after dinner and does not smoke cigarettes, cigars or a pipe." Stevenson, according to his doctor, "takes an occasional social drink at night only—prefers bourbon. Smokes cigarettes, about a pack a day."

Each worked an average of ten hours a day. The General had "very few" vacations in the past ten years, while the Governor took frequent short breaks but no prolonged vacations. Eisenhower exercised about eight hours each week, preferring golf, a rowing machine, and an electric exercise bicycle. He relaxed indoors by painting and playing bridge. Stevenson liked tennis, golf, horseback riding, and walks in the evening. He enjoyed sports as participant and spectator and could handle the controls of a plane.*

On Monday, November 3, seven weeks and a day after it started out, the campaign train returned to Penn Station for the last time. It had traveled 33,000 miles and Ike had made 230 whistle-stop talks and forty major speeches.

---

*Despite the clean bill of health, Eisenhower had two major illnesses within four years. See part 4, chapter 4. Stevenson died of a heart attack within thirteen years.

Mamie went to her home on Morningside Heights and luxuriated in a warm bath. She stayed there so long that Ike, returning from conferences, couldn't find her in the apartment and got worried. When she heard him bellowing for her, she called out where she was.

Next day, the country voted. Early in the evening Mamie went to the Hotel Commodore where she and Ike had a suite and listened for the returns. Before midnight, it was clear that Ike was registering a victory of landslide proportions. Mamie had invited a few of her closest friends, telling them she was supremely confident Ike would win. Nevertheless, tears streamed down her face as the returns were announced. At 1:45 A.M., Stevenson conceded, and fifteen minutes later Ike and Mamie stood before wildly cheering followers in the grand ballroom—the next President and his First Lady. Ike's popular vote was 33,778,963 to Stevenson's 27,314,992, a plurality of more than 6,400,000. His electoral vote was 442 to his Democratic opponent's 89.

A little more than three weeks after his election, Ike set out to fulfill a pledge made during the bitter Presidential campaign.

American fighting forces, troops, planes and ships, had been in Korea since the summer of 1950. The country was not at war, President Truman had said at a White House press conference; it was engaged in a police action, along with other members of the United Nations. Nevertheless, thousands of American soldiers had been killed and many more thousands wounded in battle.

Korea became a campaign issue and Ike, in a speech in Detroit later credited with insuring his victory, promised, "I shall go to Korea," if elected.

On Nov. 29, 1952, in the early hours of the morning while most of New York City slept, Ike was whisked by limousine from his Morningside Drive residence to Mitchell Field where two planes waited to take him and members of his staff to Seoul in Korea.

There had been elaborate secrecy surrounding the preparations to foil any possible assassination attempts. A busy agenda for the day had been prepared for newsmen to convey the impression that the General was at work in his office. The members of his entourage were picked up at obscure locations all over the city and throughout the day important figures arrived at Morningside Drive to maintain the fiction that Ike was conferring inside.

He spent three days in Korea, meeting with Generals Mark Clark and James H. Van Fleet, poring over battle plans, discussing strategy and meeting the troops. It wasn't until December 6, when Ike was on his way home aboard a Navy cruiser that Hagerty released news of the trip. The President-elect had "no panaceas, no solutions," he said, but felt "much can be done and will be done."

Inauguration Day the following January 20 dawned crisply cold in Washington but, despite a forecast of rain, the sun emerged intermittently from a hazy blue sky, bringing the temperature to the middle forties as noon approached. At 9:30 A.M. that Tuesday, the Eisenhowers and all his major appointees, with their families, went to the National Presbyterian Church for a solemn twenty-minute service. At 12:32 Ike took the Presidential oath on the platform specially built into the east plaza. After repeating Chief Justice Fred M. Vinson's words, "so help me God," Ike shook hands with the Justice and with former President Truman.

Then Ike turned and quickly crossed the platform to where Mamie sat a few feet away, her eyes bright with tears. Leaning down, he kissed her.

2. And After Dinner, They Watched TV

EVER SINCE WILLIAM McKinley entered the White House a half-century before, tall, reed-slender John Mays, in powder-blue swallowtail coat, white stockings, and patent-leather shoes, had been welcoming new Presidents and their First Ladies. Now stooped with age, but dignified as ever, he stood outside the North Entrance Hall and bowed Ike and Mamie through the glass doors.

Someone had recorded the time: precisely two minutes past seven. The ten-mile-long Inauguration parade, with its floats, whooping cowboys, marching bands, and smartly uniformed men and women, had lasted more than five hours. In 1948 Harry Truman had ordered a low stool for the platform on which he could sit from time to time, but Ike had stood all through his parade, his arm snapping salutes every few minutes when a new contingent passed with the colors. Mamie giggled, clapped and waved, and blew kisses. Beside her, 78-year-old Herbert Hoover, a lap robe tucked around him, invited her to share the warmth as the sun descended. She agreed readily and the two sat huddled together.

When it finally ended, Ike and Mamie were driven to the White House. There was no time for a celebration or even a proper dinner. Trays were sent up to the family quarters for the Eisenhowers, John and Barbara, and Mamie's mother. Then Mamie dressed for the twin Inaugural balls.

It took her three hours but when she was finished Ike blurted out, "By golly, Mamie, you're beautiful." In a Renoir-pink creation by the designer Nettie Rosenstein, bought through the Dallas department store Neiman-Marcus, she was stunning. The gown, of peau de soie, glittered with 2,000 pink rhinestones and the evening bag she carried, made of a matching pink silk and framed in pure silver, was embroidered with exactly 3,456 rhinestones, pearls, and beads, all of them pink. Beneath the gown's bouffant skirt were taffeta and crinoline petticoats; on her arms, almost to the shoulder, were silk gloves; on her feet fabric shoes. Petticoats, gloves, shoes—all were of the same pink silk.

If Mamie's gown was a big hit, Ike had a problem with his formal suit. After the quick dinner, he took off his jacket and pants and before popping into the bathroom he looked for his tails, white-tie, and boiled-shirt outfit. He couldn't find them. "Hey, Mamie," he bellowed, "where the hell is my monkey suit?"

Mamie didn't know, neither did Sergeant John Moaney, his wartime aide who had become his valet. They searched the closets and still-unpacked bags; several Secret Service men joined in the hunt without success. Ike sat on the bed in his shorts and growled that the first crisis of his administration had already occurred. Mamie, unperturbed, finally figured it all out. "You must have left it on the train," she told him.

Moaney and a Secret Service man raced down to the station, searched the car on which Ike and Mamie had come down the day before, and found another suitcase. It contained the tails and the crisis was averted.

Above: During a tour in France General Eisenhower, left, stops to chat with Lieutenant General Omar N. Bradley and Major General J. Lawton Collins, July 5, 1944. *U.S. Army Photograph.*

Right: General Eisenhower, right, discussing the bombing mission that prepared the way for the new offensive at Normandy against the Germans with Major General Edwin L. Quesada as Lieutenant General Omar N. Bradley, center, looks on, July 26, 1944. *U.S. Army Photograph.*

Left: King George of England, left, with Ike in Liège, Be!gium, October 14, 1944. *U.S. Army Photograph.*

Below: Winston Churchill and General Eisenhower, November 14, 1944. *U.S. Army Photograph.*

Right: General Dwight D. Eisenhower, Supreme Allied Commander, at his head-quarters, February 1, 1945. *U.S. Army Photograph.*

Above: President Harry S. Truman congratulates the General upon his triumphant return home after V-E Day as Mamie and crowds of excited White House employees look on. *Courtesy Dwight D. Eisenhower Library. Below:* While visiting New York upon his return from Europe, Ike leaves the official box at Polo Grounds Ball Park after being caught in a rainstorm. Mayor Fiorello La Guardia, holding a baseball bat, speaks to him as he leaves. *U.S. Army Photograph.*

Above: General Eisenhower and Mamie in New York on June 19, 1945. He is holding the key to the city. *Courtesy Dwight D. Eisenhower Library. Below:* Ike and Mamie share a ride with Lord Louis Mountbatten in London in 1946. *Courtesy Dwight D. Eisenhower Library.*

Above: Mamie and Ike attend the wedding of their son John to Barbara Thompson at Fort Monroe, Virginia, on June 10, 1947. *Courtesy Dwight D. Eisenhower Library.*

Right: The installation of Ike as Columbia University's 13th president on October 12, 1948, as Mamie, John and Omar Bradley (in sunglasses) look on. *Courtesy Columbia University; photo by Manny Warman.*

Above: Ike with the Columbia football team and coach Lon Little. *Courtesy Columbia University; photo by Manny Warman.*

Above: President-elect Dwight D. Eisenhower and Sergeant Jack R. Hutcherson eat dinner in Korea, December 1952. *U.S. Army Photograph. Below:* Dwight D. Eisenhower is sworn in as President of the United States in Washington, D.C., 1953. *U.S. Army Photograph.*

Dwight and Mamie Eisenhower as President and First Lady. *Courtesy Dwight D. Eisenhower Library.*

Above: Ike, golfing at Quantico, Virginia, in July 1953. *Courtesy Dwight D. Eisenhower Library.*

Below: President Eisenhower at his desk in the Oval Office, 1955. *Courtesy Dwight D. Eisenhower Library.*

Right: Ike and Mamie spend the weekend at their farm at Gettysburg, 1956. *Courtesy Dwight D. Eisenhower Library.*

Above: President Eisenhower poses with his various physicians at Fitzsimons Army Medical Center. *U.S. Army Photograph.*

Left: President Eisenhower convalescing after his heart attack. The stitching on his pajamas reads "Much Better, Thanks." *U.S. Army Photograph.*

Right: President Richard M. Nixon places a wreath before the casket of Dwight D. Eisenhower. Speaker of the House John W. McCormack, Spiro Agnew, and the Shah of Iran, as well as members of the Eisenhower and Nixon families stand at attention. *Courtesy Dwight D. Eisenhower Library.*

Below: The casket containing the body of President Eisenhower lies in state in the rotunda of the Capitol. *Courtesy Dwight D. Eisenhower Library.*

The statue of Ike at Gettysburg College; Mamie and David are at right, with a student of the college in the center, 1977. *Courtesy of Gettysburg College.*

The White House was the grandest home they had ever had, yet, oddly enough, neither Ike nor Mamie had ever seen where they would live or where he would work until after they had moved in.

The day after the Inauguration Mamie took a tour of the house with Katherine Howard and Mrs. Nevins, wife of General Nevins. "It was just as new to Mamie as it was to us," says Mrs. Howard. In the Lincoln Suite down the East Hall, which includes the bedroom and a sitting room, Mamie examined the lace curtains on the tall windows and remarked that they needed a cleaning. She grimaced as she took the women into Bess Truman's bedroom, where she had spent the first night; it was a small chamber where Eleanor Roosevelt had also slept, unattractively furnished with a single bed, a simple bureau and chair, and a dresser pushed into the corner. "It didn't appeal to Mamie at all," Mrs. Howard says. Midway, the tour was interrupted by a message from Ike: Would Mamie and her friends come down to the East Room and watch the Cabinet being sworn in? Afterward, the tour continued, Mamie ticking off the changes she planned to make.

As for Ike, he didn't even know where his office was located or where his Cabinet would meet.

Despite his long day and even longer night, he arose at seven A.M. that first morning on the job and boarded the elevator for the ground floor. With him was a White House usher who had signaled downstairs that the President was coming. At the elevator doors stood Rufus Youngblood, the Secret Service agent who, eleven years later, would be riding in Lyndon Johnson's car in Dallas the day President Kennedy was assassinated. Youngblood was astonished to see Ike, who hadn't been expected for hours. He was more astounded when the new President inquired: "Would you show me where my office is? I want to get an early start."

Youngblood recovered quickly and invited the President to follow him to the Executive Wing at the west end of the building where he showed Ike to the Oval Office. Ike went inside, then popped out a moment later. Hooking a thumb toward a closed door, he asked Youngblood what was behind it. "That's the Cabinet Room, sir," the Secret Service man replied. Ike thanked him and went to work.

When Ike and Mamie lived there, the White House, for all its grandeur and historical significance, could have been a split-level in any suburb. The occupants lived that kind of private life.

After the stay-at-home Trumans, Washington hostesses had expected the great war hero and his wife to be glamorous guests at their dinner parties. They were disappointed; if anything, the Eisenhowers were even bigger homebodies than their predecessors. Ike had had enough of the roving life. "At last I've got a job where I can stay home nights and, by golly, I'm going to stay home," he said.

And he did, as often as he could.

Elegance was to come in the next Administration, with the Kennedys; this one was homespun middle-America. After work, Eisenhower came "home," which was upstairs. Like most men who put in a hard day, he kissed his wife, put on an old sweater, and waited for dinner. Afterward, also like millions of others, he and Mamie sat in their living room and watched television.

By then, families around the country, on average, were looking at the screen between four and five hours a day. Mamie came close, because she watched daytime shows. In the evening both she and Ike liked "I Love Lucy," "You Bet Your Life," and "Talent Scouts," all of which consistently hit high ratings. Ike was a fan of Arthur Godfrey, the host of "Talent Scouts," because although he was an Easterner, born and bred in Hasbrouck Heights, New Jersey, the redhead's show-business persona was that of the simple country boy and Ike still identified with that.

They disliked anything smacking of the incoming new music, rock 'n' roll; Ike was baffled by Elvis Presley. Westerns were more to his liking.

Mamie was an unabashed soap-opera fan. Once the designer Mollie Parnis was showing Mamie her collection from which the First Lady would select a new wardrobe. Mamie looked at her watch and saw that one of her favorite serials was just beginning. Says Miss Parnis, "So we had to stop and wait until the program was over before we could continue."

Color television was just coming into popularity and Ike and Mamie became the first First Family to have a color set. One Sunday it stopped working. A hurried call came to Traphes Bryant, the electrician on duty, whose expertise in color television was somewhat limited. Ike, apparently angered at the instrument's eccentricities, snapped, "Let the goddamned thing go!" Mamie, however, wanted it fixed, so Bryant poked around inside, moved some tubes, and got it working again after a fashion.

One evening they watched an audience-participation show during which an elderly lady revealed that the living person she would most like to meet was Mamie Eisenhower. "I never saw Mamie more pleased," the President told a friend the next day. "Mamie sure got a kick out of that."

The Eisenhowers went to the movies twice and sometimes three times a week. Their theater was on the ground floor of the White House off the East Colonnade, and they had their pick of any film they wanted.* Westerns were Ike's fare, love stories and musicals were Mamie's. Ike adored *High Noon,* for which Gary Cooper won an Academy Award the year Ike was elected President. He saw *Stalag 17,* which starred William Holden, the movie about American POWs in Germany, but said nothing afterward. Mamie liked *The Greatest Show on Earth, The King and I,* and *Never Wave at a WAC.* The latter was a slight little

* The long, narrow room where Ike and Mamie watched their movies was converted into an upholstery shop by Jacqueline Kennedy to repair antiques. Later, during the Nixon Administration, it was changed once again into a movie theater.

comedy but it starred Rosalind Russell, a personal friend. Andrew Tully, a Washington columnist, recalled that Ike once became so caught up in Gary Cooper's attempt to escape on horseback from a quartet of killers that he leaned forward in his chair and yelled, "Run!" Afterward, Tully says, Ike told Mamie's mother, who had been watching with him, "By golly, I never thought he'd make it." Ike's admiration for Cooper was matched by his dislike of the sleepy-eyed Robert Mitchum. "I can't stand that s.o.b.," he fumed, and if ever Mitchum appeared on the screen, Ike left and went upstairs.

Mamie was not unlike many wives who wanted their husbands home on time for dinner and worried when they stayed too late at the office. One November evening, a year after his election, Ike remained long past his regular quitting time, deep in conference on a science-and-security speech being prepared by Arthur Larson, one of his aides. When darkness was setting in, the telephone rang. Mamie was calling to ask when he'd be up. He told her it wouldn't be long, and continued to work on the speech. She called repeatedly every few minutes, concerned that Ike should not go too long without eating.

"Now, honey, I'm all right," Ike assured her. "I'll just get something when I get back." Mamie offered to have a tray sent down to him, but he told her it wasn't necessary. Much later, the speech was finished to his satisfaction and he went upstairs.

Ike and Mamie were dining alone the first week of March 1953, when Moscow Radio broadcast news of the death of Premier Joseph Stalin. The next day, discussing with his advisers the course of future relations with the Soviet Union, Ike made it clear that he was more interested in pressing for peace and disarmament than in continuing the cold war.

In a major speech before the American Society of Newspaper Editors on April 16, which he called "The

Chance for Peace," Ike stressed this position. Widely applauded in this country, the address also met with the strong approval of the Chinese Communists who were as anxious as he was to end the fighting in Korea. Eleven days later, the stalemated negotiations to bring the conflict to a close were resumed and finally, after three more hard months of talks, an armistice was signed on July 27.

Many nights the President retired as early as nine P.M. and Mamie either continued to watch television or read for another two hours—she was especially interested in books about other First Ladies.

Sometimes the Eisenhowers had some friends in for dinner and an evening of cards—bridge for Ike, canasta for Mamie. These evenings often ended with Mamie thumping the piano and the others harmonizing sentimental ballads and old Army songs. Once, one of the guests recalled, Mamie stopped momentarily, before starting "Tears in My Eyes," to issue a warning. "Now Ike," she said, "please, no bellowing."

Mamie doted on her grandchildren and in early March brought Dwight David Eisenhower II, who was five, Barbara Ann, three, and Susan fifteen months, to the White House for their first visit. They were accompanied by their mother. John was serving in Korea.

David, a square-jawed, serious youngster, with an engaging grin reminiscent of his grandfather, entered the elegant front hall and looked about him quizzically. "Mimi," he asked—the name Barbara Eisenhower had bestowed years ago on her new mother-in-law which was subsequently adopted by the grandchildren and even Julie Nixon when she married David—"why did you build yourself such a big house?"

Mamie explained carefully: "This isn't my home. It belongs to Uncle Sam." The next day she told members of the newspaper corps at her first press conference, "I think it's really livable for as large a house as it is."

The children visited at the White House often, occupying bedrooms on the third floor, where a huge closet stored their playthings. Christening ceremonies for Mary Jean, born in 1955, were held in the Blue Room. However, Mamie laid down strict rules for the children's behavior—no riding up and down the self-service elevator, smudgy hands were to be kept off the walls, and romping and horseplay was forbidden on the first two floors.

Mamie's Western upbringing and her itinerant life with Ike developed in her an informality and openness which she carried right into the White House. She was breezy, unaffected, and had a naturalness which charmed and disarmed even the most critical.

Shortly after she became the First Lady, she left an all-female gathering, waving and calling out, "Good-bye girls!" A few weeks after Ike's election she greeted a reporter friend with a handshake and a cheerful "Hello, kiddo, I haven't changed a bit."

Accustomed to mingling with royalty and high-ranking diplomats, she was not fazed by the protocol and formalities of White House entertaining. She did, in fact, eliminate some of the stodginess and did away with some traditional customs.

Mamie didn't like the table arrangements for state dinners which found her sitting opposite Ike at a horseshoe-shaped table, her back to the guests. She ordered a change. At the next function, guests sat around an E-shaped table with President and Mrs. Eisenhower, side by side, on high-backed mahogany chairs at its head.

Some months after the Inauguration the Eisenhowers gave a formal white-tie reception for the diplomatic corps, the first such affair to be held in the White House for years. The guest list of almost fifteen hundred persons included ambassadors, ministers, Cabinet officers, and members of Congress.

In keeping with tradition, the gentlemen wore tails; the ladies, fancy ballgowns, many of the diplomatic wives chosing creations of leading designers of their country. Mamie appeared in the pink rhinestone-embroidered peau de soie she had worn to the Inaugural balls. On the receiving line, however, Washington ladies noted only her left hand and arm were gloved; the right was bare. Shaking hands, Mamie had decided, was not a high-hat gesture.

She loved her role as First Lady. Unlike Bess Truman, who counted the days until she could return to Missouri, Mamie thoroughly enjoyed the teas, receptions, and luncheons which occupied a large part of her day. When a friend asked if she wasn't bored, Mamie exclaimed: "Bored? Why, no! These women from all over the country are so interesting, and you know they can scarcely name a place that I haven't visited or campaigned in with Ike. We never run out of things to say."

The first few months of Ike's Presidency, Mamie shook about 600 to 700 hands a day—more, according to veteran White House aides, than any other First Lady in so short a time.

Her handshake was not the quick, casual, pass 'em-along of professional politicians. She would look the person straight in the eye and grip a hand firmly, sometimes even placing her own left hand over the other's right in a warm clasp. She never seemed to run out of small talk; she had something special to say to each woman, telling one, "I love your bracelet," and another "I was in Des Moines last year and thought it was so pretty."

She was so busy shaking hands that Ike protested. "I've got to get Mamie out of the White House," he grumbled to an aide. "She's shaking hands with seven hundred women a day." When a friend asked Mamie if her hand didn't hurt, Mamie laughed. "It's not my hands, it's my feet."

Ike, accustomed to early rising, was up at six, but since the kitchen staff was not ready to begin serving before eight he brewed his own coffee in an electric percolator in his bedroom. Later, he had a small kitchen installed in the family quarters, where on Sundays he made his vegetable soup. The cabinets and counters were built to his height, a fact that disconcerted Tricia Nixon when she came to live there. Tricia, a trace over five feet tall, said everything was too high up.

Mamie's day began at eight. She had turned Bess Truman's tiny bedroom into a dressing room and converted the larger sitting room next to it into her bedroom, adjoining Ike's. Bess's single bed was banished to the basement and a king-size one brought in. Mamie had the room painted in pale pink. Outside her window, which commanded a view of the South Lawn, officially the President's Park, was a magnolia tree planted by Thomas Jefferson.

After studying Bess's bedroom, she had gone to Woodward & Lothrop, the Washington department store, and bought two small cabinets and a glass top. She had the cabinets painted, placed the glass across them—and created a dressing table as attractive and serviceable as any that could be purchased at far greater price. A White House carpenter built closets along one entire wall; Mamie kept all her dresses here.

After breakfast, usually just dry toast and coffee with an occasional half-grapefruit, Mamie settled back against the pink pillows to handle her paperwork.

J. B. West, then assistant to Chief Usher Howell G. Crim at the White House, tells of his astonishment when they answered a call to the First Lady's bedroom the morning after Ike took office.

"Mr. Crim and I walked into the room and stopped in our tracks," he said. Mrs. Eisenhower was still in bed. "We managed to say 'Good morning,' as Mrs. Eisenhower pushed away her breakfast tray. She was wearing a dainty pink-ruffled bedjacket and had a pink satin bow in her hair."

Mamie met with the chief usher and housekeeper every morning to go over the day's schedule, select menus, and make household decisions. Although it had been years since she did housekeeping chores herself, she had an eagle eye for burned-out bulbs, rugs that needed cleaning, and frayed sheets. She gave orders that only the best linen was to be used on White House beds, which were changed whenever occupied, no matter how short a time. "I don't want to see mended linens again," she told the housekeeper.

When Mamie first arrived at the White House, says Eileen Archibold, she was appalled at the condition of the curtains in the family bedrooms.

Told there were no others in the mansion to replace them, Mamie tightened her lips and said, "We'll see." Having learned a thing or two about requisitioning materials in her years as an Army wife, she made a few telephone calls to the right places. Soon, yards and yards of fabric arrived from the Air Force. Several of the maids were put to work sewing new curtains.

One day a Weimaraner named Heidi, a gift to Ike, piddled on a fabulously expensive green oval carpet in the Diplomatic Reception Room, a gathering place for the President and his guests at state functions. The Aubusson rug, specially woven for the room, had the seals of all the states in its border. Now it also had a yellowish stain.

Mamie was fit to be tied. She spent hours on her hands and knees with the White House housekeeper, trying to eradicate the stain. Nothing worked. Finally she decided to send the carpet out to be dyed, which reduced but did not completely eliminate the discoloration. Mamie brooded about the incident for weeks, even complaining to Ike. "Mamie," he said finally, "I've got a few other things more important than that to worry about."

Rugs which showed footprints became a fetish with Mamie who insisted they be vacuumed or hand-brushed before guests were expected to eliminate all signs of steps.

Once she came to the office of the White House dentist to

have her teeth cleaned and found one of Ike's aides sprawled in the chair, cigarette ashes and newspapers strewn on the floor. Shocked at the disorderly condition of the room, she demanded sternly: "What is this? What are you doing here?"

The aide explained that he was waiting for Steve Martini, the President's barber, to cut his hair. The chair Martini customarily used was broken and he had been told that he could take his clients there until it was repaired. Mamie sternly rebuked the aide for the mess and told him to get his hair cut elsewhere.

Martini, the official White House barber for four Presidents, began his tenure with Ike. He would come to the Oval Office once a week to trim the Presidential hair, always close, as Ike had requested the first day.

One time, however, Martini cut it differently. Robert Montgomery, the former actor who was Eisenhower's adviser for his television appearances, suggested that Martini allow the President's hair to grow out more fully at the temples. Ike looked in the mirror afterward and demanded, "What's this?" Martini explained his instructions from Montgomery.

"Never mind him," Ike said, his temper rising. "I don't want to look like a goddamned movie star. I'm just a GI, so cut it that way!" Martini did.

After she had settled housekeeping matters, Mamie conferred with her social secretary, Mrs. Mary Jane McCaffree (later Monroe) on plans for the teas, receptions, dinners, and luncheons to be held at the White House. In addition to menus, seating plans, entertainment and floral arrangements were discussed.

Each day there were also hundreds of letters to answer. The first week after the Inauguration, Mamie received seven hundred letters a day. Although this tapered off, her correspondence remained heavy. She insisted on answering many of the letters personally; the others were handled by Mrs. McCaffree's staff of fifteen.

Mamie's public day sometimes began with a series of "coffees" in the midmorning, a custom which she adopted from the English. She went to innumerable luncheons for charitable organizations—in addition to those held at the White House—posed with crippled children for fund-raising drives, entertained Girl Scout leaders, clubwomen, and political wives. She saw groups ranging from a half-dozen persons to sixteen hundred wives of members of the United States Chamber of Commerce and two thousand Daughters of the American Revolution.

A few gaffes were inevitable. Once she offended the General Federation of Women's Clubs when she turned down a request for a large reception because the social season had ended. Instead, she invited the ladies to visit the White House, then miffed them even more when she failed to show up. The women complained they were shown no more attention than the tourists who visited the mansion.

More serious were the diplomatic blunders when she invited Mrs. Lopez Mateos, wife of the President of Mexico, for lunch. The day started badly when Mrs. Lopez arrived, accompanied by an entourage of about ten women. Mrs. McCaffree, who had not expected them, explained that there simply wasn't time to make preparations for so many. The ladies left.

During the lunch, Mrs. Mateos presented Mamie with a magnificent pin, entwined Mexican and American flags set in precious gems. Mamie thanked her, and tossed the unopened box to a waiter. "Put this on my desk," she said. Mrs. Mateos was stony-faced and, soon after, departed.

Mamie had not known that in Mexico gifts are opened at once, and the donors profusely thanked. Not to do so is considered an insult. News of the incident spread quickly south of the border where, for a while, diplomats worried that a coolness in relations could result.

Mamie made an ardent rooter, however, of one little old lady on a receiving line who confided that it was her birthday. The First Lady smiled and, leaning over, kissed the woman on her cheek. Word of the incident got around and many other elderly ladies made it to the White House on their birthdays. Mamie kissed them all.

Her popularity was not as high with the White House staff who thought many of her orders dictatorial, demanding homage paid in some parts of the world only to royalty. Mr. West affirmed this in his memoirs. "She could be imperious," he says.

When Mrs. Eisenhower left the White House, he wrote, she insisted that "I am to be escorted to the diplomatic entrance by an usher. And when I return, I am to be met at the door and escorted upstairs." She found a houseman using what she called the "family" elevator and she gave orders that it was not to be used by the staff. "But fifteen minutes after she left the White House, George was riding the elevator again," says West. "The servants had a long history of skirting around a First Lady's wishes."

Although she was a tough boss, Mamie was also keenly interested in the welfare and personal lives of staff members, asking many questions about relatives, homes, and outside activities. Secret Service men working late were reminded to call home, sick employees and their families received flowers from the White House and, on birthdays, each employee received a card from the First Lady and a cake baked in the White House kitchen.

At Christmas, Mamie personally wrapped presents for every member of the staff, gifts which ranged from handkerchiefs and neckties to portable radios and household accessories of silver and crystal.

Traphes Bryant recalls that "Mamie endeared herself to me because, when she gave a little gift, she actually wrapped it and wrote the card herself. She really knew how to pick a present that you would cherish and use."

Although described elsewhere as cold and indifferent employers, the Eisenhowers were the first occupants of the White House to throw a party for the staff at their Gettysburg farm.

Mamie had originally planned one party, to which she invited every cook, maid, butler, and telephone operator on the White House staff—including members of the Secret Service assigned to the White House who had never visited Gettysburg. But when it came time to work out the logistics, she realized they could not accommodate all of them at the same time. Undaunted, she broke up her list and made plans for two parties.

"We had tents set up on the lawn and we had all the food served there," she recalled. "We couldn't get them all in there at once and so we had two."

Holidays were a great source of fun—a throwback to Mamie's childhood when Min and John Doud used every occasion to festoon the house with banners and party favors and invite relatives and friends to celebrate. Mamie did the same at the White House, utilizing traditional, albeit corny, symbols.

Wives of White House staff members, invited to lunch on Halloween, found cornstalks, pumpkins, and apples heaped against the marble columns in the corridors, chalky-white skeletons dangling from the lighting fixtures in the dining room, and black witches riding broomsticks along the table. Papier-mâché black cats, goblins, and ghosts were scattered throughout the state rooms and huge bowls of yellow chrysanthemums, Indian corn, nuts, gourds, and dried leaves on the table.

Mamie went all-out for Christmas with a tall, shining tree in the East Room and many others all over the White House—one year there were twenty-seven. Holly wreaths, tied with red ribbon, hung at every window and on the front door. Green ropes of leaves were twined around the white columns and red carnations tied with green ribbons dangled from the wall fixtures.

For the Congressional wives invited to tea a week before St. Patrick's Day, Mamie tucked green-and-white candy canes and green top hats into green ribbons which wound around the hall columns. Shamrocks and green carnations decorated the mantel of the dining room and hung from the chandeliers. Mamie, wearing a green brocade gown, greeted her guests in the Green Room.

Next day, when she hosted a luncheon for Senate and Cabinet wives, she added green-jacketed leprechauns to the luncheon table and a corsage of green carnations and shamrocks for each guest.

During Ike's two terms, they entertained over seventy official foreign visitors, more than any of the previous White House occupants, including Queen Elizabeth of England and Prince Philip, Soviet premier Nikita S. Khrushchev and Mrs. Khrushchev, Madame Chiang Kai-shek, Winston Churchill, Emperor Haile Selassie of Ethiopia, King Baudouin of Belgium, Princess Beatrix of the Netherlands, and West German president Theodor Heuss.

When Queen Elizabeth visited Washington in 1957 President Eisenhower dispatched his own plane, the *Columbine III*, to fetch the young Queen and Prince Philip from Colonial Williamsburg where they had joined in the 350th anniversary celebration of the founding of Jamestown. The royal couple debarked at Washington National Airport to a 21-gun salute followed by the British and American national anthems, played by an Army band.

Waiting at the foot of the ramp were President Eisenhower, members of the Cabinet, and representatives of the British Commonwealth. Ike greeted the Queen with a courtly bow and a broad grin and led her along a newly laid red carpet to the speaker's stand, also carpeted in red. Along the path to the stand, in places carefully marked by Clement Conger, Assistant Chief of Protocol, were the ambassadors of the Commonwealth nations and their wives.

When the official greetings and picture-taking were concluded (with Ike introducing the photographers as "the nearest we have to a dictatorship") the Queen and Prince joined Ike in his bubble-topped Lincoln for the ride to the White House along a route lined with a million spectators.

Mamie, who had been watching the proceedings on

television with her grandchildren, went to the north portico as the motorcade approached. She had changed her mind about her costume at the last minute. The White House had announced earlier that the First Lady would wear a peony-red wool-jersey dress by Nettie Rosenstein, who had designed her Inaugural ballgown, and a matching pillbox hat with velvet bows. Instead, Mamie appeared in a green wool dress with a fitted bodice, pleated skirt, and three-quarter sleeves.

Hospitable and homey, she reached for the Queen's hand and shook it. "Welcome!" she exclaimed. "We have been watching you on television. We have been wanting you to come for so long. My, you look pretty." A four-day round of dinners, teas, receptions, and visits began with a luncheon at the White House, at which the President and Mrs. Eisenhower and the royal visitors were joined by John and Barbara Eisenhower.

That evening, the Queen and Prince Philip were the guests of honor at a dinner for ninety-seven persons in the State Dining Room. Ike, in white tie and tails, escorted the radiant Queen along the red-carpeted hall where Mamie had ordered masses of pink carnations banked against the walls and vines wound around the white columns. The Marine Band, resplendent in scarlet coats and blue trousers, played background music.

Mamie's full-skirted pink satin gown matched the decor. She also wore pink gloves and slippers and carried a pink handbag, embroidered with crystals, rhinestones, and pearls. A diamond necklace and earnings completed her costume.

The Queen was regal and lovely in a green satin gown with a full skirt on which green velvet maple leaves were appliquéd with crystals and emeralds. Her glistening jewels included a fringed tiara of diamonds, a pearl-and-diamond necklace, and the Garter sash, which she had fastened with a diamond brooch.

The guests dined on gold-rimmed service plates bearing

the President's Seal, using gold flatwear engraved with "The President's House." The menu included chilled pineapple, cream-of-almond soup, roast Long Island duckling, and frozen Nesselrode cream with brandied sauce. Some two hundred other guests were invited to a post-dinner musicale by Fred Waring and his Pennsylvanians, followed by a champagne reception.

State dinners in the Eisenhower White House were always "white tie" and the one given in September of 1959, during Ike's second term, in honor of the visiting Soviet premier Nikita Khrushchev was no exception.

Mamie wore an elaborate gold brocade gown with a full skirt and train, diamond necklace, and earrings. Ike and most of the male guests, both American and Russian, wore formal white tie and tails. There was one dissident. Premier Khrushchev, apparently unwilling to don capitalist garb even for one evening, wore a dark business suit and light gray four-in-hand, his decorations pinned, Soviet fashion, to his lapel. Madame Khrushchev was somberly clad in a full-length gown of a bluish-black fabric, a jeweled brooch at her neck.

The dinner that evening was the largest yet held by the Eisenhowers, bringing together such diverse representatives of both countries as Keith Funston, the president of the New York Stock Exchange; the president of the United States Chamber of Commerce, Erwin D. Canaham; Soviet Foreign Minister Andrei Gromyko; Vice-President and Mrs. Nixon; Secretary of State Christian Herter and Mrs. Herter; Milton Eisenhower; and Perle Mesta.

The menu, announced by the White House, follows:

Melon with Prosciutto Ham
Curry Soup
Whole Wheat Melba Toast
Celery Hearts
Green and Ripe Olives

Molded Crab Louis
Coleslaw in Tomato Basket
Boston Brown Bread
Sandwiches
Roast Young Turkey
Corn Bread Dressing
and Gravy
Whole Cranberry Sauce
Scalloped Sweet Potatoes
and Pineapple
French Green Beans
Almondine
Breadsticks
Tossed Bibb Lettuce
Parmesan, Green Goddess
Dressing
Toasted Sesame Crackers
Vanilla Ice Cream Ring with Strawberries

The Eisenhowers gave two memorable parties to celebrate purely personal events. On the eve of their thirty-
eighth wedding anniversary, about one hundred members
of the West Point class of 1915 and their wives, and a few
widows of class members, came to dinner at the White
House.

It was a sentimental, nostalgic get-together. The Marine
Band played song hits of 1915, including Ike's favorite,
"Down Among the Sheltering Palms." The dinner was
followed by a concert by the Air Force Symphony Orchestra
after which Ike distributed West Point songbooks and led
the guests in a community sing. At midnight the orchestra
played the "Anniversary Waltz." Ike got up, bowed low
before Mamie, and carefully guided her over the polished
dance floor. It was the first time they had danced together in
sixteen years, he confided to a friend later.

One of the most endearing moments of Ike and Mamie's

White House years came on the night they staged a mock wedding. It was their forty-third anniversary and the event brought tears to the eyes of those who watched.

Two other couples, old friends, were also celebrating their wedding days: Secretary of Defense Neil McElroy and his wife, and General Leonard Heaton, commander of Walter Reed Army Hospital, and Mrs. Heaton. Ike and Mamie invited them to the party.

Shortly after ten o'clock, the United States Marine Band, in one corner of the East Room, broke into the Lohengrin Wedding March. Mamie, wearing a white veil and carrying a bridal bouquet, flanked by the two women similarly attired, appeared in the doorway and walked slowly toward Ike. The President, McElroy, and Heaton met them in the center and, as the band switched to a waltz, danced their ladies around the large, formal chamber.

Afterward, the three couples stood before a clergyman and repeated their marriage vows. There were audible sobs from some of the guests.

When Mamie wanted a change of scenery—or to shed unwanted weight—she made for Main Chance, Elizabeth Arden's luxurious beauty resort in Phoenix, Arizona, where a seven-room cottage was made available for her use. The cottage had ample space for her personal maid and her Secret Service agents, as well as a garden and screened porch in front, a patio in the back, and a private swimming pool. The bedroom, decorated in Mamie's favorite pink and green, had a direct phone line to Washington.

After her first visit there, Mamie confided to reporters that she had lost five pounds in two weeks. Here is the diet she followed:

Breakfast: Black coffee or tea, half a grapefruit.
11 A.M.:   One cup of clear vegetable broth
1 P.M.:   One scrambled egg, garnished with juli-
                enne of green pepper and mushrooms,

	jellied raspberries topped with yogurt, small coffee.
4 P.M.:	Small glass of buttermilk or skimmed milk.
7:15 P.M.:	Fresh vegetable juice cocktail.
7:30 P.M.:	Broiled calf's liver, steamed broccoli with mock hollandaise, stewed tomatoes, baked apple, small coffee.
9:30 P.M.	One cup herb tea.

Additional details were provided by Emma Jackson, widow of the publisher of the *Oregon Journal*, who was a Main Chance guest at the same time.

She said that Mamie wore a blue tank suit, as did all the other guests, a white terrycloth robe, avoided the "more strenuous treatments," delighted in low-calorie chocolates, and missed Ike.

"One night when pianist Alec Templeton played 'When You and I Were Young, Maggie,' Mamie sighed. 'That's his favorite song!'"

When it came to clothes, Mamie was more Gimbel's than Givenchy.

After she became First Lady, she purchased some dresses from the *haute couture* houses because she felt it was expected of her. But at heart she always remained an off-the-rack woman. She felt she got good value there, and good looks, and who could ask for more?

She was not, in consequence, the darling of the designers, who sniffed at her tastes and never voted her onto any best-dressed list. Mollie Parnis, who made many of Mamie's clothes when she came to the White House, says candidly: "You know, she really didn't have much fashion sense. She didn't know how to put things together. I used to bring all the accessories she would need—scarves, gloves, pearls, handbags—when I went to the White House, to make sure that Mamie would be put together correctly."

Miss Parnis was recalling her association with Mamie in her quiet, carpeted office adjoining her showroom at Thirty-ninth Street and Seventh Avenue. Photographs of some of her famous clients surrounded her: Lady Bird Johnson, Pat Nixon, Betty Ford—all First Ladies—among them.

"I made Mamie her first really expensive dress," she said. "She was like a little girl about it, touching and feeling it. This was different from anything she ever had. Before that, she had been buying her clothes mostly at the Army post exchange."

Mamie understood the importance of looking, as she said, "high class," but as First Lady she still held onto her charge accounts in the Washington department and specialty shops. Early in Ike's administration, she would go into the stores and pull things right off the racks. When other customers recognized her and crowded around, the Secret Service ruled this out. Still, Mamie did not stop shopping the local stores. She would scour the newspaper ads and when she saw something she liked would either call and ask to have it sent or dispatch her sister Mike or her maid to pick it up.

In Denver, when she and Ike visited in the summer, Mamie had more freedom. Eyes popped in a downtown store one morning when attendants opened the door at ten o'clock to find the First Lady and her mother patiently waiting to get in. The two spent about three hours walking around the counters, examining the merchandise, and buying "mostly things for the house." The Secret Servicemen discreetly trailed behind them.

Mamie was also a familiar browser in the five-and-dime variety stores in Gettysburg and in Aiken, South Carolina, not far from the Augusta, Georgia, golf course where Ike played several times a year. She collected costume jewelry avidly—on one trip to the C. C. Murphy Company store on Baltimore Street in Gettysburg, she selected a choker costing thirty-seven cents, a pair of pearl earrings for fifty-seven cents, a bottle of nail polish, and the day's candy special, a twenty-nine-cent bag of assorted sourballs.

She was not recognized the day she went into a shop in the Hotel Gettysburg Annex, accompanied by her mother and Mrs. Gruenther. It was raining outside, so the ladies took their time shopping.

Mrs. Doud tried on and purchased three dresses. Mamie picked a pearl necklace for one dollar and a pink quilted dressing gown. "I don't really need it but it's so pretty, I can't resist it."

When Mrs. Gruenther, who wanted to buy a dress, asked, "Will you cash a traveler's check?" Mrs. Anna Bierer, the proprietor, said, "Well yes, but where are you from?"

A salesgirl who had been hovering nearby whispered in Mrs. Bierer's ear and the hapless woman blushed and apologized.

Next to her bangs, Mamie's hats got her the most attention from the press. Designed mostly by Sally Victor, they were flowered, veiled, beribboned, and completely feminine, perching jauntily atop those famous bangs. Her legs, encased in red, purple, green, or blue stockings imported from Paris to match her costumes, brought groans from the fashion world but endeared Mamie to millions of American women who thought high fashion was stuff and nonsense and that she looked simply great in the colored hose.

As First Lady, Mamie never ceased worrying about money. She fretted about all the entertaining she and Ike were called upon to do, and kept a careful account of all disbursements. "After all," she told Ike, "we've only got twenty-five thousand dollars a year to spend on entertaining, and that won't go very far."

Once she complained to Katherine Howard about the

Presidential aides who were using the swimming pool. "Do you know," she said, "that all these people come over here and swim, and they use my towels, and I have to pay for having them laundered out of my allowance?"

3. A Place in the Country

In 1980, WHEN the Eisenhower Gettysburg farm was opened to the public, a young boy and his mother emerged after a tour of the stone-and-brick house on the edge of the Civil War battlefield. The boy looked puzzled and disappointed. As he walked down the path, a green uniformed Park Service ranger heard him blurt out to his mother, "But it looks just like Grandma's house!"

It does, and it did. To Ike and Mamie, their Gettysburg farm was the first permanent dwelling they had ever known in their married life. Although they envisioned it as a retirement home, it eventually evolved into part-residence and part-museum, recalling key events of their public and private lives.

When Ike was president of Columbia University, he and Mamie had sought a summer place where they could escape the city's heat, and perhaps retire when the time came. On Sundays, they had driven along the Hudson River, gone into Connecticut and New Jersey, poked around dozens of

215

possible homes, but everything they saw was too big and thus difficult to staff—"too estate-y," Mamie said.

One day in 1950, returning from a visit to Mamie's mother in Denver, they met George S. Allen on the train at Kansas City. Allen and his wife, Mary, old and close friends, had just purchased a home in Gettysburg and they persuaded the Eisenhowers to look further south. Ike had never forgotten the lush Pennsylvania farmlands from his Camp Colt days and Mamie remembered the friendly townspeople. They didn't need much convincing. They went to Gettysburg.

A century-old brick farmhouse on 189 acres, owned by a farmer named Allen S. Redding, had just been put up for sale. It was down the road from the Allen property and about three miles from the town. Ike sent Mamie to look at it first.

"Mrs. Allen brought me over and she sort of slurred my name so they didn't know it was Eisenhower," she said, an apparent reference to the fact that land values in an area leaped when it became known that Ike was settling there.

The big square kitchen, its window lined with red geranium pots through which she could see the foothills of the South Mountains eight miles away captured Mamie's heart.

"I said, 'I must have this place,'" she recalled. "I went back and Ike said, 'Well, Mamie, if you like it, buy it.'"

But the Reddings had decided not to sell. Mamie was keenly disappointed. Three months later, however, the owners changed their minds again and early in 1951 the deal was closed, with Ike paying forty thousand dollars for the land, two-story brick farmhouse, thirty-five Holstein and Guernsey dairy cattle and five hundred white leghorn chickens. (In 1954–55 the Eisenhowers bought two farms on either side to insure their privacy.)

The house and farm were now theirs, but they were not to move in until they were settled at the White House. In the spring of 1953 Mamie said to Ike: "Now, look, we have the place. We bought and paid for it. I've never had a home. Let's fix it up."

Ike didn't agree. He was not going to run for a second term, he said, and he wanted to postpone work on the house until he left office.

"No, I want it!" Mamie insisted. Then, as she recalled later, "I did all the things ladies do when they want their own way. I wept and argued and I did everything. I finally got my way."

The Eisenhowers had hoped to make only minor changes but contractors told them that part of the brick house was built over the remains of a log cabin, possibly two hundred years old, the wood now wormy and decaying. Major remodeling was necessary and Mamie worked with architect Milton Osborne of Pennsylvania State University who drew plans for a two-story Georgian-style farmhouse with two new wings to be built around a narrow brick section, the only part of the original structure to be retained.

Mamie knew what she wanted, insisted on getting it and irritated Ike frequently as renovation went on.

She told construction engineer Charles H. Tompkins that the bedroom windows must be made lower so she could view the fields from her bed. They were. When the old Dutch oven, which had been in the kitchen of the Redding house, was installed in the brick wall of Ike's den, she did not like the effect made by the new bricks used by the masons. She ordered the wall knocked down and rebuilt with old brick from the farmhouse. The construction men sighed, one admitting he was getting "a little fed up" with Mamie's changes but adding, "My wife was the same when we bought our place."

The bright red barn, containing stalls for cattle and storage space on the upper floor for hay and straw, seemed just a little too close to the house, Mamie thought. Mamie wanted it moved but knew it would be a major undertaking.

Still, she suggested it to Ike, who exploded. Absolutely not, he told her; it was more than a hundred feet away, far enough. He suggested instead that she tone down the color so that it would not stand out, and even mixed the paint himself to show her what he meant. He came up with a pale grayish green.

Ike was watching one day as workmen tore down one section of the roof which would be replaced with something different. Sighing, he said, "I'd have been satisfied living in the old house just as she stood."

From time to time, Ike put his foot down. When the bathtubs she ordered arrived, Mamie looked at them in their crates and said, "Oh, my, they're too short." Ike told her, "Mamie, you said you wanted them short." They stayed.

When she inspected the original kitchen, Mamie pronounced it too small and began talking about how she wanted it enlarged. Ike did not agree at all. He looked at her steadily and, military-order style, clipped out four words: *"Mamie, it's big enough!"* The size of the kitchen was not altered.

On balance, John Eisenhower admits, Mamie got her way most of the time. She made countless trips between Washington and Gettysburg to check on the progress of the work, which was scheduled for completion in 1955. And she kept ordering so many changes that finally, John says, his father threw up his hands and told Tompkins, "For God's sake, get her what she wants and send me the bill."

While work was progressing, the Secret Service checked the area and suggested protective measures. A guardhouse was constructed at the foot of the long driveway leading to the house, with devices which would be tripped if crossed by intruders. Fences were equipped with electronic eyes and infrared scanners for nighttime surveillance were ordered. Special screens were placed on the windows of rooms to be used by the Eisenhower grandchildren to guard against kidnap attempts.

By November 1955 "Mamie's Dream House," as the nation's press now called it, was finished. The elegant white brick-and-fieldstone house, with its green shutters and dark slate roof, bore little resemblance to the original farmhouse. The old section, in the center, was identifiable, only upon close inspection, by the unevenness of the brick.

There were fifteen rooms and eight baths, including a 37-foot-by-21-foot living room, an oak-beamed study for Ike (the beams came from the old house), dining room, kitchen and butler's pantry, an office, a bedroom and three baths on the ground floor. Upstairs were the master bedroom and dressing room, a small room where Ike napped called the "General's Room," a maid's room, and four guest bedrooms.

The open porch of the old house had been glassed-in and the red barn, staying put, shone with two coats of Ike's gray-green paint.

Mamie had their furniture, in storage during the White House days, shipped to the Gettysburg farm. Housewarming gifts came from all over the world, some forty thousand dollars' worth from the American people alone, including a tractor and several head of cattle. The front driveway was lined with trees, evergreens, and flowering shrubs, one from each of the forty-eight states. Although Mamie herself said it was "no decorator's dream" the decor was eclectic, a mix of treasures and gifts assembled during their marriage.

The wallpaper of the hallway combined the seal of the forty-eight states in its design. At the end of the living room was a white Italian marble fireplace which had been presented to Ike and Mamie on their thirty-eighth wedding anniversary by the White House staff. The fireplace had been in the Executive Mansion from 1853 to 1873, put into storage during renovation, and eventually sold at auction. Members of the staff had tracked it down. Facing the fireplace was a traditional quilted beige and orange and brown floral-printed couch, purchased by Mamie in 1937.

A grand piano, covered with many family pictures, stood

in the front window; nearby were oil paintings of Ike in the uniform of a five-star general and Mamie in her pink Inaugural ballgown.

The gold-leaf trimmed glass curio cabinets against the wall containing priceless Wedgewood plates and Boehm birds, as well as sentimental objects like the carved wooden figure of Ike golfing, had been presented by the painters, carpenters, and finishers who worked at the White House. A mustard-colored velvet ottoman, a duplicate of the red one in the East Room of the White House, and several Dutch and Victorian chairs and tables were placed about the room.

The dining-room furniture which Mamie had bought in San Antonio and the silver tea service, for which Ike had saved his cigarette and lunch money, were across the hall. And the den had a hand-drawn map of the Battle of Gettysburg presented to Eisenhower by John J. (Jock) Whitney, Ambassador to the Court of St. James during Ike's administration.

The upstairs was mostly pink and green, the colors Mamie had used in every one of her bedrooms. Light green walls and a green rug were set off by deep pink bedspreads and draperies, and by filmy white curtains. The bathroom, including the tub, tile, toilet, and towels, were pink.

Mamie's very feminine dressing table had a pink telephone, numerous lipsticks, and bottles of cologne and toilet water and Ike's first gift, the silver jewel box. Next to it was a framed picture of Cadet Eisenhower, autographed "For the dearest and sweetest girl in the world."

They began to spend weekends and holidays at the farm. Sundays they would often attend the services at the Gettysburg United Presbyterian Church on Baltimore Street, sitting in a sixth-row pew on the right side. Two rows in front, a plaque marked the pew where Abraham Lincoln had worshiped on November 19, 1863, when he came to Gettysburg to consecrate the cemetery. It had been reported that church members offered the pew to the Eisenhowers but Ike declined.

One of the things they enjoyed most about Gettysburg was the frequency with which they could see their grandchildren. John and Barbara had purchased a former one-room schoolhouse, converted to private use, on the edge of the farm. Ike had a special road put in between the Pitzer Schoolhouse and the main house so they did not have to go off the farm property to go from one place to another. He kept ponies for the children's use in the stables, along with his two Arabians and two quarter horses.

The Eisenhowers loved to entertain at Gettysburg and often brought visitors from Washington or Camp David. A strobe light, under the eaves of the barn roof, could be seen miles away at the camp, guiding the pilots who would land the passengers, who included some of the world's great leaders, right on the front lawn.

Mamie kept a guest book on a hall table and everyone who came to the Gettysburg farm, including family and friends, had to sign in each time. Among the signatures are those of Winston Churchill, Charles De Gaulle, Nikita Krushchev, Konrad Adenauer, Jawaharlal Nehru, and Eisenhower's wartime rival who flamboyantly signed as "Montgomery of Alamein."

Ike would drive his guests around the battlefield in a fringe-topped Army-green Crosley runabout, neatly initialed "Ike" and "Mamie" on the driver's side. Afterward, Mamie would serve tea or cold drinks on the porch.

The Eisenhowers spent much time on the porch. Ike liked to sit on the white wicker couch and watch the cattle grazing just beyond the rose garden. To the left of the garden was his putting green and straight ahead, beyond the green rolling pastureland was a stand of trees, marking Seminary Ridge where the fighting took place.

Ike's tour included a stop at the schoolhouse to show his guests a typical American home. John said that, on one occasion, Ike used the schoolhouse as a ruse to cool off a British prime minister who was becoming visibly upset.

In 1959 and 1960, crises erupted over the partitioned Berlin, with Russia rattling sabres as it insisted that the city be returned to the control of East Germany.

Krushchev, growling ominously, warned that unless the Allied powers freed the city by May of 1959, he would use military force. Secretary of State John Foster Dulles hurried to Europe to confer with Allied leaders, Harold MacMillan, the British Prime Minister; Charles de Gaulle, France's Premier, and the aged Konrad Adenauer, the West German Chancellor. When word came back that Britain was wavering, Ike's temper flashed. John Eisenhower reports: "Dad picked up the phone and called Dulles while I was sitting there, and Dulles was able to report that this particular piece of news had been refuted by MacMillan, and also that the heat was off for the moment." It was, but not for long; Berlin continued to be a potential flashpoint for world conflict through the remainder of Ike's second term.

Mr. MacMillan, invited to Camp David for discussions, had become overwrought over the Berlin problem. A divided city, he warned Ike, was intolerable, a situation that could present grave international complications sooner or later. Ike quickly changed the subject by suggesting a tour of the farm and the schoolhouse. MacMillan, still grumbling, agreed and was soon diverted. En route to the school, Ike and MacMillan came upon young David who was shooting baskets into a backyard hoop. As they approached, David sank a hook shot. Both men applauded.

Next morning, when the talks resumed, the British prime minister was in a much more amiable mood.

In 1960, toward the close of his second term, Ike took de Gaulle to visit John's home. *Le grand Charles,* who rarely unbent or spoke English even in private conversations, did both during this at-home, family-type visit. He and Ike were sitting in the breezeway and chatting when four-year-old Mary Jean came skipping out of the house.

De Gaulle was wearing thick lenses because of a cataract operation and the glasses attracted the little girl. She reached out and grabbed them, put them on her tiny nose, and, rocking her head from side to side, murmured, "Oh, poor me, poor me!" At that point, the General retrieved his glasses and put them back on.

Khrushchev ended his unprecedented thirteen-day tour of the United States in 1959 with a visit to the Gettysburg farm. The Soviet leader had been feted in New York, engaged in a debate in Los Angeles with Spyros P. Skouras, president of 20th Century-Fox over the respective merits of communism and capitalism and sulked when he was not permitted to go to Disneyland because of security reasons. He also expressed stern disapproval of a can-can dance for a new film which was performed for him on a Hollywood movie stage, terming it "immoral." He added: "A person's face is more beautiful than his backside." During this busy tour, the Russian premier was assailed countless times for his celebrated statement to capitalist nations: "We will bury you."

Back east, he met with Eleanor Roosevelt at Hyde Park and laid a wreath on the grave of President Franklin D. Roosevelt. Then he went to Camp David for discussions with President Eisenhower.

Inevitably, he was taken to the Gettysburg farm where he charmed all three of Ike's grandchildren and even tried to spread some Soviet propaganda among them. When he translated their names into Russian, John says, he "had them sold."

"He was a rotund little guy," David recalls. "His handshake was soft and clammy but his demeanor was extremely pleasant. We all liked him very much. We exchanged small talk about his own grandson, who he said was about my age, and the farm and dacha he had in the Soviet Union. Khrushchev promised that there would be a place for us if we were to go to the Soviet Union with Grandfather in 1960, when he was scheduled to return the visit."

In class next day David, who was in the sixth grade, was asked to tell about his experiences. "I said something like, if I didn't know any better I'd be a Communist because Khrushchev was such a nice guy." Since David had become something of a celebrity, he was trailed frequently by reporters, who interviewed his classmates and printed his remarks. "It caused quite a flap," David says. "It made the family kind of unhappy with me."

John Eisenhower was even unhappier when David appeared for breakfast wearing a small round button with a red star and a picture of the Kremlin. The Soviet premier had given it to him. "I got that off him in a hurry," John says.

It was at Gettysburg that Ike grew close to his grandchildren, especially David. Away from the pressures of Washington, he had time for long talks with the growing boy, especially about sports. Ike underscored their importance and sought to infuse David with his own very real passion for games. Some of his advice and teaching took. Some did not, with occasional disastrous results.

Ike did manage to get David excited about football and basketball but hit into the rough when it came to golf. The team sports were fine, Ike explained, but golf was special: it would be important socially and moreover could be played at any age. Ike himself glowed for months when he shot a hole in one in 1967 at the age of seventy-seven. Unfortunately, David rebelled.

"He felt that I would approach the game the same way he did," David says. "But there aren't very many people who play golf at age ten, eleven, and twelve, so I was usually alone or I was the odd man out of the foursome, and so I came to dislike golf very much." At fourteen, David gave up the game entirely, then rediscovered it when he was twenty. "Now," he says, "I can go out and play eighteen holes and not disgrace myself."

Ike tried to teach David to hunt for pheasant but had

little luck with his pupil. He had even less with his hunting dogs. Eisenhower owned four, two pointers and two Weimaraners, the latter named Art and George for his friends Arthur Nevins and George Allen. While all four were friendly animals they were not especially bright. As hunters, David recalls, they were utterly useless.

"He used to send them off for six months of training," David recalls, "and then they'd come back. He would tell them to point, and they wouldn't do it. Grandfather would get furious, and then he'd pack them off for another six months in exile. They'd come back again and still wouldn't respond." Ike, who never tolerated incompetence, would explode with frustration. Finally, he gave up on the dogs and got rid of them.

David admits he didn't exactly delight his grandfather on hunting trips. "I never shot a bird," he says, while Nevins, Allen, and the President "got everything." Once, however, he did manage to hit something—a field mouse. "That was about the best I ever did, and I don't brag about it much because Granddad was pretty mad when he found out that I wasted a couple of shells."

Ike also tried to instruct David in the art of angling. When the boy was only seven, Eisenhower took him trout fishing at his friend Aksel Nielsen's ranch in Colorado. Ike and Aksel, a Denver investment banker, favored the dry fly technique which calls for one-hand casting. David, too small and too impatient to master the technique, gripped his rod like a baseball bat and sent the line and bait winging into the stream. Ike grimaced and tried again, but David wasn't an apt pupil.

In less than an hour, David had caught two beautiful trout, one about a foot long. Ike sighed and let him do it his way.

One of David's worst experiences with his grandfather at Gettysburg occurred when he was about fourteen years old. Ike had earmarked three horses for the use of each of his grandchildren, quarter horses for David and Anne and a graceful Arabian for Susan. One foggy afternoon, Susan was saddling up her mount and David had just returned from a ride across the fields.

A short distance away, Ike was on his glassed-in porch with two visitors, pointing out the sights, in which he proudly included his sleekly smooth putting green which he insisted had to be tended like a rare camellia. Suddenly, David says, one of the horses "spooked." He dashed to the edge of the green, stopped, and then, as though knowing full well that here was something special, ran all over it, ripping the unmarred turf, destroying it completely.

Ike could only watch, speechless and horrified. Afterward, he wanted to exile the offending animal but David and the others in the family pleaded in his defense that he was a first offender and it would never again recur. The punishment was not carried out but it took two years before the putting green regained its original billiard-table look.

Much later, when David became engaged to Julie Nixon, he admits he was "bashful" about discussing the subject with Ike "because I had good grounds to believe he would oppose the marriage." His grandfather, David knew, was "very traditional."

"He wanted me to go through high school and college," David says and get an M.B.A. and a Ph.D. and then a law degree and go to work and make a million dollars—and then get married, you know, God knows when I was forty years old or whatever."

David was nineteen and had no intention of waiting that long, or very much longer. He had told Mamie and his parents in November of 1967 at the Gettysburg farm that he intended to marry Richard Nixon's younger daughter, but had not yet informed Ike. However, David was convinced that his grandfather knew.

One day that November Ike told David he wanted to see him after lunch. "I didn't want to hear what he had to say,"

David admits. "I wasn't going to bring it up. I knew he'd found out from Mamie and I could expect a blowup."

The young man and his 77-year-old grandfather sat in stony silence, and the meeting ended without a discussion of David's marriage plans. Later, Ike wrote to David expressing regret at their inability to communicate.

David and Julie were married in Marble Collegiate Church in New York City on December 22, 1968, but neither Ike nor Mamie were able to attend. Both were in Walter Reed General Hospital in Washington, he recuperating from several heart attacks and she a flu victim. However, they were able to watch the wedding. The ceremony, which was performed by the Rev. Dr. Norman Vincent Peale, pastor of the church, was televised exclusively for them on closed circuit TV by the National Broadcasting Company.

Mamie sent the young couple a brass plaque bearing the inscription "God Bless This Home." On the back she had written, "This hung in the White House during the eight years your grandfather was President."

The Gettysburg townsfolk were proud of the Eisenhowers, but they treated them as neighbors, not as the President and First Lady.

Their comings and goings made news, but no more than the other important personages who lived there. On a typical occasion, Mary Louise Callahan, society editor of the *Gettysburg Times,* recorded the day's social events. In her column of twenty-four items, the eleventh one read: "Mrs. Mamie Doud Eisenhower, the White House, Washington, arrived in Gettysburg Wednesday afternoon to spend the weekend at the Eisenhower farm here. Her husband, President Eisenhower, was expected to arrive Friday afternoon to spend the weekend."

4. A Medal for Mamie

"THIS GIVES ME the answer once and for all. He isn't going to run again, and I'm going to take him to Gettysburg, and we're going to lead our own lives in our own way from here on out."

An anguished Mamie Eisenhower was speaking her mind in the late afternoon of September 24, 1955, after Ike had suffered his major heart attack in Denver. If there ever was any doubt that Mamie did not want her husband to seek a second term in 1956, those words, spoken to General Howard Snyder, the White House physician, settled the question. General Snyder repeated them to Ellis D. Slater, president of Frankfort Distilleries and an Eisenhower intimate for years, who recorded them in his diary. Slater's revealing record of his relationship with the Eisenhowers from 1950 to Ike's death in 1969 was published privately in 1980 under the title *The Ike I Knew* and made available to us. Slater, eighty-five years old when his diary was published, told us in his North Palm Beach home: "Mamie's first reaction was as definite as could be. It was a firm 'No, not again!' "

The day before Ike was stricken, an overcast Friday, Mamie had slept late, as she had done since she and Ike arrived in Denver for a long vacation in mid-September. By the time she woke, the sun had cut through the morning haze; a bright, warm day was promised. At breakfast in her room, she told her mother she was expecting some friends for a little card game. She was hoping to hear from Ike soon. He had gone on a four-day fishing trip to the rustic ranch owned by Aksel Nielsen near Fraser northwest of the city. With them were George Allen and General Snyder.

Mamie planned to spend the day quietly with her friends and her mother. Elivera had been fretting about Mamie's health lately and was insisting that she rest as much as she could. She was happy Mamie and Ike had been able to come out to Denver that fall for their vacation. Elivera, who spent the winter months in the White House, had noticed that there had been times when Mamie had strength enough to leave her bed for only a few hours each day. Her strenuous schedule had built up a bone-weariness that could be relieved only by prolonged rest. Six months before, Mamie had fought off a severe bout of influenza and in early September Dr. Snyder, concerned over her pallor, weakness, and inability to shake off constant colds, had ordered her to bed at Gettysburg.

"Life in the White House is just too hard on that poor child," Mrs. Doud had said that summer. (Mamie was then fifty-eight, going on fifty-nine.) Another time, she said, "Mamie can't stand another four years in the White House," setting off a buzz of speculation that Ike might not run for a second term.

But the vacation had done wonders for Mamie. There was color in her cheeks and her weariness had ebbed. She looked forward to Ike's return that afternoon and asked the cook to prepare one of his favorite meals, roast leg of lamb with pan-roasted potatoes and fresh vegetables.

While she was finishing her tea, Ike came home and in an

hour prepared to leave for Lowry Air Force Base outside
Denver, where he maintained an office. He was feeling fine,
he told Mamie. There was nothing like the bracing air up
there, and surely nothing to equal the taste of fresh-caught
trout from the cold mountain streams in the foothills of the
Rocky Mountains. He had about an hour's work, then he'd
head out to the Cherry Hills Country Club, closer to the
city, for golf and some lunch before going on home. Expect
him about three with George, whom he had invited for
dinner that evening. Mary Allen would be along later.

Ike arrived home on time, complaining of a little indiges-
tion. His appetite good as ever, he had not been especially
judicious in his choice of food that day. The breakfast he
himself had cooked early that morning on Byers Peak was
not the most digestible. The fried mush, pork sausage, and
the bacon, accompanied by his own specially mixed pan-
cakes, and several cups of scalding coffee, sat heavily on his
stomach. At lunch, after eighteen holes of golf, he had piled
another dietary indiscretion on top of that—two large slices
of onion on a huge hamburger. Still, he had felt good
enough to go out for another nine holes before heading for
home with George Allen.

Feeling somewhat queasy, Ike spent the rest of the
afternoon painting in the paneled basement, then dined
with the Allens. The discomfort increased and, shortly after
ten, the Allens left and Ike went upstairs to his bedroom at
the top of the stairs. Because Ike rose early, Mamie slept in
the second bedroom a few steps to the left. Both rooms
faced Lafayette Street but there was no traffic to disturb
them because the Secret Service had placed saw horses on
both ends of the block, diverting all cars except those of the
people who lived there.

Mamie talked to her mother as Ike removed the yellow
bedspread, took his pajamas from a closet where he had
hung them the night before, and undressed. Before getting
into the bed, he took some milk of magnesia from the

medicine chest for his stomach distress, which hadn't stopped. The room was hardly Presidential in size, only fifteen feet square. The fireplace on the wall opposite the double bed was already stacked with wood because winter came early in Denver. Shortly before eleven, Mamie went up too, stretched the velvet-covered rope across the head of the stairs, and entered her bedroom.

At two-thirty she was aroused from a light sleep hearing Ike toss and turn. It was unusual; Ike always slept heavily. Mamie put on a robe and went into his room. Standing above him, she touched him gently and asked: "What's the matter, Ike? Are you having a nightmare or something?" He said he was all right, turned, and tried to get back to sleep. Mamie left.

Within minutes, he felt a crushing, squeezing pain in his chest, a few inches below his throat. He had had heartburn a few hours before, but it was nothing like this. He rose and walked the few steps into Mamie's room. He was pale and beginning to perspire. Mamie told him to sit on the bed while she went for the milk of magnesia. She gave Ike a large tablespoonful in some water and he returned to his room. Meanwhile, Mamie, now concerned, called General Snyder, who was at Lowry, described what was happening, and asked him to come over.

Snyder, although four miles away, was at Ike's side in fifteen minutes, a robe over his pajamas. Mamie had described the classic symptoms of a coronary thrombosis, a blocking of an artery carrying nutrients to the heart muscle. He found the President flushed and perspiring with an agonizing pressure-pain in front of his chest. Before he had even placed his stethoscope on Ike, Howard Synder was quite certain what he would discover. His tentative diagnosis, pending verification by an electrocardiogram, was that Ike had suffered a myocardial infarction.

He followed the correct medical procedure. He gave his patient three injections, then standard for heart-attack victims: morphine to sedate him and prevent shock; papaverine hydrochloride to widen the coronary arteries; and heparin to thin the blood and help prevent the formation of new clots on the inner arterial walls that would cut off the blood supply to the heart.

Snyder was in a quandary. Mamie herself had a damaged heart valve; telling her, and the world, could be a severe emotional shock. So he said nothing, remaining with Ike as he slept until after dawn. Later he said he deferred making a public announcement "because I wished the President to benefit from the rest and quiet induced by the sedation incident to combating the initial manifestations. This decision also spared him, his wife, and mother-in-law emotional upset upon too precipitate announcement of such serious import." So until the diagnosis could be confirmed, Snyder called Ann Whitman, Ike's secretary at Lowry, and told her to attribute his absence from his office there to a "digestive upset."

As the hours passed, Ike's heart sounds became stronger and steadier, and his blood pressure stabilized. Newspersons in Denver had received word of his "digestive upset" and were clamoring for more information. Tall, ruddy Murray Snyder, a former reporter for the *Brooklyn Eagle* who was Ike's assistant press aide, called the Doud home and asked General Snyder—to whom he was not related—if there was anything more he could tell them. General Snyder still insisted it was a "minor illness."

Just before noon, General Snyder took Mamie downstairs and told her, as gently as he could, what had happened. She took the news calmly and listened as he picked up the telephone to call Fitzsimons Army Hospital in the city of Aurora, seven miles east of downtown Denver.

Major General Martin R. Griffin, commanding general of Fitzsimons, was about to leave for lunch when his secretary told him General Snyder was on the wire. Griffin, a tall, spare man with a Lincolnesque face, was shocked at what he heard. When Snyder hung up, he kept the phone in his ear and cleared the line with his index finger. He asked the operator to get him Colonel Byron E. Pollack, the hospital's chief of cardiology services. Pollock got the news and dashed out of his office carrying an electrocardiograph, a box about the size of a toaster oven. At the hospital entrance he met General Griffin, whose car was already waiting.

As they raced to Lafayette Street, the Presidential suite on the eighth floor was unlocked, swept clean, disinfected, and made ready under the supervision of Colonel Donald E. Carle, the deputy commander. Specialists and technicians who were off duty were telephoned and told to come in. Lieutenant James P. Baugh, the assistant provost marshal, was barking orders: double the number of guards at the gates, and all internal patrols, station an MP at the two elevators in the main lobby and pair them with Secret Service agents. On the eighth floor, detail MPs to work with Secret Service men to check identities of all purported hospital personnel and others coming to the floor, and to keep a close watch on the freight elevator and occupants when supplies were being delivered to the President's kitchen. One of the passenger elevators was designated to take only persons bound for the President's suite, but it would stop on the floor below; the visitors would walk to the eighth. This measure had a twofold purpose: to eliminate unnecessary noise on the President's floor and to provide additional security. When a passenger emerged, he would be checked once again, and if cleared a signal light would be flashed between this post and the one above to alert the MP at the head of the staircase.

The Secret Service received the names of every doctor, nurse, dietician, medical technician, orderly, and corpsman—every person who would have anything to do with the care of the President—and their personnel files were studied for security clearance. On the ground floor, a special room was set aside by the Secret Service as a "package search center" where all incoming parcels were opened and checked for explosive devices before being cleared for delivery.

The nursing department was alerted to assign round-the-clock staffs. Lieutenant Colonel Edythe Turner, the chief nurse, was not about to call the Denver registry for the "best qualified" people; she felt she had good ones on her staff and "what was good enough for Army patients was good enough for the Chief Executive." So she made calls and assigned shifts. Captain Margaret M. Williams, who would be the eleven-to-seven, washed and set her hair twice. After finishing her regular tour, she had shampooed but, glancing in a mirror, she decided once was not enough when it came to attending a President.

At home, Ike was dozing when the two doctors arrived. Mamie, a robe over her night clothes, was asking General Snyder if the President should eat something. He told her to wait. The electrocardiograph, which could operate on regular house current, was plugged into an outlet, electrodes were attached to Ike's chest, wrists, and leg and the electrical pattern of his heartbeat was traced on a long thin strip which clicked from the instrument. The procedure, which took only a few minutes, confirmed Dr. Snyder's tentative diagnosis of a coronary thrombosis. A portion of the heart muscle, deprived of blood by the closing of an artery, had died.

Eisenhower was told and accepted the information calmly. In a move that would later be criticized, General Snyder and the two doctors walked Ike, clad in a bathrobe, down the stairs, through the foyer, and down the front steps into a waiting limousine. Mamie watched as Ike was eased into the car, sitting between General Snyder and Colonel Pollock. Deeter B. Flohr, the chauffeur assigned to the President, drove to Fourteenth Avenue, turned east to Yosemite Street, then went up Colfax to the hospital, where a wheelchair was waiting at a back entrance. Within minutes, Ike was in his suite, where nurses changed him into hospital pajamas and affixed an oxygen tent.

An hour later, General Snyder released the news to Murray Snyder, and the story flashed around the world. Reporters besieged the hospital and by five P.M. the ordinarily peaceful atmosphere of the main lobby was shattered. The media was to turn most of the ground floor into its special domain for the next forty-seven days.

At seven-twenty that evening Mamie arrived at the hospital with her suitcases, entering through the same rear entrance as Ike. On the eighth floor she talked briefly with her husband, who was awake, but she was allowed to remain only a few minutes.

Ike's suite consisted of a small antechamber, a room where a doctor was on duty around the clock, and a white-and-yellow-walled twenty-by-ten-foot hospital room, with a huge sun porch measuring sixty by forty feet.* From a window, snow-capped Pikes Peak, seventy-five miles away, could be seen on days when the haze cleared.

Across the hall about twenty-five feet away was another suite, this one with a sitting room and a twelve-by-sixteen-foot bedroom, also with a large sun porch. Mamie looked at it, pronounced it fine, but made one request. Could she have a pink toilet seat?

The First Lady's wish was relayed downstairs where it caused some consternation. The hospital had extra toilet seats, but none were pink. Of course, one could be painted but it would be risky if it didn't dry on time. Hospital officials called Denver stores, none of which stocked pink seats. Someone suggested that since Mamie had doubtless obtained one in Washington, there must be others there. A call was made to the White House, and a pink toilet seat for

---

*The room Ike occupied is now the office of two hospital chaplains, Captain Samuel Adamson and the Reverend Thomas F. Foley.

Mamie was purchased and airmailed to Fitzsimons. The seat is still on the john in the former Mamie suite, which is now a hospital office.

Ike had instructed Jim Hagerty, who flew in from Washington, to give newspeople the full story of his illness—"Hold nothing back," he said—and the press secretary, a former reporter for *The New York Times*, complied. Correspondents got the latest blood-pressure reading, results of urinalyses and X-ray studies, and reports on everything he ate and drank. When he issued the order, Eisenhower hadn't foreseen the candid bulletins which Dr. Paul Dudley White, the eminent Boston cardiologist who was summoned as a consultant, would issue. One of the earlier ones, duly released by the press and wired around the world, ended with, "He had a good bowel movement."

For nineteen days, Mamie never left the hospital. As Ike's heart mended, she sat at his bedside for as many hours as the doctors permitted. While he was in the oxygen tent, she would sit holding his hand. After the third day the tent was removed and she began reading to him some of the messages that flooded the hospital from heads of state and just plain people, including wires from Churchill, Khrushchev, Soviet Marshals Georgi Zhukov and Nikolai Bulganin. She and Ike would listen to recorded music together and, as the days passed, she read the newspapers to him. He worked crossword puzzles as she read. And, as his sixty-fifth birthday neared on October 14, he asked for his easel and paints and began painting again. On nice days she sat with him on the sun deck and looked at the spectacular front range of the Rockies, Mount Evans, Longs Peak, and Pikes Peak.

On November 4, his recovery nearly complete, Ike was visited by Ellis Slater. Howard Snyder greeted the industrialist in the reception room and asked him to wait a few minutes because Ike was busy.

The President was helping Mamie balance her checkbook.

Later Slater returned to the hospital, at Mamie's invitation, to have dinner with her in her suite. Ike had eaten earlier and was napping. Mamie was annoyed. Her birthday was coming up in ten days, she complained, and some newspapers had called it her sixtieth. "I'll only be fifty-nine!" she said.

During her long vigil at the hospital, Mamie undertook a gigantic task—dictating and signing more than eleven thousand letters of thanks in response to the letters, telegrams, flowers, and gifts Ike received from all over the globe.

As the days passed, the sacks of mail multiplied. The messages were placed in large baskets and carried into Mamie's room where they soon covered almost every square foot of space. Mamie had a moveable table placed across her bed and, when she wasn't with Ike, read them all. "It's so wonderful," she told one of the nurses. "They love him too." She brought many of them to Ike's room to read to him.

For hours on end, Mamie dictated replies to Mary Jane McCaffree, Ann Parsons, Ann Ward, and other White House secretaries, stopping only when she could no longer keep her eyes open. Before she and Ike left the hospital, she had read almost every message and telegram—tens of thousands in all—although she could not send answers to everyone. Those she had to omit later received prepared cards of thanks sent from the White House.

On his return to the White House, Ike decided to show his gratitude and love by presenting Mamie with a "military medal" for her devotion to the nation's Commander in Chief. It would, of course, be quite unofficial. He decided on a jeweled medallion to be worn on a chain or as a brooch and when he was in New York City he visited Tiffany & Company and explained to Walter Hoving, its board chairman, what he had in mind. Knowing it would be expensive, he asked if the store offered discounts to Presidents of the United States.

Hoving, perplexed, said he did not know. He excused himself and ran next door to the company's offices and asked William Lusk, the store's president, if there was a policy covering the circumstances. Hoving, recalling the incident, said that Lusk thought for a moment, then replied, "Well, we didn't give a discount to Lincoln." Abraham Lincoln had presented his wife, Mary Todd, with a pearl necklace and earrings, from Tiffany's. Hoving returned and told Ike he was sorry but not even Presidents get discounts. Eisenhower ordered the medal and paid full price.

Mamie capitulated on a second term for Ike despite her own strong desire for private life and her fears that the strains of office would be too intense for him. She came to realize that even though he had told her privately during his first term that he would not seek office again, he needed and wanted the challenge of work. Not being President, she finally understood, would harm him more than the strains of the office.

"All she wanted was Ike—alive," says Eileen Archibold. "She very definitely was against his running again. She never really cared for all the to-do of being First Lady, didn't like the panoply and wasn't at all impressed by the prestige. She just wanted to live a simple, uncomplicated, comfortable private life. She felt they both had earned it."

But after their return to Gettysburg, something alarming had happened to Ike. Dr. Paul Dudley White had told Mamie that many heart-attack survivors commonly become depressed during recuperation when they realize that death has been close and that they must alter their life styles, but all hoped that Ike would be too busy to worry. The doctors were wrong. Ike fell into the deepest depression he had known since the death of Icky thirty-five years before.

(Years later, in 1967, the wife of Lou Little, Columbia University's football coach, had become depressed following a coronary. Ike wrote to tell Little that the intense, crippling feeling of isolation and sadness would soon lift and that he understood it well because he too had undergone the same kind of "depression, almost despair" after his first attack.)

Watching his alternating moods of gloom and restlessness, listening to him voice worries that the work of government was not getting done in Washington, seeing him slump into his chair after saying he could do nothing about it, Mamie began to realize that quitting was not the answer for her husband. While her son John and Ike's brother Milton still opposed a second race because they feared the physical strain, she began to waver. Moreover, Howard Snyder was telling her that retirement for a man of Eisenhower's drive and temperament would be a greater risk than another term as President.

So, when Ike came to her one day in late December and asked what she thought, she thrust aside her own strong wish for private life. "I told him I wanted him to follow his own wishes," she said.

For most of that winter, Ike agonized about the decision. In January, on Friday the thirteenth, he was host at the now-famous dinner to which he invited twelve close friends and advisers, asking them all one by one to give him their candid views.* Most thought he should make the race. On February 14, following a series of tests at Walter Reed, Dr. White announced that "medically the chances are that the

---

*The guests were Secretary of State John Foster Dulles; Sherman Adams, Assistant to the President; Senator Henry Cabot Lodge of Massachusetts; Treasury Secretary George M. Humphrey; Press Secretary Jim Hagerty; Tom Stephens, who had been Ike's appointments aide; Postmaster General Arthur E. Summerfield; Attorney General Herbert Brownell, Jr.; Leonard Hall, chairman of the Republican National Committee; Howard Pyle, a White House aide; Wilton B. (Jerry) Persons, Ike's Congressional liaison man; and his brother Milton.

President should be able to carry on an active life satisfac-
torily for another five to ten years."

Then, on February 27, Ike invited General Lucius Clay
and his wife, Marjorie, to dinner at the White House. There
were no other guests present to hear a momentous announcement.

In his oral history on file at Columbia University, General
Clay, a close friend who had been Ike's deputy for military
government in Germany after the war and later the hero of
the Berlin airlift, says that after dinner the quartet went
upstairs to the living quarters.

There Ike told them, "Tonight's the night I'm going to
make my decision as to whether I'm going to run."

Mamie said, "It's your decision, not mine. I'm not going
to have anything to do with it."

After a moment's silence, Ike spoke again. "I've made up
my mind. I am going to run again."

Mamie said nothing.

"We were the first people who knew about that, that
particular time," says Clay.

Two days later, Ike told the world.

Ike's decision to run had the overwhelming approval of
the American voters. When the ballots were counted he had
again triumphed over Stevenson, this time by an even
greater plurality than in 1952—a total of 35,590,472 votes,
more than any former American President. Mamie and Pat
Nixon joined their husbands on election night in the huge,
crowded ballroom of Washington's Sheraton Park Hotel as
Ike, flinging both arms upward in a victory salute, thanked
"Republicans, friendly Democrats, and Independents" for
their support.

The pattern of their White House lives did not change
during Ike's second term. While Ike "ran the country,"
Mamie continued to make it possible for him to do so.

"Mamie's biggest contribution was to make the White

House livable, comfortable, and meaningful for the people who came in," Ike said. "She was always helpful and ready to do anything. She exuded hospitality. She saw that as one of her functions and performed it, no matter how tired she was. In the White House, you need intelligence and charm—to make others glad to be around you. She had that ability."

With the inauguration of John Kennedy on January 20, 1961, Ike and Mamie's White House days came to an end. While the new President and his glamorous wife waved to paraders marching down Pennsylvania Avenue, a Secret Serviceman drove the Eisenhowers from the White House grounds, past mounds of snow left from the storm of the previous night, to their Gettysburg farm.

They used Mamie's five-year-old car. Ike had recently complained to an aide, somewhat ruefully, Mamie drives a 'fifty-five car and she won't part with it.

"So how can I buy her a new one?"

PART FIVE

Later Years

1. Tattoo

On Christmas Eve in 1967 Ike and Mamie, who were spending the winter at the El Dorado Country Club in Palm Desert, California, were invited to dinner at the palatial ranch home of Jacqueline Cochran and her husband Floyd Odlum, in Indio.

Ike's once-robust health was plainly deteriorating. He told Ellis Slater that he felt "punk" and had been that way for some time. Ever since his heart attack in 1955, he had been through bad times. One year later he had been rushed into emergency surgery to relieve a blockage in the ileum, the narrowest portion of the small intestine. He had been troubled by stomach upsets after that and, on November 25, 1957, suffered a mild stroke in the Oval Office. There had been no major illnesses for the next eight years but it was clear that his health was a problem. In 1965 came his second heart attack in Augusta, Georgia, followed two days later by a third in the United States Army Hospital at Fort Gordon.

The problems multiplied. Out of the hospital less than a year, he was back at Walter Reed in May 1967 for removal of his gallbladder. Less than four months after his discharge, he was back again at midsummer for gastroenteritis, returning on October 6 suffering from the same ailment. Less than two months later, he was hospitalized yet again with a urinary tract infection.

Still, there were times when his appetite returned to its formerly impressive level, and this evening at the Odlum house Ike arrived ravenous. Jacqueline Cochran, aware that he had been instructed to remain on a low-cholestrol, bland diet, had her cook prepare a special dinner for him—roast turkey without seasoning, tomatoes stewed without seeds, plain steamed broccoli, baked apple. Ike, who knew the dishes were not nearly as tasty as the spread for the other guests, walked right past them.

"He didn't touch any of those special things," Miss Cochran recalled. "He went over to the table where the other dishes were and ate everything in sight. He had pecan pie, mincemeat pie, and, of course, seasoned turkey and roast beef. And Mamie didn't see any of it because she was at another table.

"I just didn't have the heart to tell on him."

It was one of the few times after his retirement that Ike eluded Mamie's watchful eyes. She saw to it that he dressed for the weather, followed the doctors' orders explicitly, rested when he should, exercised, and ate—no more and no differently—than he was supposed to. Lieutenant General Leonard Heaton, commanding general of Walter Reed, and later U.S. Surgeon General, who had operated on Eisenhower for ileitis in 1956, had cautioned him not to bolt his food but chew more slowly. Mamie, ever on the alert, would nudge her husband and whisper, "Ike, don't eat so fast."

Once, on a winter's day, he walked out to the barn, returning in a few minutes. It was clear and cold, with no wind blowing, but inside the entrance Mamie waited. "Why," she demanded, "did you go out like *that* in the morning when there's snow on the ground?" Like *that* meant hatless and without rubbers or boots. An aide who observed the scene, said Ike sighed and walked upstairs.

Retired or not, Ike went to work daily. Up at six-thirty, he arrived each morning at eight A.M. at his offices in a large brick building at 300 Carlisle Street on the campus of Gettysburg College three miles away.* There, in a northeast corner room on the second floor, at a desk that was once used by Sherman Adams in the White House, he wrote his memoirs on yellow legal-size pads, which he handed to Mrs. Ethel Wetzel, his administrative assistant, to have typed. After lunch and a brief rest, he continued working until five, occasionally six P.M., then headed home.

Mamie, who arose several hours later, called him daily, often two and three times, to relate news, ask how he was, and even what he wanted for dinner. Once she showed up at the office in midmorning with his overcoat, explaining to Mrs. Wetzel that colder weather was expected and he'd best have it to ward off a chill.

Mamie was sometimes surprisingly petulant with other members of the family. When Barbara was planning the wedding of her daughter, Susan, she asked Mamie if she could borrow Mrs. Wetzel to help with the arrangements. Mamie refused pointblank, telling her daughter-in-law, "I'm sorry, but Mrs. Wetzel is my secretary, not yours."

Most days Ike was driven to his office in a chauffeured car but from time to time he got behind the wheel of his station wagon and headed down Steinware Avenue to Baltimore Street and into Carlisle himself. One afternoon in winter, Mamie called and said she was sending the driver to bring him home when he was finished for the day. Ike sighed. "I drove myself in this morning," he said to Mrs. Wetzel. "I don't know why I can't drive home."

His patience had a snapping point. Once he strode into

---

*The building is now used by the Gettysburg College admissions staff.

the house, red-faced with anger. *"Mamie,"* he bellowed, *"I want to talk to you!"* They disappeared upstairs. History may never learn what Mamie did to blow Ike's fuse, but Ethel Wetzel, who relates the incident, says she emerged after several minutes looking chastened.

Ike's office at 300 Carlisle was furnished simply with a desk, several chairs for visitors and, on the floor, an Oriental throw rug over gold carpeting. Behind him, on the right, was the American flag, as it had been in every office he had occupied including the White House. He put family pictures and some pieces of Steuben glass on the shelves and desk; in the bookcases he wanted reference volumes and a set of the *Encyclopaedia Britannica.* In the second-floor hallway leading to his office, a recess of shelves contained many of the awards and honors he had received as General and President. On a table just outside his office was a bronze statue of Abraham Lincoln, another President whose name, the college had noted, was linked to Gettysburg.

World figures such as Chancellor Konrad Adenauer of West Germany, India's first Prime Minister Jawaharlal Nehru, and former Secretary of State John Foster Dulles came to this small office to visit Ike. Yet he was just as available to graduate students who were engaged in research on his Presidency and the conduct of the war.

If John D. Rockefeller, Sr., gave away shiny new dimes some forty years earlier, Dwight Eisenhower handed out dollars, although not in such great numbers. In his desk Ike kept rolls of silver dollars bearing the date 1890, the year he was born. He handed one to each student who interviewed him as a memento of the visit.

Ike and Mamie spent their winters in California, but by the time the first crocuses opened back East they were at the farm and on their glassed-in, sun-drenched porch. "We lived in that room," Mamie said. Nearly all their free time was spent on the porch, with its magnificent view.

Most days they had their dinners served on trays there instead of using the formal dining room. Ike kept his easel and paints in a corner and many evenings he would work while Mamie watched television. Sometimes General Nevins and his wife would visit. "The men would sit at one end and discuss Angus cattle," recalls Mrs. Nevins, who still lives in Gettysburg, "while Mamie and I played two-handed solitaire in the other. We gave it a real silly name, and I don't think anybody knew that game except us."

As a private citizen, he delighted in informality, for which he had longed, for the most part unsuccessfully, during his Presidency. A few of his most intimate friends were reminded strongly of this just before he left the White House. To a score of them Eisenhower sent notes, telling them that throughout his entire life, until his return from Europe in 1945, he had been known to them as "Ike." After that, circumstances changed and protocol demanded he be addressed "Mr. President." But now that he was no longer in office, he wrote, he demanded *"as my right"* that when he left Washington they all address him by that old nickname. "No longer do I propose to be excluded from the privileges that other friends enjoy," he told them.

And all of his friends obliged.

Bridge, along with golf, fishing, cooking, and painting, remained one of Ike's consuming interests in his retirement. Friends visited him from all over the nation for a weekend on the farm—and, of course, a few rubbers. But sometimes he wanted to play and nobody was available. Then Mamie was pressed into service.

Mamie, it must be said, was not his favorite partner in the game to which he brought the logic, judgment, and analytical power of the military mind. She possessed none of these attributes; she was given to talking instead of concentrating, and as a result made some monumental blunders. On several occasions, Ike would squirm when he heard her bids. Other times, he would explode with, "Oh, Jesus!"

Once, when she made a play he thought was particularly dumb, he threw down his cards and stalked away from the table.

With more time to spend on hobbies, Ike cooked with increasing frequency. Most times his guests liked his creations but on some occasions an Eisenhower dish was received with pretended enthusiasm. Once, for his birthday, he prepared a magnificent dinner of prime ribs of beef for a few friends, among them Brigadier General Henry J. Matchett and his wife. Mrs. Matchett, recalling the occasion, says that after the main course was served Ike beamed at his guests. "I have a treat for you," he told them. Then he handed each a huge bone to chew on.

"What are you going to do?" Mrs. Matchett says. "You've got a long evening dress on, but you're going to gnaw on that bone if he tells you to gnaw on the bone." That evening, Ike served sauerkraut with the beef. "Henry doesn't like sauerkraut, but he loved sauerkraut that night," she said.

On an earlier occasion Ike had made a gaffe at a dinner party hosted by Mrs. Matchett but got out of it gracefully. She had spent days collecting special ingredients to prepare what she called "a real fancy dish" and served it with considerable pride. After dinner, Ike and his men friends retired to another room for bridge. Some time later, Ike came out and asked, "Can I have some more stew?"

Mamie chided him. "Ike, for goodness sake," she said. "That's not *stew*. That's a wonderful dish." Ike thought fast, then replied, "Mamie, when I tell anybody that it's a good stew, I'm giving them the greatest compliment you can imagine."

When it came to his famous charcoal-grilled steaks, Ike kept his family in a state of high nervousness. John remembers, "He was a perfectionist in that as well as other activities. His steaks were very, very artistically done. The big hazard of the whole exercise was that when those steaks were ready, he would give a yell for the family. We might be finishing a cocktail or something like that, but forget it, you went to the table and you sat down. There was no fiddling around about it."

At Gettysburg Mamie once again began to do her own food shopping, as in earlier years. Driven to the A & P on Carlisle Street in the limousine, she would pick a cart and wander through the aisles, indistinguishable from all the other shoppers.

Price-conscious as always, she would compare costs and select only what she considered the best values. She read the food advertisements carefully and, like most housewives, shopped the "specials." Once she was irritated because she had bought a London broil a few days before it went on sale for forty cents less a pound. In the fruit-and-vegetable section, she would squeeze the tomatoes to test for ripeness, thump on the watermelons, and inspect the vegetables before buying. If she was finished, she stood on the checkout line with the others. When she was recognized and invited to move ahead, she insisted on waiting her turn. In later years, as inflation mounted, the former First Lady saved discount coupons clipped from newspapers and magazines and presented them to the cashier with payment for her purchases. Among the more memorable recollections of Gettysburgers was the sight of Secret Service men loading Mamie's paper bags of provisions into the back seat of the limousine.

Mamie, who celebrated her golden wedding anniversary in 1966, always tried to remain youthful-looking and attractive for Ike, whom she called "my boyfriend" and "my best beau"—and she succeeded remarkably well. Nearing seventy, she kept her hair a reddish blond, the bangs intact, of course, and wore bright-colored dresses, or occasionally a suit brightened with a red or pink scarf.

"Ike knew he was dying. He had been in the hospital almost a year and had no illusions about recovery. He knew he would never leave Walter Reed alive.

"But he had no fear of death. He sensed only an unworthiness, and that was characteristic. For he was a man of humility. He had never aspired to fame or great popularity. He accepted what came, but what emerged from my talks with him in those days was the conviction that Ike felt himself most undeserving of the greatness that had come to him."

Dr. MacAskill, pastor of the United Presbyterian Church of Gettysburg, recalling the last year in the life of his famous parishioner, describes a side of Eisenhower the world rarely saw.

Ike had been taken to the hospital in northwestern Washington early in May of 1968 after suffering a comparatively mild heart attack in Palm Desert, California. Three others followed within two months, on June 15, August 6, and August 16. In February of the following year, he underwent surgery to relieve another intestinal blockage.

As the months passed, Ike would gain strength but, as one doctor said, it was always one step forward and three backward. He lost strength and his once husky body, 176 pounds when he was elected President, shriveled to less than 120 by year's end. His lips were blue, the white skin of his face taut against his skull.

Dr. MacAskill drove in from Gettysburg to pray with Ike and for discussions on literature, philosophy, and faith. "Ike's knowledge of the classics was extensive and sound," Dr. MacAskill told us in his study in Calvin House, adjoining the church building on Baltimore Street in Gettysburg. "He knew Shakespeare and could quote lengthy verses from even the obscure plays. He was well acquainted, too, with the writings of the great philosophers and theologians, figures such as Karl Barth, the Swiss Protestant reformed scholar, and with the works of Plato and Aristotle. This was a great surprise to me. Quite obviously General Eisenhower had read a great deal more than western stories!

"He had always been an excellent Bible student, something that has not been stressed by historians and biographers. As we talked, I discovered that he was thoroughly familiar with the military campaigns as described in the Old Testament, and I found myself wondering to what extent he had applied this knowledge to the conduct of his own campaigns during the war.

"Beyond these, Ike studied the Bible because he had a deep faith in a sovereign God as a creator, a sustainer, and a redeemer of life. He lived in that hope and that assurance."

Ike's favorite biblical passages were Psalms 23, 46, and 121, Dr. MacAskill says. Almost every time they met, they would recite together from Psalm 121: "I lift up my eyes to the hills. From whence does my help come? My help comes from the Lord, who made heaven and earth. The Lord will keep your going out and your coming in from this time forth and for evermore."

Ike had never attended church regularly nor was he even a member of one until midlife, when he was baptized as a Presbyterian. Nonetheless, faith had been bred into him in childhood. "I realize that a strong spiritual experience has literally been the staff of life to me." He prayed before making a command decision in war; in the Oval Office he would shut his eyes in a moment of silent prayer before signing a major executive order or making an important judgment; he opened every Cabinet meeting by calling for a minute of unspoken prayer.

"A lifetime of soldiering and public service," Ike wrote, "only confirms my conviction that I am as intensely religious as any man I know. Nobody goes through six years of war and two terms of the Presidency without faith. And, although I have seldom discussed my religious philosophy with anyone, a deep Bible-centered Christian faith has colored my life since childhood."

On the morning of his first Inauguration, he had asked his entire Cabinet, the leading officials of his administration, and several dozens of his relatives—some 140 persons in all—to join him at a special service at the National Presbyterian Church on Nebraska Avenue. No other President has ever sought divine guidance for himself and his entire administrative staff, said the Reverend Edward L. R. Elson, pastor of the church who conducted the services.

Directly afterward, at his hotel, Ike reached for a pad and began to write. Five minutes later, he told Mamie he had composed a short prayer which, he said, he would like to say to the nation before his address. Those hastily written words, heard by millions, are now engraved on a wooden tablet in the crypt where he lies:

> Almighty God, as we stand here at this moment my future associates in the executive branch of government join me in beseeching that thou will make full and complete our dedication to the service of the people in this throng, and their fellow citizens everywhere.
>
> Give us, we pray, the power to discern clearly right from wrong, and allow all our words and actions to be governed thereby, and by the laws of this land. Especially we pray that our concern shall be for all the people, regardless of station, race or calling.
>
> May co-operation be permitted and be the mutual aim of those who, under the concepts of our constitution, hold to differing political faiths; so that all may work for the good of our beloved country and thy glory. Amen.

When Ike was flown to Walter Reed from California, Mamie followed by train. On May 13 a white orchid corsage he had sent her for Mother's Day caught up with her at Harrisburg, Pennsylvania. Mamie pinned it on and wanted her photograph taken. As she posed, smiling radiantly, on the train steps she said to the cameraman: "Now make sure

Ike sees this picture. I want him to see how happy I am with his white corsage."

Ike and Mamie spent the final ten months of their life together in Ward Eight on the third floor of the ivy-covered main building at Walter Reed, the VIP area for generals and high Government officials. As the most famous patient, Ike occupied a lavish five-room suite. He lay in a custom-made double bed in an eighteen-by-twenty-foot room, richly carpeted, which faced out on the rose garden of the 147-acre hospital complex in northwest Washington. Directly outside was a large dining room and beyond that an immense 25-foot square conference chamber with a table in its center, a fireplace along one wall, and silk-upholstered sofas and chairs.

His food was specially prepared in an L-shaped kitchen with chrome counter tops, white cabinets, several stoves, and a huge refrigerator. And outside the suite, hidden from onlookers, a balcony was constructed so that, on nice days, he could sit in the sunshine.

Just as she had done in Denver, Mamie moved into Walter Reed too, occupying a large room in Ward Eight—painted pink of course—only a few steps from Ike.

At the hospital Mamie kept her vigil as she had in Denver thirteen years before. She talked to Ike, tended to him, read to him, sat quietly with him as he slept, and never showed her concern to him or anyone else. Yet, when she was alone in her room, the nurses saw her weep.

Ike was not doing well. He was not permitted to sit up. Doctors were only allowing the bed to be cranked up slightly so that he could read and converse with his family. Intermittently, he was given oxygen through a nasal catheter, a narrow-diameter tube inserted into one of his nostrils. Electrodes, taped to his body, transmitted his heartbeat, blood pressure, and breathing rate to a bank of instruments outside; Ike never saw them but nurses were watching twenty-four hours a day. The instant an abnormality was detected by the monitors, a warning light flashed.

The light flashed often; Ike was stricken by attacks of ventricular fibrillation, the chaotic, uncontrolled flutter that can occur when the heart muscle has been damaged and, unless quickly corrected, cause death. Defibrillating equipment, at the nurses' station, would be rushed in to stabilize the heartbeat with a brief jolt of electric current. The outlook was not good; Ike himself said it seemed as though "I might cash in my chips."

Then, in September, he bounced back. The fibrillations ceased. General Heaton, the Surgeon General, calling it a "miraculous turnabout," said he could have visitors but cautioned that they should not tire him. None of Ike's military policemen were as rigid in their guard duty as was Mamie at the door of his hospital room. She screened all visitors, and told them how long they must remain, including close members of the family, high Government officials, and even Lyndon Johnson and Lady Bird, the President and First Lady.

It was at Walter Reed that Mamie, talking with Lady Bird in her room, confided that, if Ike were to die, she would be fearful of returning to Gettysburg and living alone. The designer Mollie Parnis, a close friend of Lady Bird, reveals that Mrs. Johnson told the President what Mamie had said. Johnson acted fast. He asked for, and quickly got, legislation enacted which for the first time gave widows of Chief Executives protection for life by the Secret Service.

Mamie began to have hope again. Late in September, she made one of her few appearances outside the hospital, visiting the campaign headquarters of the Richard Nixon-Spiro Agnew ticket at the Willard Hotel. Everyone wanted to know about Ike's condition. Mamie smiled and said he was "much better." The chairman of the campaign committee, Charles S. Rhyne, gave her pins which, he said, would admit them to headquarters at any time of the day or night, and she said she would affix one to Ike's pajamas.

She did exactly that, and more. She gave him a Nixon-Agnew button which he taped to one of his electrodes. She handed out buttons and campaign bumper stickers to all visitors. As his birthday neared, she watched happily as Ike took his first few steps in months by himself. And on October 14, his seventy-eighth birthday, the hospital's chefs baked him a huge cake and the United States Army Band serenaded him from beneath his window.

Ike's recovery continued, amazing his doctors, though he was still allowed only limited activity. The newly elected President, Richard Nixon, Vice-President Agnew, and each member of the Cabinet came to the third-floor suite for short visits and there was guarded talk that, perhaps after the New Year, Ike could be taken home to Gettysburg.

But there was a setback. Adhesions had developed from the ileitis surgery in 1956 and a new operation was performed late in February to correct the intestinal blockage. It was risky, yet Ike survived.

But his heart had been weakened by the repeated attacks, after each of which more of the cardiac muscle was destroyed. Lacking the strength to talk, he spoke only occasionally; but once he whispered to Mamie, who remained constantly at his beside: "I've always loved my wife. I've always loved my children. I've always loved my grandchildren. And I have always loved my country."

His final words, spoken on March 8, 1969, were: "I want to go. God take me." That day, at twenty-five minutes before one o'clock in the afternoon, with Mamie holding his hand, Ike died.

2. "I Miss Him Every Day"

MAMIE EISENHOWER NEVER spoke publicly about her husband's reputed romance with Kay Summersby. Because of the sensitivity of the subject, not to mention her advanced age when the story broke in the mid-1970s, the matter apparently was not discussed by family members in her presence.

Not even her son John was certain how Mamie felt or what she thought. Just before the television mini-series was broadcast, he was quoted in the *Philadelphia Inquirer* as saying: "She's not terribly exposed to it [published reports of the relationship]. She hadn't read the book. I don't know if she is aware of the television broadcast."

Mamie, nearing eighty-three, was not only aware of the television series but eagerly awaited it and, when it was broadcast, did not miss a single segment of the three-part series.

On May 2, 1979, a Thursday evening, she had her dinner, then settled in a chair before the TV set in her upstairs sitting room-bedroom at Gettysburg. Even before eight o'clock, the scheduled hour for the start of the show, she had switched it on, ready to watch Robert Duvall enact the roll of Ike and Lee Remick portray Kay.

The following evening she was there again; and on Saturday she saw the concluding segment.

"Mamie," confirms Mickey McKeogh, "saw it all. Every night, after an episode ended, we would call each other— Pearlie and I would telephone her, and then she would call us—for long talks about what we had seen.

"We would ask her, 'Well, what did you think of that one?' And she would laugh and say, 'Mickey, it doesn't bother me one way or the other.' Once, after a scene we were afraid might upset her, we called and said it couldn't possibly have happened that way, and she said: 'Now don't you bother your pretty little heads about it for one minute. We both know it just isn't true.'

"All through these talks, she would say things like, 'It's ridiculous' and 'I know it isn't true, you know it isn't true, so why do we worry about it?' She wasn't just talking to hide her hurt. We knew Mamie and we knew she was saying what she really felt.

"The important thing is that she simply never believed there had been a romance or anything close to one." (Mary Jane Monroe, her former social secretary, agrees. "She just pooh-pooed the whole thing," says Mrs. Monroe.)

Dr. Sterrett, who was seeing her regularly, says she had not only watched the show but he suspects she also read the memoirs.

"In one section in the book," Dr. Sterrett asserts, "Ike was supposedly so infatuated with Kay that, when he returned home to the States on leave, he mistakenly kept calling Mamie Kay. Ike is quoting as telling Kay that this made Mamie furious.

"Mamie was certainly furious, but not for the reason given. She told me: 'Ike is dead. Kay is dead. No one can

prove a thing. But I know that did not happen. I know that
part is false. Ike never, *never* called me Kay or anything else
but Mamie!'"

Less than four months later, Mamie brought up the
subject again to Dr. Sterrett. Earl Mountbatten of Burma
had just been killed by a bomb, placed aboard his fishing
boat off the village of Mullaghmore by Irish terrorists.
Mamie recalled the long friendship she and Ike had had
with Lord Mountbatten after the war.

"We knew him so well. He was such a perfect English
gentleman, so witty, so charming, and so cultured. And so
handsome in his English hand-tailored suits."

Then Mamie added with an impish smile: "If I had one
thought that there was an iota of truth in the Kay Summersby affair, I would have gone after Monty. And believe
you me, my friend, I could have gotten him!"

The loneliness hit Mamie only a few days after she
returned to Gettysburg. She had chosen to live at the farm
instead of Denver because the latter's altitude was too high
and, in addition to her heart problems, she had developed
asthma. She and Ike had slept in twin beds, with one
headboard, Ike on the right, Mamie the left. At night, when
she looked at the next bed, the emptiness there was
overwhelming. She couldn't sleep, she told friends; she
missed him so much.

One night she rose and piled books, boxes of candy,
newspapers, magazines, anything she could find on top of
the bed beside hers. That took away the emptiness and
made her feel better. She slept.

She rarely went on the big glassed-in porch anymore,
preferring to remain upstairs in her large bedroom and her
sitting room, surrounded by the furnishings and the pictures
she had lived with all her life. "There's too much of Ike
down there," she explained.

A year after Ike died, she went by train to Abilene to visit his grave but she was too tired to see the museum, filled with Eisenhower memorabilia, only a few hundred feet across the lawn. Each year thereafter, on his birthday, she came, most times being driven the fifteen hundred miles from Gettysburg by Secret Service men. The journey would take five days; Mamie would travel only three hundred miles daily, remain overnight in a motel, and start out in mid-morning.

She spent most of her winters at the white-painted six-room brick house on the grounds of the Augusta National Golf Club in Augusta, Georgia, which Ike had used on his golfing vacations. Dubbed "Mamie's Cabin," title to the home was held by the golf club but it had been made available to the President and his family. She was there on the first anniversary of Ike's death, visited by three of her grandchildren. While she was in Georgia, Jimmy Carter, then the Governor, invited her to his Atlanta mansion and she accepted. Later, when Carter was President, he visited her at Gettysburg and, on leaving, kissed her. Mamie was flustered. "My Lord," she told Dr. Sterrett, "I didn't know what to do. I hadn't been kissed by a man outside of the family since Ike died."

Secret Service men who guarded her set up their headquarters in the barn. She became very close to them, and they to her. She called them "my boys" and joked, "They've got to keep me alive until they retire."

At Gettysburg she spent mornings working on her correspondence with her secretary, answering every letter she received. The cooking and housework were done by a sleep-in couple. Afternoons, she would play cards, watch television, talk on the telephone, or have visits from old friends, like Mrs. Arthur Nevins. Occasionally, she would pop in at some of the town's loosely organized bridge luncheons, or she would go downtown to shop.

Six months after Ike died Mickey and Pearlie wrote to her that they were having a big party on their silver anniversary at their home in Bowie. They reminded her that Ike had been at their wedding in Versailles and they would love to have her at their twenty-fifth celebration. Mamie wrote back that she probably would not be able to make it, and Mickey answered that they would send her an invitation anyway.

The party was scheduled for a Friday evening. The Tuesday before, Mamie's secretary called. "Mrs. Eisenhower," she said, "is waiting for an invitation."

Says Mickey: "Golly, we didn't send it because we were so sure she wouldn't come. So we rushed one to her and, when Friday came, our doorbell rang. It was the Secret Service men who checked out our house, then the whole neighborhood, including the church, and then said she was on her way. We left for the church and there she was, waiting for us, with that wonderful smile.

"Afterward, we all came back to the house and went downstairs to the rec room, where the party was, and she stayed and had a grand time."

She made a few public appearances, which tapered off through the 1970s. Dearest to her heart was Eisenhower College at Seneca Falls, New York, whose students impressed her enormously.* Once she attended commencement exercises and wept when she saw four seniors who were so crippled they were unable to walk to the platform to receive their diplomas. "Just think of all the hardship and sacrifice they went through to get an education," she said. "It's like a family there. The girls wait on tables and the boys work."

At a time when students were rioting on campuses, Eisenhower College was peaceful. "There have been no

*Before he died, Eisenhower turned over the $50,000 Atoms for Peace prize toward the construction of the four-year liberal-arts college.

confrontations," Mamie said, adding: "And no one has even painted a mustache on any of Ike's portraits. They don't even have to put glass over the pictures."

Once in a while, she went to see David and Julie in their Washington apartment and enjoyed—she insisted bravely—the dinner Julie cooked, curried hot dogs. She even spent a night once again in the White House, as President Nixon's guest.

Ike remained constantly in her thoughts. She had never become used to being alone, even as an Army wife. "He was my husband," she said in the mid-1970s. "He was my whole life."

After he died, she said, "I miss him every day."

In 1970 a statue of Ike was placed in front of his former office on Carlisle Street. Sculpted by Dr. Norman Annis, once a member of the college's art department, the bronze shows a bareheaded Ike in civilian clothes, a hat held in his hand.

"I always speak to him when I pass it," she told Steve Neal of the *Philadelphia Inquirer*. "During the winter I don't like seeing the snow covering his head."

As the years went on, money, always one of Mamie's prime concerns, became an almost constant preoccupation. "She had a fixation on finances," says Dr. MacAskill.

Her total income amounted to about $40,000 annually—$20,000 she received from the Government as the widow of a President and another $20,000 from Ike's estate. Before he died, Eisenhower had realized, regretfully, that the financial burden of maintaining the farm had become too heavy. He had wanted to keep it in the family and hand it down to his children, David says, and was disappointed that he could not. The value of the property, the taxes, and the cost of maintaining it kept rising over the years and, moreover, the animal-raising yielded no profit. In 1967 he deeded the farm to the Government as a historic site with the stipulation that he and Mamie could live there for the remainder of their lives.* Under the agreement, the Government paid property taxes but the Eisenhowers were responsible for insurance, heat, light, and general repairs.

With Ike gone, Mamie had to reorder her life style dramatically. As a five-star general, Eisenhower had been entitled to domestic servants, paid by the Army, but they were withdrawn after his death. Mamie kept paying for her own live-in help but soon dispensed with a secretary. She planned her meals more carefully than ever, keeping an even sharper eye out for specials, saving more grocery coupons. She bought few clothes, and only if they were on sale. Sixteen years after Ike left the Presidency, she was still wearing the same things she had when she was First Lady. "I took care of them," she said, "and they are very nice."

When the water pipes began to leak one year, she telephoned John and worried about how much the plumber was going to charge. "But, Mother," John told her, "you've got the home tax free." But, seeing that his mother was still apprehensive, John agreed to pay for the repairs.

She attended church often, though not regularly, and each night before retiring she read a passage from her Bible. "I stayed with her and I know," says Mrs. Nevins. "But religion was always a private matter with her. She never spoke about it."

She was also intensely patriotic. She would always wear an American flag pin, affixed somewhere on her person. "She was never without it," Mickey says. "Actually, she had two—one with diamonds and rubies, very expensive, the other a cheap imitation. She wore the phony a lot more often because she was afraid the real one would be stolen." Each night at dusk, Mamie would stand and watch the flag being lowered at the farm. "Heaven help the fellow who let

---

*The farm is now operated by the National Park Service of the Department of the Interior and attracts many thousands of visitors annually.

that flag touch the ground," Mickey says. "He'd catch it from Mamie."

She was unable to understand what she called "this crazy young generation," with its relaxed moral standards and, to her, bizarre view of marriage and its responsibilities. She and Mrs. Nevins spent many hours talking about young people and their live-in arrangements, and wondering why the divorce rate was so high among those who did marry. "She couldn't understand," says Mrs. Nevins, "why marriages broke up so quickly and so easily."

Deep into her seventies, she was vain about the way she dressed. Says Pearlie McKeogh: "She was very much 'the lady' at all times. Every time she went someplace, she chose her clothes with the greatest care. She called them her 'costumes,' not dresses. Everything had to match, her shoes, purse, coat, gloves, stockings, hat—always a hat. She would never go without one. Most women in the 1960s and 70s would mix and match their outfits, but not Mamie."

And always she would insist on high heels, even when women her age would wear "sensible shoes." Ladies, she felt, always wore them. As a result, she was, at times, unsteady on her feet.

This wobbliness was just one of the reasons for the persistence of the stories that Mamie Eisenhower was an alcoholic. Here are the facts, verified once and for all, by Dr. Sterrett and supported by Mamie Eisenhower's medical record at the Walter Reed Army Medical Center.

Reports about Mamie's drinking followed her into retirement. "When the Eisenhowers first moved to Gettysburg, the story was all over Adams County that she was an alcoholic," Dr. Sterrett says.

Throughout the White House years and afterward, the cruel stories continued, despite repeated denials by persons who had close contact with the Eisenhowers. One tale, typical of all the others, will suffice. In Mamie's house on Lafayette Street in Denver, the velvet rope at the head of the stairs was really not the signal to the Secret Service that the Eisenhowers had retired for the night. It was there to protect a tipsy Mamie from falling down the stairs!

As Mamie's personal physician, Dr. Sterrett had received her medical history from Walter Reed. The record, combined with his own evaluation, confirms Mamie's own explanation and that of her friends and associates of the occasional unsteady gait which gave rise to the rumors that she was drunk.

"The stories," Dr. Sterrett told us, "were simply not true. As her doctor, I will vouch for that one hundred percent."

Dr. Sterrett said Mamie had suffered for years from two conditions which could cause symptoms that mimic intoxication. "To the casual observer this may have appeared to be tipsiness but it was not," he says. In earlier years, according to her medical record, she had vertigo from an undetermined cause. Later, after further testing, she was diagnosed as having vestibulitis, a disturbance of the inner ear. This disease, also known as Ménière's Syndrome, is characterized by attacks of deafness, ear noises, dizziness, nausea, and vomiting. Doctors say the exact cause is unknown and it is difficult to treat.

Dr. Sterrett said that Walter Reed's records also confirmed that Mamie had a problem with her carotid sinus, an area in the large artery of the neck which contains sensitive nerve endings. In some individuals, the sinus is too close to the skin surface. Pressure on the neck from a heavy necklace, a tight collar, or even a sudden turning of the head may be sufficient to set off a reflex which would constrict facial and brain blood vessels, bringing on temporary giddiness. There is a classic story in medical annals of a trolley motorman who was about to be fired because his continual dizzy spells were thought to be a hazard to his passengers. No reason could be found until one day a doctor observed that he wore a high, stiff celluloid collar which dug into his neck as he swiveled his head to observe side-street traffic. When he switched to a soft collar which lay low on his neck, the problem disappeared.

Mamie's drinking, as has been noted, had virtually ceased many years earlier. According to Mrs. Nevins, the stories that the problem still existed got their impetus in 1951 at Marnes-la-Coquette in France when Ike was Supreme NATO Commander.

"We were attending a diplomatic reception on New Year's Eve," says Mrs. Nevins. "Mamie was descending the marble staircase very carefully, clutching the railing for dear life because her inner ear problem caused her to sway. Ike turned to her and said, 'Can you make it all right?'

"Well a darned-fool second lieutenant overheard and came home to New York and told everybody that she was tight and Ike was afraid she couldn't get down the stairs."

When Ike was president of Columbia University, Mrs. Nevins said, she and her husband lived only a block away but Mamie would not walk even that block without someone to hold her arm and make sure she would not fall.

Friends felt the gossip was politically inspired. "You heard the accusation made during the campaign that Mamie was an alcoholic," said General Matchett. "There could be nothing further from the truth."

"We'd have cocktails, but I could never get her to take a second."

The question was put to Jim Hagerty.

"Was she an alcoholic?"

"No," he replied hotly. "She would have a drink before dinner, a very little one."

Kevin McCann told us, "I saw her for years from early morning until late at night and I never saw any evidence that she was drunk." He said Mamie would have a drink occasionally with friends and "could nurse a drink for hours and hours."

Maxwell M. Rabb, who served as Secretary of the Cabinet in the Eisenhower Administration, had an office in the White House and saw her constantly. "I never saw her drunk," he said in an interview in his law office on the twenty-second floor of a Wall Street skyscraper. "I heard those stories, too, at Washington cocktail parties, but I thought they were nuts. I was with the President and Mamie in their living quarters, at dinner parties and on the road and I never saw any sign of that. I couldn't put it together with what I knew."

Mamie acknowledged the stories which had circulated only once, in a television interview with Barbara Walters. "I'm going to ask you something, because it's been a rumor for years and I want to finally put it to rest," said Miss Walters. "You know what it is."

"Oh, yes, that I'm a dipsomaniac," said Mamie frankly, explaining that her carotid sinus condition caused her to stumble and bump into things. "I'm black and blue from walking about my own house," she declared. The stories did not bother her, she said, "because I lived with myself and I knew it wasn't so. And my friends knew it wasn't so. I don't think there's anybody who drinks less than I do."

In November of 1978 Mamie had packed her clothes and some kitchen utensils and, leaving everything else behind, moved back to the Wardman Towers of the Sheraton Park Hotel in Washington, formerly the Wardman Park Apartments, where she had lived during the war. Her apartment, Number K 300 on the third floor, was an elegant two-bedroom, two-bath suite with a balcony and a steep rental which was never disclosed. Because she had resided there formerly, Mamie was given a discount.

"Mamie's boys" rented an apartment on the same floor. She had wanted to live at Army Distaff Hall on Oregon

Avenue, a nonprofit residence for wives of retired officers, where she would have the companionship of women who shared her military background. But space could not be found for her Secret Servicemen.

Mamie left Gettysburg because she thought she would be happier in a less isolated setting, closer to the places she once knew. She had loved the Wardman Park; it was there that she and John first received word that Ike had been appointed Supreme Allied Commander; and Ike had returned there during the war on his secret visit to the States.

As the weeks passed, Mamie realized that almost everything had changed.

Washington in the late 1970s was nothing like the old city of the 1940s: things moved faster, old, familiar buildings had been torn down and replaced by tall, shining glass ones, and, worst of all, most of the people she had known were gone, some retired, most dead. "She found the social life too frenzied, too hectic, not as gracious as she had known it," says Mr. MacAskill. "There was too much of the new, not enough of the old, too much hubbub, not enough gentility."

Mamie began to long for the peace of Gettysburg, and before the winter was over she had moved back.

At the farm, she remained close to home. She had lost thirty pounds and looked frail. "I always wondered whether I'd be a fat old lady or a thin old lady," she said. "I guess I'm finding out."

The sleep-in couple had gone and she had a succession of housekeepers or day workers. But for many hours during the day and weekends, and nights, she was alone. "We used to go up there to visit," says Pearlie, "and there was nobody: the Secret Service men, out there in the barn, couldn't know what was going on inside the house, though they would come in to check on her from time to time. If she needed help, or wanted the men for any reason, she could call them by phone. There was also an alarm system;

if a door was opened that should have been closed, it would trigger a signal and they would come."

One day, while she was in the kitchen, her legs buckled and she fell. She was alone in the big house. Despite a broken right wrist, Mamie crawled slowly along the floor to the telephone, pulled it down, and called the agents. They came running, picked her up, and brought her to her bedroom. It was the second time she had fallen.

After that, the Secret Service men insisted that she engage somebody to stay with her constantly. John, seriously concerned about her safety and welfare, wanted her to live with him and his family, not far away, but she would not go. "She was too darned independent," Pearlie says. "She didn't want to be a burden. She didn't want to mess up anybody's life. She wanted her own home. She had her own way of living and they had theirs.

"It was also hard for her to find someone she could relate to, who would be willing to stay with her as women had done in years gone by, on call twenty-four hours a day. It wasn't that kind of world anymore. People didn't want to put in those kinds of hours.

"Finally she got two fine persons she liked. One came in at four in the afternoon and remained until eight A.M., and then another arrived at eight and stayed until four in the afternoon."

Mamie was astonished that she was truly old. "I am still that little girl skating up and down the sidewalk," she wrote to her childhood friend, Eileen Archibold in mid-May of 1979. She described the old days they spent together and wished that she could go back to Denver once more for the "fun" they would both have recalling the past.

She told Eileen about her two falls that year, and the present intruded into her reveries. "It is h—— to get old and be in pain a lot this year," she wrote.

Eileen Archibold put the letter on her writing table,

intending to answer it; but her own personal affairs intruded, and she never did.

Mamie's family came to visit her but there were few others. "I think she was a very lonely lady," Dr. Sterrett says, and Mrs. Nevins agrees. "You don't live that long—she was eighty-three—and have many contemporaries," she says.

"People didn't come to the farmhouse often," Dr. Sterrett declares, "partly because she was shielded by the Secret Service and partly because she was not feeling well at all. When I went to see her, I would always plan on spending plenty of time because we'd always have a long confab about everything and anything. She loved to chat and her subjects were wide and diverse."

By midsummer, Mamie could no longer get out of bed. Her heart, enlarged from chronic valvular disease, was failing. But she remained cheerful, even chipper; she read a great deal, she still watched television. "I've lived a good life," she told Dr. Sterrett.

On September 25 Dr. Sterrett received a call from the farmhouse. Mamie was very ill. He rushed over and quickly saw she had had a stroke. A volunteer fire department ambulance raced eighty miles with her to Walter Reed Hospital. Dr. Sterrett, who rode with her, says she was awake during the hour-and-twenty-minute trip, though the stroke had affected her right side.

Mamie was taken to the VIP suite where Ike had been treated and where he died. Six days later, on a Sunday, she fell asleep and never awakened.

She was buried beside her husband and her first-born son in the Place of Meditation, the thin-spired chapel on the grounds of the Dwight D. Eisenhower Center in the small city on the plains of Kansas.

APPENDIX A

WHERE THEY LIVED

Mamie Eisenhower has said that she and Ike had thirty-seven separate residences during their married lives. However, this number includes hotels and other lodgings which they occupied only for brief periods. Here is a list of the places in which Ike and Mamie kept house for a year or longer. Their "homes," rented or assigned, ranged from furnished rooms and Army barracks to a French chateau, a New York City mansion and—the White House:

1916–17	Fort Sam Houston, San Antonio, Texas
1917–18	Fort Leavenworth, Leavenworth, Kansas
1918–19	Camp Colt, Gettysburg, Pennsylvania
1919–22	Camp Meade, south of Baltimore, Maryland
1922–24	Camp Gaillard, Panama
1925–26	Fort Leavenworth
1926	Fort Benning, south of Columbus, Georgia
1927–28	Wyoming Apartments, Washington, District of Columbia
1928–29	Quai d' Auteuil, Paris, France

1930–35	Wyoming Apartments
1936–40	The Manila Hotel, Manila, Philippines
1940–41	Fort Lewis, south of Tacoma, Washington
1941–42	Fort Sam Houston
1942	Fort Myer, Arlington, Virginia
1942–1945	Ike—Telegraph Cottage, Kingston upon Thames, Surrey, England
	Mamie—Wardman Park Apartments, Washington, District of Columbia
1945–48	Fort Myer
1948–50	Columbia University, 60 Morningside Drive, New York City
1951–52	Villa St. Pierre, Marnes-la-Coquette, France
1952	Columbia University
1953–61	The White House, 1600 Pennsylvania Avenue, Washington, District of Columbia

APPENDIX B

FAVORITE EISENHOWER RECIPES

Ike had several dishes he liked to prepare for guests. One was quail hash which he often served at Gettysburg, using birds he had hunted himself. Another was his famous beef stew.

Mamie, who did not like to cook, nevertheless collected recipes for family favorites which she gave to her cooks. These and President Eisenhower's recipes are presented below.

Quail Hash

2 quail   1 tablespoon flour
1 cup chicken stock   Salt and pepper to taste

Put quail in saucepan with 1-2 cup of stock. Cover and steam for 10 minutes. Add the remainder of the stock and simmer until tender. Remove from burner and dice the quail. Add the flour to stock remaining in pan and make a gravy. Return the diced quail to the pot and simmer, covered, 10 minutes longer.

President Eisenhower's Old-Fashioned Beef Stew

20 pounds stewing meat
    (prime round)
8 pounds small Irish
    potatoes
6 bunches small carrots

5 pounds small onions
15 fresh tomatoes
1 bunch bouquet garniture
3 gallons beef stock
    Salt, pepper and Accent

Stew the meat until tender. Add the vegetables and bouquet garniture (thyme leaves, garlic, etc., in cloth bag). When vegetables are done, strain off two gallons of stock from the stew and thicken slightly with beef roux. Pour back into stew and let simmer for 1-2 hour. Serves 60.

Danish Tomatoes

Slice the tomatoes. Add dark brown sugar, a layer of tomatoes, and a layer of brown sugar. Add vinegar and salt and pepper to taste. Put in refrigerator for a couple of hours.

"Perfect Steak"

(a) Get a sirloin tip four inches thick. (This makes it as thick as it is wide).
(b) Make a dry mixture of salt, black pepper, and garlic powder. Put it in a flat, wide bowl.
(c) Roll and rub the steak in the mixture until it will take up no more.
(d) Two hours before ready to start cooking, build, on the ground, a bonfire on which dump a goodsized basketful of charcoal. Keep fire going well until charcoal has formed a good thick body of glowing coals.

(e) Forty minutes before time to eat, throw the steak into the fire (use no grates, grills, or anything of the kind).

(f) Nudge it over once or twice but let it lie in fire about thirty-five minutes.

(g) Take out, slice slant-wise (about three-eighths-inch thick). Serve hot. (One steak will serve three persons generously.)

Devil's Food Cake

2½ cups sifted flour
1 teaspoon soda
1 teaspoon baking powder
    (rounded)
¼ teaspoon salt
½ cup butter

1 cup sour milk
3 eggs
1 teaspoon vanilla
⅔ cup cocoa dissolved in
½ cup boiling water
2 cups sugar

Sift flour, soda, baking powder, and salt. Cream shortening, slowly beat in milk. Add beaten egg yolks, vanilla; add cocoa. Add flour mixture alternately with sugar. Fold in stiffly beaten egg whites. Pour into 2 greased layer cake tins, bake 25 minutes in a 375° oven. Or use greased 9-inch square tin and bake 45 minutes in a 350° oven.

Seven-Minute Frosting

2 egg whites, unbeaten
1½ cups sugar, finely sifted
5 tablespoons cold water

½ teaspoon cream of tartar
    or 2 teaspoons light corn
    syrup
Few grains of salt
1 teaspoon vanilla

Combine all ingredients but vanilla in top of double boiler. Stir until sugar dissolves, then place over briskly boiling water. Beat with egg beater until stiff enough to stand up in peaks (6 to 10 minutes). Add vanilla. Beat until thick enough to spread. During cooking, keep sides of double boiler cleaned down with spatula. With an electric beater, the process may take as little as four minutes.

Cold Curry Soup

⅓ cup butter	⅛ teaspoon pepper
¼ minced onion	¼ cup flour
¼ cup diced celery	1 quart milk
1½ teaspoon curry powder	2 chicken bouillon cubes
1 teaspoon salt	Flaked coconut

Melt butter in saucepan over low heat. Sauté onions and celery in butter until transparent. Blend in seasonings and flour. Add milk, stirring constantly. Cook until smooth and thickened. Add bouillon cubes; stir until blended. Chill thoroughly. Pour into chilled bowls and sprinkle with flaked coconut. Serves 6.

BIBLIOGRAPHY

Ambrose, Stephen E. *Ike/Abilene to Berlin*. New York: Harper and Row Publishers, 1973.

Brandon, Dorothy. *Mamie Doud Eisenhower, A Portrait of a First Lady*. New York: Charles Scribner's Sons, 1954.

Brodie, Fawn M. *Thomas Jefferson*. New York: W. W. Norton & Company, 1974.

Bryant Traphes, with Frances Spatz Leighton. *Dog Days at the White House*. New York: Macmillan Publishing Co., 1975.

Butcher, Harry. *My Three Years with Eisenhower*. New York: Simon and Schuster, 1946.

Childs, Marquis. *Eisenhower: Captive Hero*. New York: Harcourt, Brace & World, 1958.

————. *Witness to Power*. New York: McGraw-Hill International Book Co., 1975.

Cooke, Alistair. *Six Men*. New York: Alfred A. Knopf, 1977.

Davis, Kenneth S. *Soldier of Democracy*. New York: Doubleday, Doran & Company, 1945.

Eisenhower, Dwight D. *At Ease: Stories I Tell.* New York: Doubleday & Company, 1967.

———. *Letters to Mamie.* Edited with commentary by John S. D. Eisenhower. New York: Doubleday & Company, 1978.

———. *Mandate for Change.* New York: Doubleday & Company, 1963.

———. *The Papers of Dwight D. Eisenhower: the War Years.* Alfred D. Chandler, Jr., editor, Stephen E. Ambrose, associate editor, and others. Baltimore: Johns Hopkins Press, 1970.

Eisenhower, John S. D. *Strictly Personal.* New York: Doubleday & Company, 1974.

Eisenhower, Julie Nixon. *Special People.* New York: Simon and Schuster, 1977.

Eisenhower, Milton S. *The President Is Calling.* New York: Doubleday & Company, 1974.

Gammon, Roland. *All Believers Are Brothers.* New York: Doubleday & Company, 1969.

Gulley, Bill, with Mary Ellen Reese. *Breaking Cover.* New York: Simon and Schuster, 1980.

Gunther, John. *Eisenhower.* New York: Harper & Row, 1951.

Hatch, Alden. *Red Carpet for Mamie.* New York: Henry Holt & Co., 1954.

——— *Young Ike.* New York: Julian Messner, 1953.

Howard, Katherine G. *With My Shoes Off.* New York: Vantage Press, 1977.

Kornitzer, Bela. *The Story of the Five Eisenhower Brothers.* New York: Farrar, Straus and Cudahy, 1955.

Larson, Arthur. *The President Nobody Knew.* New York: Charles Scribner's Sons, 1968.

Lyon, Peter. *Eisenhower: Portrait of the Hero.* Boston: Little, Brown and Company, 1974.

Manchester, William. *American Caesar.* Boston: Little, Brown and Company, 1978.

McCann, Kevin. *Man From Abilene.* New York: Doubleday & Company, 1952.

McKeogh, Michael J., and Lockridge, Richard. *Sgt. Mickey and General Ike.* New York: G. P. Putnam's Sons, 1946.

Miller, Merle. *Plain Speaking.* New York: G. P. Putnam's Sons, 1973.

Neal, Steve. *The Eisenhowers: Reluctant Dynasty.* New York: Doubleday & Company, 1978.

Nicolay, Helen. *Born To Command.* New York: D. Appleton-Century Company, 1945.

Parmet, Herbert S. *Eisenhower and the American Crusades.* New York: MacMillan Company, 1972.

Pinkley, Virgil, and Scheer, James F. *Eisenhower Declassified.* Old Tappan: Fleming H. Revell Co., 1979.

Pogue, Forrest C. *George C. Marshall, Organizer of Victory.* vol. 3. New York: The Viking Press, 1973.

Slater, Ellis D. *The Ike I Knew.* Privately published, 1980.

Smith, Mary D. *Entertaining in the White House.* Washington, D. C., Acropolis, 1967.

Snyder, Marty, *My Friend Ike.* New York: Frederick Fell, 1956.

Summersby, Kay. *Eisenhower Was My Boss.* New York: Prentice-Hall, 1948.

————. *Past Forgetting: My Love Affair with Dwight D. Eisenhower.* New York: Simon and Schuster, 1977.

Ter Horst, J. F., and Albertazzie, Col. Ralph. *The Flying White House: The Story of Air Force One.* New York: Coward, McCann & Geoghegan, 1979.

Truman, Harry S. *Memoirs: Years of Trial and Hope.* New York: Doubleday & Company, 1956.

West, J. B. *Upstairs at the White House.* New York: Coward, McCann & Geoghegan, 1973.

Youngblood, Rufus W. *20 Years in the Secret Service.* New York: Simon and Schuster, 1973.

Index

Waldorf-Astoria Hotel, New York
 City, 172–73
Wallace, Robert, 178
Walter Reed Army Medical
 Center, Washington, 239–40
 Ike in, 227, 243–44, 249–50, 252–55
 Mamie in, 80, 112, 227
 Mamie's medical record at, 263, 264
Walters, Barbara, 266
War Plans Division, 101, 102
Ward, Ann, 237
Wardman Park Apartments (later
 Wardman Towers), Washing-
 ton, 101, 104, 109–22, 266–67
Waring, Fred, 208
Warren, Earl, 101*n*
Washington, George, 128, 179
West, J. B., 200, 204
West Point, *see* United States Military
 Academy
Wetzel, Ethel, 245, 246
Wheaton, Anne, 170
White, Paul Dudley, 236, 238–40
White House, Ike and Mamie's life in,
 106, 193–214, 240–41
Whitman, Ann, 82, 232
Whitney, John J. (Jock), 220
Williams, Captain Margaret M., 234

Williamson, William, 60
Wilson, Woodrow, 68, 73
Windsor, Duchess of, 128
Windsor, Duke of, 128
With My Shoes Off (Howard), 181
Wolcott School for Girls, 32, 34, 174
Woman's Air Force Service
 Pilots, 85*n*
Woman's Army Corps (WAC), U.S.,
 102, 148–50
Women's Auxiliary Corps,
 British, 125
Women's Motor Transport Corps,
 British, 143, 144
World War I, 67–72
 Ike's work on battlefields of, 96–97
World War II
 Ike in, 108–9, 113–14, 116–25, 137,
 143–57
 Mamie's life during, 101, 111–26,
 158–61

"You Bet Your Life" (television
 show), 194
Youngblood, Rufus, 193–94

Zhukov, Marshal Georgi, 237